PIRATES & PATRIOTS

PIRATES & PATRIOTS

Tales of the Delaware Coast

Michael Morgan

Algora Publishing
New York

ISBN: 0-87586-337-X (softcover)
ISBN: 0-87586-338-8(hardcover)
ISBN: 0-87586-339-6 (ebook)

Library of Congress Cataloging-in-Publication Data —

Morgan, Michael, 1943-
Pirates and patriots, tales of the Delaware coast / Michael Morgan.
    p. cm.
Includes bibliographical references and index.
ISBN 0-87586-337-X (Paper : alk. paper) — ISBN 0-87586-338-8
(Hard cover : alk. paper) — ISBN 0-87586-339-6 (ebook)
1. Delaware Bay (Del. and N.J.)—History—Anecdotes. 2. Atlantic
Coast (Del.)—History—Anecdotes. 3. Atlantic Coast (Del.)—
History, Naval—Anecdotes. I. Title.

F172.D3M67 2004
910'.9163'46—dc22

                        2004017647

Front cover: Man walking on the beach —
© The Lewes Historical Society. Used by permission, all rights reserved.
Back cover: Photo by Tom Morgan.
All other pictures in this book: Photos by the author.

Printed in the United States

MAPS

1. Delaware, as of 1796.
2. The State of Delaware today.
3. Rehoboth Beach.
4. Detailed map of Rehoboth Beach.

All maps are courtesy of the Delaware Department of Transportation.

DE 1796

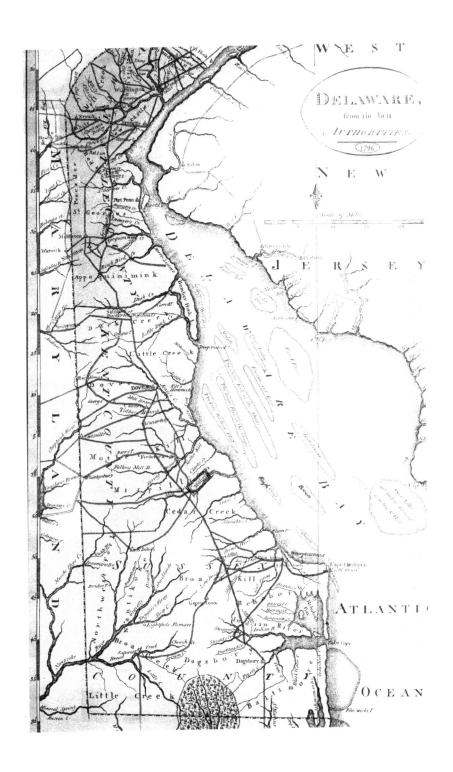

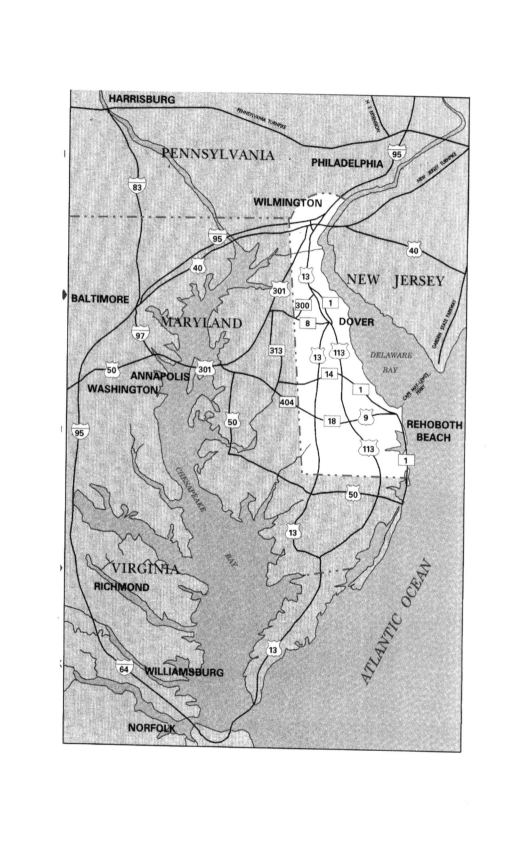

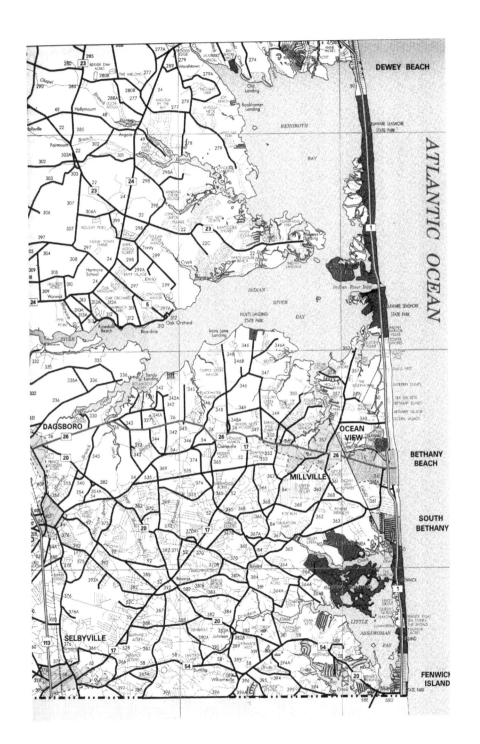

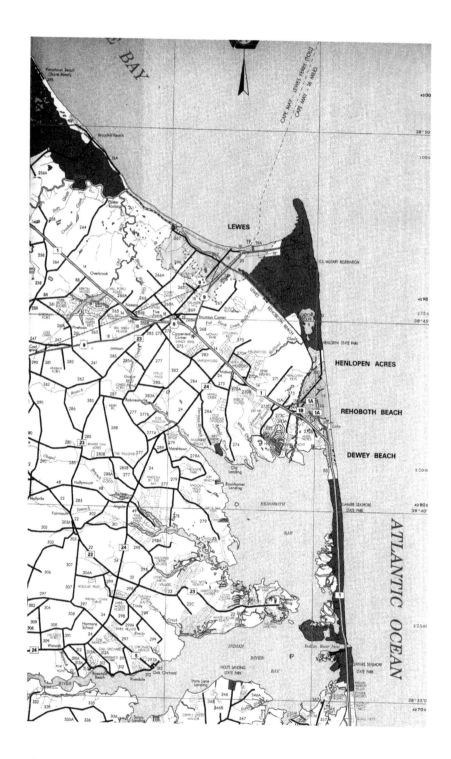

TABLE OF CONTENTS

INTRODUCTION

The people of Sussex County (Delaware's most southern county) breathe the salt spray of the Atlantic Ocean; and these hearty people's lives match the brawly nature of the sea. Many of these folks, such as the intrepid patriot Henry Fisher, the infamous serial killer Patty Cannon, and the clever witness, Noah Burton, are not known beyond the boundaries of southern Delaware. Others, such as William Penn and Captain Kidd, enjoy more widespread reputations. This kaleidoscope collection of tales provides a colorful portrait of life in southern Delaware from the Europeans' first arrival at Cape Henlopen until modern times.

The tales of the Delaware coast lie buried in numerous libraries, archives, and museums; it would not have been possible to write this work without the assistance of the dedicated caretakers of these records. I am deeply grateful for the help that these librarians and archivists have given me over the years.

In addition, I would like to thank Mike Mills, Terry Plowman, Bruce Pringle, Ashley Dawson, and the other editors of the *Delaware Coast Press* who have supported the "Delaware Diary" for the past fifteen years. Writing this weekly column enables me to probe the details of the history of the coastal region; and this experience provides the foundation for *Pirates and Patriots, Tales of the Delaware Coast*. Also, I would like to thank the faithful readers of the "Delaware Diary" who have supplied tidbits of coastal history that I would have otherwise missed.

Finally, I would like to thank my wife, Madelyn, for her assistance in producing this work. She is the only person who has read every word that I have written; and she has spent countless hours correcting my spelling, punctuation, and grammar. Without her help, this book would not have been possible. Whatever errors remain are mine.

Chapter 1. Colonists and Cutthroats

A Great Bay is Named

In 1610, the English captain Samuel Argall sailed around the gentle curve of a dune-covered cape and into a wide bay. Argall was not the first European to sail these waters. Nearly a century earlier, Giovanni da Verrazano had sailed up the North American coast from Cape Hatteras to Canada; but the Italian explorer kept so far from shore that he failed to notice the bay that Argall had entered. A year before Argall arrived, Henry Hudson had also sailed into the bay. Hudson was leading a Dutch expedition looking for the fabled Northwest Passage across America; Hudson surmised that the bay would not lead to an opening that crossed the continent and after a brief stay, he sailed on.

Captain Argall was looking for food. Thomas West, the governor of the Virginia colony, had dispatched the English captain to the north in an attempt to locate supplies for the Jamestown settlers, who were so short of provisions that they wanted to return to England. When Argall sailed past the high dunes that lined the cape on the southern shore of the bay, there were no European settlements in the region; and he decided to continue northward. But he was impressed by the wide waterway, and decided to give the bay a proper name. At the same time, Argall hoped to curry favor with Governor West.

Thomas West was born on July 9, 1577, in Hampshire, England. He studied at Oxford, but he failed to earn a degree. After traveling abroad for a few years, West returned to England where he became active in politics and was elected to Parliament. At about the same time, West also became interested in the colonization of America. West was a member of the Virginia Company of London that established the Jamestown colony in 1607. When the colonists sailed to Virginia, he remained in England where he organized additional expeditions to the New World. West's efficient work earned him a seat on the colonial company's ruling council. When news reached England that the Jamestown settlers were having difficulty maintaining an adequate supply of food, West was appointed governor of the weak colony.

At that time, ships bound for America followed the path first sailed by Christopher Columbus in 1492. They sailed southward toward Africa until they encountered the easterly winds that would carry them across the Atlantic Ocean to the West Indies. After they reached the islands, British captains sailed northward to the mid-Atlantic region, where the first British colonies were established. Although this dependable route took excellent advantage of the prevailing winds, it took almost a year to complete a round trip voyage to America. In addition, the route took ships through waters controlled by Spain, which was often at war with England. Twenty-two years earlier, the lack of a safe and quick route to North America had delayed supply ships to the Roanoke colony that Sir Walter Raleigh had established on the coast of North Carolina. When the ships finally arrived, all of the settlers were gone; and Roanoke became known as the "Lost Colony."

West was determined to find a dependable and fast way to provision the Virginia settlement. When he sailed for America, West took with him one of the most renowned English mariners of the day, Samuel Argall, who did, indeed, provide an answer to West's supply problem and at the same time left his mark on Delaware.

To prevent Jamestown from becoming England's next "Lost Colony," Samuel Argall embarked on a bold plan to reach America more quickly. Instead of sailing southward to reach the easterly winds off Africa, Argall sailed from England on a westerly course that led him directly across the Atlantic. It was commonly believed that such a route would lead Argall into the center of destructive storms that would sink his ship. When his ship disappeared over the horizon, many people thought that they had seen the last of the impetuous Samuel Argall.

Five months after setting sail from England, Argall returned home with the electrifying news that he had reached America! He had proven that the Atlantic Ocean could be crossed in as little as six or seven weeks. To nearly everyone's surprise, Argall's most difficult problem was a lack of wind that left his ship nearly stationary for two weeks.

In the spring of 1610, West and Argall set sail for America at the head of a major supply expedition that was to re-provision the weak Jamestown colony. Argall's expedition was able to make the Atlantic crossing quickly and without incident; but the winter had been a disaster for the colonists. During a period that is now known as "The Starving Time," the settlers had scoured the ground looking for "wylde and unknowne roots" to eat. Other colonists were reduced to eating "doggs, Cats, Ratts, and myce." At least one settler had resorted to cannibalism. Of the 500 Jamestown colonists who began the winter, only 59 survived until the spring. They decided to abandon Jamestown when the weather cleared, and the settlers had already boarded a ship to return to England when Argall's supply ships appeared in the Chesapeake Bay.

Governor Thomas West quickly took command of the colony. The settlers returned to their huts at Jamestown; and West began to distribute the supplies that he had brought. He then dispatched Argall to search for additional food. The resourceful captain returned to the Atlantic, where he sailed northward along the coast. When he passed a cape marked by some of the highest dunes along the coast, Argall turned westward and drifted into a broad bay. It is not known if Argall was aware that Henry Hudson had visited these waters a year earlier. Hudson had named the wide estuary the "South River."

After a brief stay in the South River, Captain Argall returned to the Atlantic, and continued northward until he encountered European fishermen near Cape Cod. Argall secured a cargo of fish and returned to Jamestown. Governor West sent Argall on several more expeditions; and the English captain was able to gather enough food so that the Jamestown colonists could face the coming winter without fear of starvation.

Argall spent several years in America; and during this time, he helped secure England's hold on the Atlantic coast. At one point, he attempted to bring the Dutch settlements along the Hudson River under British rule. Argall failed to gain control of the Dutch colony; but he did succeed in changing the name of Henry Hudson's prosaic "South River." Argall decided to christen the waterway after Governor Thomas West; but he used West's title, Baron De La Warr, and "Delaware Bay" began to appear on English maps.

No Peace in the Valley of the Swans

In 1631, Captain Pieter Heyes followed in the wake of Samuel Argall as he guided the ship *Walvis* around the easy arc of Cape Henlopen and entered Delaware Bay. Aboard his ship were a score of Dutch colonists who hoped to establish a settlement on the South River that would rival the Dutch trading posts along the Hudson River. Heyes and others aboard the *Walvis* watched the shoreline for a suitable place to land. Someone spotted the mouth of the wide creek, and the captain edged the *Walvis* toward shore. After the settlers scrambled onto land, they surveyed the shoreline from a small bluff opposite where the creek emptied into the bay. Here, they decided, was the perfect place to begin construction of a new settlement, which became known as Zwaanendael, or "Valley of the Swans."

Following Henry Hudson's brief visit to the wide estuary, the Dutch had established Fort Nassau, far inland on the northern bank of the Delaware River, near the mouth of the Schuylkill River. In addition, the Dutch had been busy on the Hudson River. Colonists had journeyed far up the river to establish Fort Orange (now absorbed into the city of Albany) where the Mohawk River comes in from the west to join the Hudson, which enabled them to trade with Native Americans from the interior of the continent. And at the mouth of the Hudson River, Peter Minuit had purchased Manhattan Island for $24 worth of trinkets.

The Dutch trading posts along the Delaware and Hudson Rivers were flanked by Lord De La Warr's Virginia colony to the south, and a struggling Plymouth colony to the north. If the settlers aboard the *Walvis* could expand the Dutch presence on the South River, they could drive a wedge between the two fledging English colonies.

After the Dutch colonists were satisfied that the bluff provided a clear view of the bay where ships from rival European nations might appear at any time, they began work on the new colony's first structures. Bricks carried in the hold of the *Walvis* were used to erect a small building, around which they then constructed a rough wooden stockade. After the small fort had taken shape, the Dutch colonists set up a small metal plaque to indicate their ownership of Zwaanendael. Such plaques were not uncommon — a similar sign was reportedly erected on Fenwick Island (in southeastern Delaware), and Sir Francis Drake nailed a similar sign to a tree in California during his epic voyage around the world.

The promoters of the new Zwaanendael colony were confident that they had found a nearly ideal location for their settlement. The land was fertile, there was fresh water close by, and the bay provided easy transportation. As they saw it, "New Netherlands is the flower, the noblest of all lands." The Native Americans of the Lenne Lenape and Nanticoke tribes were friendly, and they appeared eager to trade with the new settlers.

Coastal Delaware may have been "the noblest of all lands," but soon after the *Walvis* anchored near Cape Henlopen, Captain Pieter Heyes concluded that his expedition had already lost a great opportunity. At that time, whales were often spotted near the mouth of the Delaware Bay, and the organizers of the Zwaanendael venture believed that the colonists would be able to establish a shore-based whaling station. It was hoped that whaling would be as profitable as fur trading had been to the other colonies.

Hunting whales was hazardous work that required men with strong backs and stronger nerves. When whales were spotted, the whalers would race to their small boats, which they launched through the surf. Straining at every stroke of the oars, the men rowed after the great beasts. As they approached their prey, a single slap by the whale's great tail could smash their vessel into splinters. *whales*

Once a boat drew close enough, the harpooneer would lift his long spear and take aim. He had to drive the metal shaft into the whale's body in one single, steady motion. If the harpoon was delivered with sufficient skill, it would pierce a vital organ and the whale would die quickly. If not, the massive, wounded beast would likely upset the boat and the seamen would be killed; and the precious quarry would be lost, as well. In a successful hunt, the dead whale was then towed to shore, where the blubber would be sliced from the carcass and rendered into oil.

Whaling was difficult and dangerous, but the high price of whale oil made the effort worthwhile. The Dutch backers of the Delaware colony expected the settlers to begin shipping valuable whale oil to Europe shortly after they landed near Cape Henlopen. The profits from the whale oil was expected to begin flowing long before farming and fur trading could generate income to pay for the new colony.

During the 17th century, when most of the coastal waters of North America had not yet been charted, most colonial expeditions consisted of several vessels. The larger ships, carrying the bulk of the colonists and supplies, were in constant danger of running aground on unmapped shoals. The smaller vessels often sailed ahead and measured the depth of the water so that bigger ships could avoid the shallows. When the *Walvis* set sail from the Dutch port of Hoorn, the *Salm* accompanied the ship as its escort.

When the colonists for Zwaanendael boarded the two ships, all of the harpooneers crowded aboard the *Salm*. After the two ships set sail, the smaller *Salm* cruised ahead of the *Walvis*; the two ships soon became separated. Several weeks later, the *Walvis* arrived in Delaware Bay; but there was not a sign of the *Salm*, or the harpooneers who were vital to the success of the whaling station at Cape Henlopen. Although the colonists held out hope that the sails of the *Salm* would appear over the horizon, it soon became apparent that something dreadful had happened. It was not uncommon in those days for ships to disappear without a trace; some were swallowed up by ocean storms, and others were captured by pirates.

The loss of the *Salm* forced the *Walvis* to navigate the dangerous shallows of Delaware Bay alone. In all likelihood, Captain Heyes lowered one of his ship's small boats soon after rounding Cape Henlopen. The crewmen in the small boat could measure the water depth and alert Heyes to any hazards, and could scout out a safe anchorage for the *Walvis*. Although Heyes managed to negotiate the waters of Delaware Bay, the harpooneers aboard the *Salm* could not be replaced. Without these skilled men, there was little hope of establishing a whaling station on Cape Henlopen.

After the *Walvis* returned to Europe for supplies, the settlers finished work on their houses and on Zwaanendael's protective stockade. Fields were cleared in the surrounding area and planted with seed. In addition, the colonists began trading with the Native Americans.

Davids Perterzen de Vries had been one of the organizers of the Zwaanendael expedition, but he was unable to accompany Heyes on the *Walvis*. Eager to see the new American colony, he was aboard the first supply ship that was dispatched to the Dutch settlement. When he arrived at Zwaanendael on December 5, 1632, de Vries was devastated by what he found. Scattered about the deserted stockade were the bleached bones of the Dutch settlers.

After questioning the Native Americans, de Vries deduced what had happened. One day, the settlers discovered that their metal plaque was missing. They questioned the Native Americans, who discovered that one of their own had taken the sign. A short time later, several Native Americans returned to the stockade with a bag. When the Dutch settlers gathered around to see what they had brought, the Native Americans lifted from the bag the head of the man who had taken the metal sign. The colonists reacted in such horror that they upset the Native Americans, who returned to their village to ponder what to do next. A few days later, the Native Americans returned to the stockade. Everything seemed to have returned to normal, until a signal was given. Instantly, knives and tomahawks were drawn; and within minutes, the surprised Dutch settlers were slashed, stabbed, and bludgeoned to death. The lifeless bodies of the massacred colonists were left to rot in the small stockade that sat on the low bluff overlooking Delaware Bay.

A golden opportunity to establish a colony in "the noblest of all lands" was gone.

A CASTAWAY AND A DREAMER

A few years after the destruction of Zwaanendael, Helmanus Wiltbank's ship foundered on a shoal lurking beneath the water off Cape Henlopen. After struggling through the waves, Wiltbank's feet finally touched the sandy bottom, and he was able to make his way through the surf to dry land. Wiltbank's wife and sons also reached shore safely; with his family intact, Wiltbank refused to travel any farther; and he became the first permanent settler of the Cape Henlopen area.

Wiltbank was born in Sweden in about 1625. In the 17th century, Sweden's fine army complemented Holland's excellent navy; and the two countries were often allies. Both nations had established extensive trading empires that included settlements in America. For Wiltbank, the close relationship between the two countries made it easy for him to move to Holland, where he switched his allegiance to the Dutch.

At that time, it was not unusual for people to shift their allegiance from one country to another. The modern concept of nationalism was only beginning to develop. Medieval practice called for average folk to swear to serve their local lord. If that person died or was replaced, it was not difficult for his subjects to shift their loyalty to a new lord. Wiltbank would have ample opportunity to practice such swift changes in allegiance in America.

When Helmanus Wiltbank survived the shipwreck that dumped him on the sandy beach of Cape Henlopen, he held title to 800 acres of land in the coastal area, and he was determined to attract other colonists to the region. To encourage others to settle in the area, Wiltbank could point to the fertile land, the bounty of the bay and the easy access to the Atlantic sea-lanes. In addition,

Wiltbank offered to educate the children of colonists who settled near Cape Henlopen. He was gratified that several families did move to the Cape Henlopen area; but he may have been a little surprised when Peter Cornelius Plockhoy arrived on the shores of the South River.

By the time Plockhoy landed, in 1662, the area around Cape Henlopen had changed little since the destruction of the Zwaanendael colony three decades earlier. A small fort had been erected near the ruins of the Zwaanendael stockade; but except for Wiltbank and a few others, most Swedish and Dutch colonists had by-passed the area to establish settlements that would become New Castle and Wilmington. Plockhoy, however, thought that the Cape Henlopen area was an excellent place for a noble experiment in community living.

For Europeans during the 17th century, social class determined the course of their lives. Those who were born into the noble and upper classes were pampered by scores of servants. In addition, theological fervor ran high and European nations routinely declared war on one another in the name of religion. People may have dreamt of a world where there would be no social classes and people could live in religious harmony, but most thought that would be only in the life to come. Peter Plockhoy, however, spent many years generating support for an egalitarian colony where social classes were outlawed and opposing religious beliefs were tolerated.

In England, a group known as the "Levelers" advocated ideas similar to Plockhoy's. Many Levelers supported Oliver Cromwell during the English Civil War. When Cromwell won that war and the king of England was beheaded, it seemed that Plockhoy's ideas would be well received by the new English government. Plockhoy wrote several letters to Cromwell to ask for his support in establishing a classless colony in America. Cromwell turned him down.

Rebuffed by the English government, Plockhoy turned to the Dutch for help. The burgermeisters of Amsterdam were more receptive to Plockhoy's ideas. The Dutch allowed him to establish a small colony in which there would be "No lordship or servile slavery," near present-day Lewes. Plockhoy's colony was to be founded "upon righteousness, upon love and upon brotherly union." Religious diversity was to be permitted in the Delaware settlement as long as "brotherhood and unity possess them all."

With the permission of the Dutch in hand, Peter Plockhoy set out to recruit colonists for his noble experiment. Although Plockhoy may have held an overly idealistic view of how society should be organized, he had the flair of a modern promoter. To attract colonists, Plockhoy wrote glowingly of Delaware, where the birds were so numerous that they "obscure the sky."

Plockhoy realized that he would need a variety of workers if his settlement were to be successful. He attempted to recruit "agriculturists, seafaring men, all kinds of necessary tradespeople and masters of good arts and science." Although it is doubtful that Plockhoy was successful in attracting all of the artisans that he had in mind, by the latter part of 1662 he and his colonists had arrived on the Delaware coast.

The egalitarian settlement was far different from the class structure of Europe. Although colonists owned their own homes, each settler was required to work six hours a day at an occupation that would produce income for the entire community. The money earned by this work would be divided equally among all the adult colonists. To prepare for this common work, children were required to work at a trade for half a day. During the other half of the day, the children attended school, where they studied the bible and the natural sciences. The school was forbidden from teaching "human formulas of religion."

There were no social classes in Plockhoy's community. All the colonists were considered equal; and no permanent settler could be a lord, servant or maid; but outsiders could be employed as servants, provided they were paid a wage. Plockhoy also decreed that if anyone tired of living in his experimental community, he was free to collect his share of the profits and leave at any time.

Peter Plockhoy had established his innovative colony in an attempt to escape the constant European quarrels over religion and politics; but these disputes soon followed him across the Atlantic. In 1664, a war between the English and the Dutch brought a squadron of British warships to the settlements near Cape Henlopen. The British had already captured the Dutch settlements to the north at Manhattan Island and on the Hudson River. Helmanus Wiltbank met with the British, who demanded that the Dutch settlers surrender immediately. Wiltbank quickly agreed and swore allegiance to his new English lords. The homes of the settlers near the site of Zwaanendael were spared, but Plockhoy's utopian community was not. The English commander boasted that he had destroyed the "Colony of Plockhoy to a nail."

After peace was made with England, the Dutch reclaimed their settlements along the South River and Wiltbank again swore allegiance to Holland; but his troubles were far from over. Lord Baltimore of England had been granted a large tract of land north of Virginia in 1632; and the Maryland authorities had always considered the Dutch settlements near Cape Henlopen an intrusion upon their land.

On Christmas Eve, 1673, several dozen travelers arrived in the Dutch village near Cape Henlopen; but they had not come for a friendly holiday visit. The Dutch settlers were alarmed as armed horsemen came thundering into town: Captain Thomas Howell and his troops had been dispatched from Maryland with orders to consolidate Lord Baltimore's claim on the Cape Henlopen area. Lord Baltimore's charter from the king of England had established the boundaries of Maryland to include all of the land between Virginia and the 40th parallel, which was north of Philadelphia. By 1673, the Maryland charter was four decades old, and Lord Baltimore's officials had decided to put an end to the impertinence of the expanding settlement at Cape Henlopen and forcibly assert his claim on the land along the Delaware Bay.

After Howell and his troops entered the Dutch town, he ordered all of the colonists to gather their weapons and turn them over. With the Dutch settlers disarmed, Howell announced that the village would be burned to the ground. The town leaders pleaded with him to leave at least one building to protect the colonists from the approaching winter, but the Maryland leader refused. The order was given, and every structure in the small village was set ablaze.

As the horrified townsfolk and Howell's forces watched the flames reduce the village to ashes, they saw that one solitary barn appeared to resist the flames. For some reason, the fire failed to consume the barn completely. Captain Howell solemnly declared it an act of God; and said he would not meddle with divine intervention. The charred structure was allowed to remain standing. With their Christmas message firmly delivered, Howell led his marauders out of town and rode back to Maryland.

The year after the Dutch settlement was burned by the Maryland raiders, the Treaty of Westminster permanently transferred the Cape Henlopen settlements to England. A few years later, William Penn was given a large tract of land west of the upper reaches of the Delaware River. The Quaker leader fretted that his new colony had limited access to the sea. After lobbying the king, Penn was also given title to the land along the south shore of Delaware Bay, as will be discussed in greater detail below.

In 1682, Penn arrived off Cape Henlopen to take possession of his new colony. He may not have stopped at the entrance to the bay, but his arrival at New Castle on October 28 is well documented. The colonists had arranged an elaborate ceremony to signal a new era for the settlements along the Delaware

River. After he landed, Penn was presented with the keys to the Dutch fort at New Castle. The keys were symbolic of Penn's power to control the colony, showing, as one settler commented, that Penn could lock the gate to the fort "himself alone."

After Penn went through the motions of locking and re-opening the fort's gate, other colonists stepped forward and presented their new proprietor with a divot of earth with a small stick in it. This represented Penn's ownership of the colony's land and all that grew upon it. Finally, the colonists gave the Quaker leader a small container of water from the Delaware River to indicate his ownership of the river. This last gift may have been the most pleasing to Penn, for the Delaware River provided the access to the sea that he had long sought for his larger colony of Pennsylvania. Hermanus Wiltbank was among the colonists who witnessed the arrival of William Penn. The old castaway had journeyed from his home near Cape Henlopen to pledge his undying loyalty to William Penn. For Wiltbank, one more change of lord would have little impact; but it was his last such oath. In January, 1683, the wily Wiltbank suffered a stroke and died a few weeks later.

By the time Wiltbank passed away, the settlements in the shadow of Cape Henlopen had coalesced into the town of Lewes. Many of the townsmen had grown familiar with the shoals and shallows in Delaware Bay, and they found ready work as pilots on vessels heading for Philadelphia.

At about this time, an old blind man and his wife arrived in Germantown, Pennsylvania. An observer commented, "His miserable condition awakened the tender sympathies of the Mennonites there. They gave him the citizenship free of charge. They set apart for him...a little house and to make a garden which should be his, so long he and his wife should live." The old man was Peter Cornelius Plockhoy, the visionary who had built the dream of an egalitarian settlement in the shadow of Cape Henlopen.

PIRATES ALONG THE COAST

After William Penn arrived in America, his holdings south of Pennsylvania became known as the Three Lower Counties on the Delaware, and they were given English names: New Castle, Kent and Sussex. The Delaware counties would play second fiddle to the Quaker leader's Pennsylvania colony; but the new arrangement gave the settlements some stability. Yet along the coast,

Sussex County still had to fend off Maryland's attempts to claim part of its territory; and while the colonial leaders were safe in Philadelphia, the people of Lewes had to be always alert to dangers from the sea.

On August 27, 1698, two dark ships flying the black flag of pirates sailed into Delaware Bay. After they dropped anchor in the calm waters behind the Cape, several dozen armed men crowded into small boats and rowed ashore. The cutthroats quickly made prisoners of eleven town leaders. The hostages were hustled back to the ships, and the pirates informed the townsfolk that if they gave them any trouble, their leaders would suffer the consequences.

During the next two days, the pirates ransacked Lewes. They broke into every house and took everything, committing "Great spoil, breaking open doors and chests, and taking away all money...to be found, as also all manner of goods...worth anything together with rugs, blankettings and all other bed covering. Leaving scarce anything in ye place to cover or wear."

After loading up their two ships, the pirates released the hostages and sailed away. The people of Lewes made frantic appeals to the colonial authorities to fortify their town against such raids; but William Penn and the other leaders of the colony were slow to respond. Many thought it was the pacifist beliefs of the colonial authorities that made them reluctant to create a military force to protect Lewes. However, it may be that some of the leaders of colonial Delaware thought that certain people of Lewes were in league with the pirates, and that the town had received just punishment for its complicity with the cutthroats.

Shortly after the raid in Lewes, Penn ordered three Lewes men arrested. George Thompson, Peter Lewis and William Orr were suspected of nefarious activities, and of dealing with pirates. After posting bail, the three men were released; and three months later Captain William Kidd arrived at Lewes with a ship full of booty. Unlike most pirates, who were social misfits who degenerated into a life of crime at sea, William Kidd was from a respectable New York family. Kidd was a successful merchant captain with a reputation for honesty and courage. Kidd's wife, who was the daughter of a New York shipping magnate, was young, beautiful and wealthy. William Kidd seemed to have everything a man could desire; but he was consumed with a passion to become a captain in the British Royal Navy.

Kidd's desire to receive a commission in the King's navy came at a time when such appointments were reserved for men of the upper class. Kidd came from an honorable family, but he was not a member of the privileged class. Undaunted, Kidd went to England in pursuit of a naval commission. He failed in that quest, but he met several politicians who outfitted him with an armed vessel to suppress the pirates who sailed the Indian Ocean.

At that time, the physical differences between a warship and a merchant ship were relatively few. An owner of a merchant ship could convert his vessel into a "privateer" by cutting gunports in the ship's bulwarks, installing a few cannon, and enlisting a crew. With the proper papers from the government, the "privateer" could sail off in hunt of enemy vessels. The crews of privateers were compensated by the sale of the ships and cargoes they captured, and the captain received the greatest share. The distinction between a legal privateer and an outlaw pirate was sometimes difficult to discern.

After a long cruise in the Indian Ocean, Kidd returned to American waters. When Captain Kidd arrived in Lewes, he was greeted by Thompson, Lewis and Orr and other residents who rowed out to his ship. The pirate captain showed the delegation from Lewes the calico, silk, muslin, sugar and other loot that he had captured. The wide-eyed men from Delaware estimated the ship held over 30 tons of gold. They also heard that each of the 130 men aboard Kidd's ship would receive the equivalent of 4,000 English pounds as his share of the loot. Before they left, Kidd sold some of the goods to the Delaware men, who quickly ferried it ashore. Several other small boats also made a mysterious trips to the sands of Cape Henlopen.

When William Penn learned of Captain Kidd's friendly reception in Lewes, he was livid. On February 2, 1700, he sent orders to the sheriff of Sussex County to arrest the men who had gone aboard Kidd's ship. Some of them were arrested immediately; but a few made their way to Accomac County, Virginia. There, they indiscreetly boasted that they had been aboard Kidd's ship; eventually, all of the men were arrested and taken to Philadelphia.

Penn demanded to know what they had been doing aboard Kidd's ship. How could they have dealings with a pirate when Lewes had just been plundered by buccaneers the year before? How could the men from Lewes ignore the recent proclamation that branded Kidd a pirate? Thompson, Lewis and Orr denied any knowledge about Kidd being a pirate. The three maintained that they had gone aboard the ship with honest attentions, simply seeking to buy goods from a passing merchant ship. None of the goods had been given to them by Kidd.

Penn was not convinced of their innocence, but he had little evidence to disprove their story. The three agreed to surrender all of the goods that they had bought from Kidd. In addition, they said they would "Give good security to behave well." The men also agreed to remain in the area so that they would be available should any other action be taken against them. When Penn finally agreed to release them, he enjoined them to move to an inland area: "It is true they are poor and married men, have children, but such men must not be endured to live near ye sea-cost nor trade, least they become receptacles and brokers for younger pirates."

Following his brief stay at Lewes, Kidd continued northward until he was apprehended by the British. Kidd was arrested and taken to England, where he was tried and convicted of piracy. While he waited for his sentence to be carried out, Kidd wrote a desperate letter to the House of Commons. Kidd's proposal was simple. In return for his life, he would reveal the location of his loot: "I have buried goods and treasure to the value of 100,000 pounds and will lead ye to it if pardoned."

The House of Commons rejected Kidd's bargain to trade the location of his treasure for his life. On May 23, 1701, William Kidd was hanged as a pirate. He died without explaining what he was doing in Lewes, or why the small boats had made so many mysterious trips between his ship and the sands of Cape Henlopen. Captain Kidd's haunting words, "I have buried goods and treasure," still inspire beachcombers who maintain a watchful eye as they walk among the dunes of Cape Henlopen.

WILLIAM PENN, PIRATE

Captain Kidd was not the last pirate to visit Lewes. The precarious position of the town became obvious again during King George's War, the third of many Anglo-French colonial conflicts in North America. On July 12, 1747, a band of marauders landed north of Lewes near Bombay Hook, and they looted several houses. As they sailed down the bay past Lewes, the buccaneers seized a ship off Cape Henlopen. In September, 1747, two French privateers entered Delaware Bay and took two ships before sailing away. These attacks so alarmed the citizens of Lewes that all free men were ordered to be armed with a fully operational musket and a dozen rounds of ammunition. In addition, patrols were established at the mouth of Delaware Bay to detect the approach of enemy warships. Shortly after these patrols were established, peace was declared. The threat of seaborne attacks may have come to an end, but the legacy of William Penn's buccaneering career would soon leave its mark on the Delaware coast.

During the colonial period, European kings granted colonists large tracts of territory that were often based on wildly inaccurate maps. When Giovanni da Verrazano explored the mid-Atlantic coast in 1524, he sailed along the Outer Banks of North Carolina, but failed to see the mainland beyond the barrier island. Verrazano reported that North America was a narrow isthmus; and for years, some European mapmakers incorporated this erroneous information into their charts. In addition, kings often made overlapping land grants. The first colonial settlements were so small and so scattered that the conflicting land grants did not seem to matter; but as more colonies were established, the inconsistent boundaries led to numerous disputes.

When the King of England granted Maryland to Lord Baltimore in 1632, the colony was bounded on the north by the 40th parallel of latitude, as noted earlier. A half-century later, William Penn received Pennsylvania, whose southern boundary was to be the 40th parallel. This left Pennsylvania nearly land-locked, and William Penn was determined to have unfettered access to the ocean.

In 1682, Penn acquired the southern shore of the Delaware Bay. The Quaker leader's new grant was to be bounded on the south by "A circle of twelve miles drawn about New Castle to the beginning of the 40th degree of latitude." Was the twelve miles a measure of the circle's circumference, diameter or radius? William Penn used the ambiguity to snatch additional land from Maryland. On December 13, Penn met with George Calvert (the third Lord Baltimore) to discuss the borders of their colonies. A surviving transcript of the meeting suggests that negotiations became heated. Penn hammered away at his contention that the 40th parallel was about 25 miles farther south than most people accepted. If that were so, then a sliver of Maryland including the head of the Chesapeake Bay and the mouth of the Susquehanna River belonged to Penn. As the arguments went on, Penn declared, "As for the land in dispute, I value it not, but barely for an inlet for conveniency of my province." Lord Baltimore smugly replied, "It is not to deprive Mr. Penn of an inlet to his province, but my interests which makes me argue so much."

At one point, Penn cited the reports of sea captains on the latitude of the Delmarva (Delaware, Maryland and Virginia) Peninsula to bolster his moving the 40th parallel to the south. The proprietor of Maryland believed that a large survey instrument was necessary to take the exact measurements needed to determine precise latitude. Lord Baltimore contended that: "The latitude of the capes was taken by a sea quadrant which by no artist will be held exact and certain as an instrument of six, eight or ten foot diameter and with such an instrument I desire to have the degree of forty taken."

Penn sarcastically replied: "I do not apprehend that a sea quadrant can have any prejudice for the Lord Baltimore more for William Penn."

After this exchange, the two leaders grudgingly agreed to work for an amicable settlement of the dispute. The problem, however, continued to fester; and in 1732, Charles Calvert (the fifth Lord Baltimore) met with the sons of William Penn to negotiate a settlement of the southern border of Sussex County. By this time, all parties agreed that Cape Henlopen marked the southern limit of Delaware. At the meeting, a map was produced that indicated Cape Henlopen in the vicinity of Fenwick Island; and Charles Calvert agreed to a boundary based on this map. When he discovered his error, Lord Baltimore complained long and loudly; but the courts ruled that he must abide by the agreement with the Penns.

On December 20, 1750, a group of six men assembled at Fenwick Island to survey the southern border of Sussex County. Ryves Holt of Lewes headed the Delaware delegation that included two surveyors, William Parsons and John Watson. Colonel Robert Henry Jenkins led the Maryland team, which included the surveyors John Emory and Thomas Jones. The surveyors laid out a line from the Atlantic Ocean to the Chesapeake Bay. The midpoint of this trans-peninsular line marked the western limit of Sussex County. To mark the beginning of the boundary, a stone incised with the coat of arms of the Penns on the north face and with that of the Calverts on the south face was erected about a quarter of a mile from the surf.

Winter weather forced the survey team to suspend their work for several months; but on June 15, 1751, they reached the shore of Chesapeake Bay. The line that forms the southern boundary of Sussex County had been accurately surveyed and marked with a wooden post every mile and a stone every five miles. While the trans-peninsular line was being determined, Charles Calvert died, and all surveyor work was suspended.

The death of Lord Baltimore led to a delay that lasted over a decade. In 1764, Charles Mason and Jeremiah Dixon were hired to finish marking the border between the colonies of the Penns and Calverts. Mason and Dixon accepted the trans-peninsular line of the earlier survey team. The two new surveyors began at the midpoint of the trans-peninsular line and worked northward to lay out the western border of Sussex County. Eventually, Mason and Dixon would survey all of the western border of Delaware and most of the boundary between Maryland and Pennsylvania; but they had little to do with the work at

Fenwick Island. The small stone that sits in the shade of the Fenwick Island Lighthouse marks the line established by the surveyors Parsons, Watson, Emory and Jones, whose fame pales against that of Mason and Dixon. The faded stone marker also stands as a tribute to the tenacity of William Penn and his sons, who were able to pirate two dozen miles of oceanfront real estate from Lord Baltimore.

A Light on the Coast

When Verrazano made his voyage along the Delaware coast, he had good reason to stay far from the beach. Coastal waters are rife with shoals and shallows, and a mariner who is unfamiliar with the changing depth of water risks disaster. Over the years, the people of Lewes became familiar with the shifting sandbars that lay beneath the surface of the bay. Ships entering the Delaware Bay stopped at Lewes to take on one of the town's residents to pilot the ship to New Castle, Wilmington and Philadelphia. The pilots were often leaders of the town, and as many of them established their homes west of Lewes, it became known as "Pilottown." *part of Lewes*

The pilots of Lewes could guide ships through the shallows of Delaware Bay, but many captains had difficulty navigating past the round hump of Cape Henlopen. Early in the 18th century, a rudimentary light was erected at the Cape. Few details have survived about this early beacon, but apparently it was little more than an open fire on some sort of raised platform.

The first light on Cape Henlopen proved unsatisfactory. In 1762, an advertisement appeared in the Philadelphia newspapers announcing "A lottery for raising 3,000 pounds to be applied to the erection of a lighthouse on Cape Henlopen." Shortly afterwards, ships with loads of ashlar granite stones began leaving Wilmington for the short voyage down Delaware Bay to Cape Henlopen. By 1767, masons had used these stones to erect the distinctive eight-sided lighthouse on Cape Henlopen.

The Cape Henlopen Lighthouse was built on the high dune line that bordered the Delaware beach. At that time, the dunes of the cape formed a lofty ridge that rose 70 feet above the surf. A covering of pine trees and coarse grasses capped the sandy bluff that stretched for nearly two miles along the cape. The high ground lifted the beacon atop the 69-foot tower to more than a hundred feet above the surface of the Atlantic Ocean. An 18th-century observer declared: "It is a handsome stone structure in the form of an octagon and 115 feet high and stands upon ground elevated nearly the same height above the level of the sea. The lantern is between 7 and 8 feet square, lighted with 8 lamps; around the lantern, at a little distance, is a strong wire network in order to prevent birds from breaking the glass at night."

The wisdom of the wire grill became evident shortly after the lighthouse was completed. On one morning alone, over 100 birds were found in and around the tower. An avian encounter with a lighthouse was usually fatal for the bird, and often for the beacon's lamp as well. When this lighthouse was constructed, it was all likelihood intended to be lit by a whale-oil lamp. This was an improvement over the tallow candles or "fire balls of pitch and ocum" that some European lighthouses used; but the open flame of the oil lamp could be hazardous if it were hit by a large bird. Once, during the lighthouse's early years, a duck was found dead in the tower's lantern. Although the incident resulted only in one cooked duck, the collision could have extinguished the tower's light at a critical time for an approaching ship. The impact of the duck also could have spilled flaming oil from the lantern and damaged the tower. Nevertheless, by the end of the 18th century, local residents (human and avian) had come to accept the Cape Henlopen lighthouse as a lasting landmark on the Delaware coast.

CHAPTER 2. PATRIOTS AND TORIES

AN HONEST, BOLD MAN

The beacon of the Cape Henlopen Lighthouse was not yet lit when John Dagworthy first confronted George Washington. At the beginning of the French and Indian War, Maryland's governor, Horatio Sharpe, had dispatched Dagworthy to Fort Cumberland, which guarded Maryland's western frontier. At that time, Dagworthy's career as a colonial leader was already several decades old. In 1732, a report to the Duke of New Castle stated: "John Dagworthy, he is an honest, bold man, well affected to the government; is of the church of England; a thriving man and present high sheriff of the county in which he resides."

On the other hand, in 1755, the 23-year-old George Washington's reputation as a military leader was marked with a heavy-handed blunder, a hasty retreat, and the surrender of his entire force. In 1754, Washington had led an expedition of Virginians over the mountains to investigate what the French were doing at Fort Duquesne at the forks of the Ohio River. Before he reached the fort, Washington stumbled onto a detachment of French soldiers. After a brief action, the Virginians beat a hasty retreat to Fort Necessity, where they were surrounded and captured. Less than a year later, Washington was part of the British army under General Edward Braddock that attempted to drive the French from Fort Duquesne. Braddock's force was surprised, ambushed, and nearly annihilated. Washington had the dubious distinction of leading the survivors back to Virginia.

Several months after the Braddock disaster, Washington led a force of 400 Virginians back into the mountains. When he arrived at Fort Cumberland, Washington announced that he outranked Dagworthy, and Washington demanded that he be given control of the fort. The experienced Dagworthy, who held a commission from Maryland's Governor Sharpe and also held a royal commission, refused to comply. The indignant Washington angrily wrote to the governor of Virginia: "I am determined to resign the commission you were so pleased to offer me...rather than submit to the command of a person who has no such superlative merits as to balance the inequity of rank."

Washington's extensive political connections enabled him to win command of the forces while he was at Fort Cumberland; but after he left, command of the garrison reverted to Dagworthy, who continued to monitor the movements of the French and their Native American allies. After one of Dagworthy's reports reached Governor Sharpe, the Maryland governor wrote to the governor of Pennsylvania to warn him of the deteriorating conditions on the frontier: "Within a few days I have received several letters by express from Captain Dagworthy, who commands the garrison consisting of 137 men at Fort Cumberland, and from some other people advising me that the Indians have since the first instant cut off a great many families who lived near Fort Cumberland and on both sides of the Potomac some miles eastward of the fort. It is supposed that near 100 persons have been murdered or carried away prisoners by these barbarians, who have burned the houses and ravaged all the plantations in that part of the country."

Following the French and Indian war, both Washington and Dagworthy left the military. Washington returned to his plantation at Mount Vernon, and Dagworthy retired to his extensive estate at the head of Pepper's Creek in Sussex County. Dagworthy had been given several thousand acres of land when it was claimed by Maryland, and his holdings were later confirmed by the Delaware colonial authorities. Dagworthy's estate bordered the Great Swamp, a large area of over 50,000 acres that straddled the Maryland-Delaware border. For both Washington at Mount Vernon, and Dagworthy in Sussex County, the American Revolution loomed ahead.

OUR NATURAL RIGHTS AND LIBERTIES

On October 5, 1764, the dull rumble of distant drums and the low peal of church bells signaled to John Hughes that the moment he feared had come. Hughes had the questionable honor of serving as the colonial official overseeing the distribution of tax stamps for the recently enacted Stamp Act. Because Delaware was still under the control of the Penn family, Hughes was appointed to distribute the stamps for both Pennsylvania and the Three Lower Counties on the Delaware.

The drumbeats and bells heard by Hughes summoned the colonists who opposed the new tax to assemble. The colonists intended to dissuade Hughes from distributing the stamps by tearing his house down. Hughes had already written to his friend Benjamin Franklin: "It seems to me that a sort of frenzy or madness has got such hold of the people of all ranks, that I fancy some lives will be lost before the fire is put out."

Along the Delaware coast, most residents had been outraged when Parliament passed the Stamp Act in 1765. Several Lewes residents organized a local chapter of the Sons of Liberty, which led the resistance to the Stamp Act. At a meeting in Lewes, the Stamp Act was condemned as "Unconstitutional, destructive of our natural rights and liberties."

The Sons of Liberty were enraged that the British Parliament would attempt to tax the American colonists directly. The British had levied numerous custom duties that were paid indirectly through higher prices, but Parliament had never passed a direct tax on the American colonists. The Stamp Act called for a tax on a large number of items such as newspapers, playing cards, and legal documents. Most of the taxed goods were paper products, and a stamp was to be placed on each item to indicate that the tax had been paid.

When news of the new tax reached Lewes, some of the colonists vented their anger by tarring and feathering the tax officials who attempted to collect the odious levy. Others refused to buy any products that had the hated stamp attached. Still others called for a general meeting of delegates from the colonies to send a protest to the English government.

In the fall of 1765, these delegates met in New York City, in what became know as the Stamp Act Congress. Simon Kollock was selected to represent Sussex County, but there is little evidence of his participation at the meeting. He may have quietly held his counsel, but some historians have suggested that he did not even attend the meeting. On the other had, Caesar Rodney, who represented Kent County, was a prominent member of the Stamp Act Congress.

Although the congress had convened to protest the new tax, the delegates soon diverted their attention to other issues. Instead of drawing up a petition of protest to be sent to the king, the Stamp Act Congress held long, theoretical debates on the nature of government and the rights of individuals. At times, Caesar Rodney despaired that the petition to the king might never be completed. Rodney wrote to his brother, Thomas, "You, and many others are surprised, perhaps, to think we should sit so long, when the business of our meeting seemed only to petition the king."

Once the delegates had decided the philosophical basis for their protest, they finally hammered out a petition. In Rodney's words, the delegates, "After arguing and debating two weeks on liberty, privileges, prerogatives, etc." finally came to agreement on the basis and the substance of their grievances with the king. According to Rodney, the writing of the resolution was "one of the most difficult tasks I ever yet saw undertaken." The work at the Stamp Act Congress may have been difficult, but the people of Lewes were pleased with the results. When they received a copy of the petition, they held a rally against the tax. At this demonstration, the Sons of Liberty and others from coastal Sussex County fired cannons, shouted hurrahs, and drank toasts to King George and liberty.

The colonial protesters then went to the courthouse in Lewes, where the petition of protests issued by the Stamp Act congress was read aloud. This demonstration intimidated the local government officials, and they agreed not to issue the hated stamps in coastal Delaware. Similar protests throughout the American colonies were so effective that Parliament agreed to rescind the tax. For several years, the Sons of Liberty in Lewes commemorated the repeal of the tax in a celebration that they dubbed "Liberty Day."

The fire that had been ignited during the Stamp Act crisis did not go out. A decade after the repeal of the Stamp Act, Delaware colonists were still determined to be free of laws that were "unconstitutional, destructive of our natural rights and liberties." The breach between the American colonists and the British had never healed, and in April, 1775, armed conflict had begun in Massachusetts.

"THAT SOUNDS LIKE A DEATH WARRANT!"

Loyalist[4]

In Sussex County, there were those who supported the war against the motherland, Great Britain (they are now known as patriots); but there were also a significant number who were appalled at the usurpation of power by the upstart colonists through the Continental Congress (most of them were Tories), and they opposed the revolution. In September, 1775, a Sussex County Tory (who was identified only by the initials "J. C.") loudly denounced the actions of Congress. In a letter to Dr. James Tilton, Samuel McMasters described what happened: "J.C., some time in the month of September, came to Lewes, and in an open, profane manner, cursed the honorable continental congress, and all those that would not curse it." The Tory's denunciation of the Revolutionary government was so vehement that he was arrested for treason. According to McMasters, "For the congress acting suitable to the power delegated, that body ought to be esteemed as king, and therefore whatever is said against the body should be deemed treason."

J. C. was arraigned before the committee of patriots who were in control of the Cape Henlopen area. There was ample testimony that J. C. had cursed the Continental Congress; and it appears that he did not deny the allegation. As the evidence against J. C. mounted, an observer in the courtroom called out: "That sounds like a death warrant!" The Sussex County Tory snapped back: "Put it in execution!"

McMasters reported what happened next: "However, upon mature consideration of the committee, some of which was no better than C., a sort of recantation was drawn up and signed by C., but by no means satisfactory to the people. Upon which, some concluded we should proceed in the new mode of making converts, by bestowing upon C. a coat of tar and feathers; but after some hesitation, and much persuasion, were prevented from using any violent measures."

Although some of the firebrands believed that J. C. was guilty of treason, the patriot court allowed the Tory to go free. When he left the courtroom, J. C. was loudly taunted, and a couple of boys tossed eggs at him; but otherwise, the Loyalist was unharmed.

HENRY FISHER DEFENDS THE DELAWARE COAST

On March 25, 1776, Henry Fisher's greatest fear was realized: a British warship rounded Cape Henlopen, and it set a course for Lewes Harbor. Fisher was a Delaware Bay pilot who had been instructed by the revolutionary government in Philadelphia to report on "Every British man-of-war or armed vessel that may arrive at the Capes of Delaware." During the first year of the American Revolution, the British had concentrated their efforts in New England. Now the war was spreading, and the British Royal Navy was determined to secure control of Delaware Bay. Fisher knew that the locals had few ships with which to oppose the powerful British Royal Navy, whom he contemptuously referred to as "pirates." Fisher also realized that some of his neighbors were British sympathizers.

When Henry Fisher first received his instructions to report the approach of any British ship, he set up certain signals and had all of the buoys that marked the shoals taken up, to deter the British from sailing past Lewes and up the bay, with its treacherous shallows and shoals. When a British ship entered the mouth of the bay, lanterns at the Cape Henlopen Lighthouse were to be lit and alarm guns fired. Finally, Fisher also set up a series of stages so that reports on the movements of the enemy warships could be relayed quickly up the coast to the Pennsylvania Committee of Safety in Philadelphia.

1774

For several months after these preparations were made, there was little activity at the mouth of the Delaware. Then in February, 1776, Fisher and the other Lewes residents were surprised by the arrival of a small squadron of eight American warships under the command of Commodore Esek Hopkins that dropped anchor near Cape Henlopen. Although it was in the middle of the winter, those on board were delighted with the warm weather. One of the officers wrote: "Tis now twelve o'clock & we are now laying at anchor at Old Keel Road at Cape Henlopen waiting for wind. Tis quite calm and like a summer's day."

While the colonial ships were anchored there, Commodore Hopkins took time to issue signals to the other ships, which he called the "First Continental Fleet." They soon disappeared over the horizon, sailing for the Bahamas, where they hoped to capture British war materiel.

The American squadron spent only a few days at Cape Henlopen, but their presence boosted the morale of Henry Fisher and other coastal patriots. A month later, patriot fortunes in Lewes began to change. On March 25, a British squadron led by the frigate *Roebuck* under the command of Captain Andrew Snape Hamond rounded Cape Henlopen and dropped anchor in Old Kiln Road.

Although Fisher's elaborate system of signals had been in place for several months, on April 1, 1776, something went wrong. Fisher reported: "The pilot boat stationed near Lewes Creek's mouth did not discover the signal at the Light House, nor see the ship that evening as it was near dark before she came to the pitch of the cape; and when the alarm guns were fired, the people on board the boat, altho' they heard them very plain, imaged, as they said, that we were cleaning the guns with a proof charge."

Fisher quickly scratched out a note which he dispatched to the colonial authorities in Philadelphia: "Gentlemen, This serves to inform you that there is a sloop-of-war coming into our road with a small tender, and as it is now night, I cannot inform you whether they are bound up the bay or not; the wind is now at south, therefore have reason to believe that they will proceed up the bay. We are apprised of the matter and shall do our utmost to prevent their getting any pilot or pilots from this place. Yours in haste, Henry Fisher."

At least the relay stages that Fisher had set up worked well. Although the British captured a boat that they suspected was carrying a message up the bay, one of Fisher's riders reached Philadelphia the next day.

Captain Hamond, aboard the *Roebuck*, knew as well as Fisher the value of a good pilot who could navigate the bay. The morning after he entered Delaware Bay, Hamond spotted what appeared to be a pilot boat near the mouth of Lewes Creek. The British captain ordered one of the *Roebuck's* small boats filled with a detail of armed men, and he dispatched this small vessel after the pilot boat. The British were only a short distance away when the Americans realized that they were in danger. They hastily launched a skiff, and frantically rowed ashore.

Several days later, Fisher sent a more detailed report on the activities of the British:

> Tuesday morning the man-of-war's boat took my pilot boat, the wind being light and northerly and ebb tide — but before they boarded her the hands in the pilot boat left and rowed on shore at the Brood kill in their skiff. The same day the man of war with their tenders and boats took a small sloop then laying the road belonging to Egg Harbour in ballast the people of whom left her first in their boats. They also took two other small sloops from Philadelphia...

The news of the arrival of the British ships caused many of the local patriots to flood into Lewes. Fisher estimated that nearly 1,000 militiamen assembled to defend the Delaware town against the British. Unfortunately, many of these men arrived without weapons. Fisher "prevailed on those who lived at a distance to leave some the best of their arms (for numbers of them want firelocks) which are not to be purchased...How long the ship intends to stay here we cannot learn."

Unable to capture a pilot, Captain Hamond had difficulty avoiding the shallows of Delaware Bay. The *Roebuck* ran aground several times, but each time Hamond was able to free the frigate from the soft sand. Although Hamond was able to capture several small merchant vessels, the Americans quickly learned that they could avoid the British warship by keeping close to shore.

On April 7, Hamond spotted a small schooner commanded by Captain Nehemiah Field of Lewes, as the vessel rounded Cape Henlopen. Captain Field was returning from the West Indies; but he had heard that the *Roebuck* was lurking in Delaware Bay. Field steered his schooner toward shore; Hamond responded by dispatching several small boats after the schooner.

In the meantime, a company of Continental soldiers who were in Lewes began a forced march toward the schooner, which Field had run onto the sandy shore. The race to reach Field's grounded schooner turned deadly when the British boats opened fire on the Delaware troops marching across the open beach. Despite their exposed position, the Delaware troops did not flinch. Their commanding officer reported: "Just before our arrival, the tender gave our guard a broadside with swivels and musquetry, which they returned. On our junction, a constant fire was kept up for some time, till we perceived the distance too great. We then left off firing, and unloaded the schooner, though several hundred shots were fired at us, to prevent it."

Another observer described the action: "A hot fire from both sides ensued, which lasted near two hours, and the tender was finally obliged to sheer off without having effect her purpose, but on the contrary, with the loss of several men, as many were seen to fall."

The quick action by the Delaware troops demonstrated to the British that the patriots of Lewes were not to be taken lightly. In addition, Henry Fisher's efforts to "prevent their getting any pilot or pilots from this place" proved successful. For the rest of the American Revolution, the British would be hampered by the lack of pilots to guide them past the dangerous shoals of Delaware Bay.

ALL'S WELL IN LEWES

Rev War

Young Enoch Anderson stood before John Dagworthy and the Council of Safety that had been convened by the patriot leaders. Following his dispute with George Washington at Fort Cumberland, Dagworthy had retired to his estate at the head of Pepper's Creek near the Great Cypress Swamp. In addition to clearing some of his land for farming, Dagworthy had begun harvesting the cypress trees in the swamp. He had them split into shingles, which were impervious to rot. He sold the shingles throughout the mid-Atlantic region, and it is believed that some of these 18th century slabs still protect many old homes. The centerpiece of his estate was a mansion that was described as "A capacious one-story house upon an eminence at the east of the town near Frankford. The approach was a broad avenue lined with trees. There surrounded by his family and a retinue of slaves he dispensed a liberal hospitality."

When the difficulties between Great Britain and the colonies degenerated into war, Dagworthy again donned the uniform of a solider to serve the American cause. When the fighting began, the British navy blockaded most major American ports. The only way to get munitions into the country was through minor waterways, such as the Indian River Inlet that provided Rehoboth Bay with an outlet to the Atlantic Ocean. The veteran Dagworthy understood that a steady supply of arms and ammunition was vital to the success of the Continental Army, which was under the command of his old rival, George Washington. For many years, Dagworthy and others had used the inlet to ship their farm produce and other items to distant markets. Early in the American Revolution, Dagworthy arranged for wagons to carry munitions across the Delmarva Peninsula and eventually to the colonial forces.

In 1776, General John Dagworthy had received reports that the British had assembled a large force of Tories from Sussex County's interior and that these English sympathizers were determined to capture Lewes. In addition, the *Roebuck* and other British warships continued to hover about Cape Henlopen. The Americans had no officers available to direct the defenses of Lewes. Young Enoch Anderson's commanding officer had recommended him for the position; and Anderson appeared before the Council of Safety and Dagworthy to gain their approval. After Anderson was introduced, Dagworthy remarked, "Why, this is but a beardless boy." Dagworthy then went on to tell Anderson: "You must be well-informed of our dangerous situation. Here are five British men-of-war in the bay right opposite us, — not more than a mile off, — and we are surrounded by

29

about fifteen hundred Tories three miles off, who, we are credibly informed, keep up a regular correspondence with the British fleet in the bay." The general went on to describe how the Tories were "mostly armed with guns, and those that have not guns have pitch-forks and down to clubs." Finally, Dagworthy said that young Anderson was to command the defenses of Lewes. The young man immediately tried to decline the assignment, but Dagworthy and the council refused to reconsider: there was no other officer available. Reluctantly, Anderson went off to assemble his men with Dagworthy's final words ringing in his ears: "Now, young man, a great responsibility is thrown on your shoulders. Be careful, — be vigilant!"

Enoch Anderson had been appointed a lieutenant in the First Delaware regiment in 1775, when he was just 21 years old. For the first year of the war, he had spent much of his time dodging British sympathizers as he traveled between Lewes and Dover. In late 1775, Anderson was given an independent command of thirty men; and he was ordered to guard the coast near Indian River Inlet. Anderson and the patriot authorities believed that this was a dangerous assignment, but the young officer discovered otherwise: "I was now for the first time in my life sent on a command to a post of danger...I had thirty men — all young fellows — with me. We traveled through rich black land and came to the place of our destination and a beautiful spot it was. I made up my quarters at Captain Hazzard's — a militia captain and a Whig. Here then I was placed at the post of danger to guard and defend, &c., but nothing happened and no vessels were driven on shore. Oysters and fish were plenty. I was stationed there for two weeks and then me and my boys returned to Lewis Town."

This foray down the Delaware coast convinced General Dagworthy that Anderson could defend Lewes. Anderson began his defense of the town by ordering all of his troops to be ready to fight on a minute's notice. He then took thirty men and placed them at intervals of a hundred yards around the town. He instructed the sentinels that if nothing unusual was observed, the first sentinel on the right was to call out "All's well!" The next sentinel was to echo the report so that the assuring word would be passed around the perimeter of guards. Anderson carefully ordered the sentinels to repeat this procedure every half hour.

As Anderson later recalled, as soon as he returned to his quarters, things began to go awry: "My boys, my sentinels, instead of crying 'All's well' each half-hour, began to cry it every ten minutes, and at last constantly on, which made a constantly bellowing and a great noise. It was thought in town that the Tories were coming."

With the constant cries of "All's well" echoing over Cape Henlopen, Anderson accompanied a second batch of sentinels to relieve the boisterous guards. "I went out with thirty new men to relieve the former sentinels and again gave each orders to cry 'All's well' every half-hour, but these were worse than the others!"

On the next night, the guards continued the cry of "All's well" and despite Anderson's efforts to quiet them, the constant caterwauling was kept up for nearly a week. The cries were also heard by the Tories, who were preparing to attack Lewes. According to Anderson, "Now, contrary to all expectation, this noise had a good effect. The Tories had conceived we were rejoicing from aid we must have got from above and which had come down the bay to our assistance, so that in a few days they were willing to make peace and to bury the tomahawk."

With the Tory threat gone, young Anderson was able to relinquish his command of Lewes and return to less demanding duties, and he was able to report "All's well," indeed.

THREE TORIES FROM LEWES

William Barry watched incredulously while three men clambered aboard the HMS *Roebuck*. Barry was an American prisoner who had been captured a few weeks earlier, and his detention on the British warship gave him a unique opportunity to observe how some people from Sussex County viewed the American Revolution.

In June, 1776, while the *Roebuck* was anchored near Cape Henlopen, three men from Lewes rowed out to the warship. Later, Barry recalled: "About three weeks after they came to Cape Henlopen, there came three men one night, in a small boat from Lewistown shore, on board said vessel, and staid on board till about ten o'clock at night." After meeting with Captain Snape Hamond of the *Roebuck*, the three visitors returned to Lewes. The next night, the three men returned. When their little boat reached the *Roebuck*, they passed a small bag aboard the British frigate. Barry learned from one of the English sailors that the bag contained letters and other documents.

Barry and the other American prisoners aboard the *Roebuck* were not allowed to speak to the men from Lewes, but he observed that they "were kindly received and entertained by the Captain and officers." Barry learned from the British sailors that the visitors had told Captain Hamond "that they had, or that there were cattle, stock, &c, for them at Indian River." Hamond dispatched one of the small British warships that accompanied the *Roebuck* down the coast to pick up the livestock, but this vessel was intercepted by two American ships and driven off.

After their last visit on the *Roebuck*, the three Tories apparently felt that they might be attacked by the patriots of Lewes. When they left the British warship, they used a small boat to row to the back of the Cape Henlopen lighthouse. As an additional security measure, one of the small British warships accompanied the boat while the men rowed toward shore.

Although Barry did not learn the names of the three Tories from Lewes, he was able to give a rudimentary description of them: "One of the people that came on board, as aforesaid, had a mark like a half-moon on, he thinks, his left cheek, and looked like a cut, a well coloured man; and had on, he thinks, a brown coat, and buckskin or leather breeches, which man he would know again. Another of said men was pale looking, and wore blue clothes, he thinks, but is not certain."

Shortly afterward, Captain Hamond reported to his superiors: "I have the pleasure to inform you that the inhabitants of the two Lower Counties on the Delaware, tired of the Tyranny and oppression of the times have taken up Arms to the number of 3 thousand and declared themselves in favour of Government: Three very sensible Men have been aboard the *Liverpool*, and declared that with a few Regulars to put them in order they would march directly to Philadelphia with 6 or 7 thousand men that they could raise in a week."

While he was held prisoner, Barry was not treated well by the officers of the *Roebuck*: "And all prisoners taken by them are forced to do King's duty, and are not reckoned prisoners of war, but Rebels, and very ill used," and he told the Captain, "a man had better curse father and mother, and be killed at once, than live such a life.'" One night, Barry took advantage of an open gunport and he slipped out into a small boat that was being towed behind the *Roebuck*. He cut the tow rope and drifted in the ocean as the *Roebuck* sailed away. The next morning, Barry reached shore. A short time later, he arrived in New Castle, where he gave a deposition that described his experiences and the collusion between the British and the Sussex County patriots.

THE MIDNIGHT RIDE OF CAESAR RODNEY

Barry's deposition, plus the reports of Henry Fisher and other patriots in southern Delaware, soon reached Philadelphia, where the Continental Congress was preparing to consider the question of independence. An alarmed Thomas McKean wrote to John Hancock: "There are a thousand Tories under arms in Sussex County...they assembled near Cedar Creek about eighteen miles on this side of Lewes, and that their intention was to proceed there and join the British forces from on board some men of war now in the Whore-kill Road."

The three Tories that William Barry saw aboard the *Roebuck* have never been identified; but these forgotten men from Lewes who collaborated with the British threatened to hopelessly deadlock the Delaware delegation to the Continental Congress.

Delaware sent a three-man delegation to the Continental Congress. Thomas McKean, who was born in 1734, near Lancaster, Pennsylvania, was a New Castle lawyer and a strong opponent to the British colonial system. He was a delegate to the 1765 Stamp Act Congress that was the first colonial protest against British taxes. McKean was an early advocate of American independence.

Delegate George Read was born in Cecil County, Maryland, in 1733. After he moved to Delaware, Read served as the attorney general for the three lower counties from 1763 to 1774. Read had a fine legal mind and he opposed many of the British policies, but he was a conservative at heart. In July, 1776, Read let it be known that he was opposed to independence.

The third member of the Delaware delegation was Caesar Rodney. Like McKean, Rodney, who was born near Dover in 1728, had been a member of the Stamp Act Congress. When fighting between the Americans and the British began in earnest, Rodney was actively engaged in quelling Loyalist uprisings in Delaware. In late June, 1776, reports from Henry Fisher and others convinced Rodney to leave the Congress and do his part in southern Delaware.

When the question of independence was raised John Adams and some others were concerned that any vacillation by the Continental Congress would derail the American cause. Without Rodney, the Delaware delegation was hopelessly divided, and unanimous support for independence seemed impossible. Thus, when the debate on the question of independence was nearing a vote, John Adams, who had been shepherding the Declaration through congress, remarked on Rodney's absence. Thomas McKean assured him that he had personally sent a rider to fetch him; nonetheless, Adams saw his hopes of a unanimous declaration fading.

As the debate on the question of independence drew to a close, Rodney had not yet appeared; Adams used every parliamentary ploy he could muster to delay the vote. When his last maneuver was exhausted, the roll call began. As each state called out its vote for independence, Thomas McKean left the room to see if there was any sign of Rodney. McKean paced up and down in front of the state house, but he was still nowhere to be seen.

Pennsylvania cast its vote for independence, and Delaware's turn was next. As McKean turned to go back into the hall, he heard the clatter of hooves. A mud-splattered Caesar Rodney had at last arrived. Rodney, who had ridden hard day and night from Sussex County, muttered to McKean, "Delayed by the storm."

Minutes later, Delaware joined the other colonies and voted in favor of American independence.

WINNING THE REVOLUTION AT LEWES

In January, 1776, Samuel Lockwood of Lewes joined Captain David Hall's Delaware regiment that was assigned to defend Cape Henlopen. Lockwood and the other soldiers were ordered to build a defensive work at the cape. Hall's regiment was also responsible for guarding the lighthouse.

After several months' work, the soldiers had nearly completed a series of gun emplacements that they hoped would dissuade the British from making a direct assault on Lewes. Although the earthworks were not finished, most of Lockwood's regiment were ordered to New York, where they joined George Washington's Continental Army. The Delaware troops would eventually earn a reputation as one of the finest regiments in the American army, but Lockwood's company would not share in that glory. Lockwood's company of less than a hundred men remained in the Cape Henlopen area for the rest of the war.

Although they were short handed, the small group of soldiers set out to complete the earthworks and guard the Cape Henlopen Lighthouse. The troops always had their muskets, cartridge boxes and other equipment close at hand while they were working to construct the earthworks. During 1776, Lewes patriots were in constant danger of attack by those Sussex County residents who sympathized with the British. In addition, a British squadron of warships led by the frigate *Roebuck* menaced the Lewes area from the sea. The soldiers kept an ear cocked for the sound of two cannons fired in quick succession. When Lockwood and the others heard this signal, they would throw down their picks, shovels, and other tools, snatch up their muskets and military equipment, and hurry to Lewes.

By the end of 1776, the Tory threat on land had subsided, but the British warships were becoming more active in the waters off Cape Henlopen. Two row galleys were dispatched from Philadelphia to Lewes to aid in the defense of the mouth of Delaware Bay. The galleys were barge-like vessels that carried a single cannon and a crew of about 20 men. They were most effective in shallow water, where the larger British warships could not venture. In addition, being propelled by oars, they could be maneuvered without regard to the wind. On the other hand, if a British warship were able to get close to one of the row galleys, the cannons would make short work of it.

When the two galleys arrived in Lewes, they carried only half the necessary crew. Lockwood and nineteen other soldiers were assigned to the small boats, and for several weeks they patrolled up and down the shore. One night, toward high tide, Lockwood's galley ran aground on a sandbar near the mouth of Lewes Creek. By dawn, the tide had fallen and the galley was left high and dry.

While Lockwood and the others struggled to get the galley refloated, a British sloop-of-war spotted them. As the warship and several smaller British vessels approached the stranded galley, Lockwood and the other Americans held a quick conference; and they decided not to give up the galley without a fight.

The Americans used oars and other pieces of wood as levers to lift one end of the galley so that they could shove wooden skids under the vessel. Years later, Lockwood recalled: "As soon as we had come to the determination to fight the British vessel, we went to work and prized up our galley and fixed skids under her so as to turn her about with tolerable convenience and in that way bring our gun to bear on her as soon as the enemy came in what they thought a convenient distance of us."

The British warship opened fire but, firing from the deck of a boat on the waves, they had difficulty finding the proper range. The Americans, on the other hand, had only a single cannon but they were able to fire from a stable platform. In addition, the Americans were able to see where their cannon balls landed and reposition the galley accordingly. After the first two or three shots, the American cannon balls began to tear into the sloop and its escort of smaller boats.

After about half an hour's battle, the British had had enough. They withdrew to lick their wounds and patch their hulls; and in the meantime, the rising tide refloated the American galley. Lockwood and the others were able to row safely ashore.

On April 11, 1777, Captain James Anderson guided the supply ship *Morris*, which was loaded with uniforms, arms, and gunpowder from France, toward the entrance to Delaware Bay. Aboard the *Roebuck*, the lookouts spotted the American vessel, and Captain Hamond ordered the British squadron to give chase. The *Morris* attempted to outrun the British warships, but Captain Anderson quickly saw that it was futile. With the enemy warship closing in on him, Anderson ran the *Morris* toward the Cape Henlopen beach. Henry Fisher described what happened next: "Captain Anderson run his Ship on shore about a half mile from the Light House, the two ships continual firing at him, and he return'd the fire for nearly three hours in a most brave & gallant manner — The ships sent three Boats, were beat off by the *Morris*. Captain Anderson, finding he could defend her no longer, he laid a train & blew the ship up, and I am sorry to tell you that so brave a Man has fell in the attempt."

Captain Hamond of the *Roebuck* described the fury of the explosion: "No sooner did she strike the ground than the crew run out to the bowsprit and jumped overboard; when she blew up with a most terrible explosion, forming a column of liquid fire to a great height, and then spread into a black smoke, showering down burnt pieces of wood etc. which covered a space round about for near one half a Mile in the Water..."

After the explosion, the Americans tried to retrieve what was left of the cargo. According to Henry Fisher: "The cargo is part blow on shore, viz, Guns, Cloaths, gun Locks. We have Number of men saving the Cargo." The shattered timbers of the *Morris* were allowed to remain in the sands of Cape Henlopen.

These small engagements were not all. The determined efforts of Henry Fisher and the other patriots who defended the Delaware coast disrupted British strategy at a critical juncture. On July 31, 1777, a powerful British fleet of over 250 ships arrived off Cape Henlopen. Captain Hamond of the *Roebuck* went aboard the flagship, where he met with General William Howe. Howe's army had been based in New York, and it had been part of a grand British strategy to split the colonies in half. Howe was to move up the Hudson River and link up with a force under General John Burgoyne, who was pushing southward from Canada.

The most direct sea route from New York to Philadelphia would have been to sail along the New Jersey coast and turn into Delaware Bay; but when Howe reached Cape Henlopen, Hamond informed the British general that a push up Delaware bay would subject the British fleet to "insult and danger from the enemy's Row Galleys & fire Vessels." With the wind favoring a voyage southward, the British fleet therefore continued down the Delmarva coast to the entrance of Chesapeake Bay.

The British ships sailed northward up the bay to the Head of Elk in Maryland, where Howe's army disembarked, and the British began an overland march to Philadelphia. At the battle of the Brandywine, Howe handily defeated George Washington's army. The British occupied Philadelphia and put the Continental Congress to flight. Howe had apparently won a great victory; but his failure to support Burgoyne and the British strategic plan was costly. Burgoyne and his entire army were captured at Saratoga; and this victory convinced the French to enter the war on the side of the Americans. Although there would be few actions along the Delaware coast and the Revolution would drag on for another five years, the downstream impact of these events was considerable. And in the meantime, troops from Sussex County fought the British on many more distant battlefields.

THE NARROW ESCAPES OF LITTLE JOHN LEARMONTH

No record has been found that indicates how tall John Learmonth was, but the Lewes native was certainly a little man. He is almost always described as "small" or "short." What Learmonth lacked in size, he made up in tenacity. During the American Revolution, the Sussex County officer was often at the head of the Delaware troops, leading them into battle against the British. In nearly every action, Learmonth fought like a giant. On several occasions he was nearly captured; but he used his wits and a little help from his friends to escape.

Learmonth was born in Lewes, and his family owned a significant amount of land in Sussex County. At the beginning of the American Revolution, he and other local patriots enlisted in the Continental Army. In August, 1776, Learmonth first saw action at the battle of Long Island, where he was nearly captured. The Delaware troops were part of a rear guard action that held back the advancing British so that the rest of the American army could escape. When Learmonth and the rest of the Delaware troops were eventually ordered to retreat, their path to safety was blocked by a stream. After the rest of the troops had begun to cross the stream, the diminutive Learmonth plunged into the water. The British were approaching quickly. Several times, Learmonth became mired in the mud. Each time he got stuck, the other Delaware troops gave the plucky little officer a tug and freed him. Learmonth was the last Delaware soldier to reach safety; but he was not concerned about his narrow escape. He immediately directed his troops to open fire on the British. The Delaware troops fought with such ferocity and sustained such heavy casualties that George Washington said to have exclaimed, "Good God! What brave fellows I must this day lose!"

Learmonth also fought at the battles of Brandywine, Germantown, and several others. Once, finding himself on the battlefield with the British fast approaching, he found a hiding spot no one else could use: a dead horse. Having no other cover to choose, he slit open the animal's belly and squeezed himself inside. Amid the carnage on the battlefield, no one spotted him. After the enemy had left, Learmonth emerged from his grotesque hiding place and made his way back to the American forces.

After fighting for several years in the Mid-Atlantic region, Learmonth and the Delaware troops were dispatched to the south. The Delaware Continentals were among the American forces that harassed the British in a series of battles that were noted for the casualties suffered by both sides. Although the British won some of these battles, when a member of Parliament saw the long casualty lists, he commented, "Another such victory would ruin the British Army."

On August 16, 1780, Learmonth stood with the rest of the Lewes company in a field near Camden, South Carolina. To the right of the Delaware troops were the veterans of the Maryland line; but on the left were raw recruits from North Carolina and Virginia. Ahead of the American forces and approaching in good order were the British troops, with muskets loaded and bayonets fixed. As the British line drew near, the North Carolina and Virginia troops broke ranks and ran. With half the army streaming to the rear, Learmonth and the Delaware troops, plus the contingent from Maryland, remained to face the British.

Although he and his men were hopelessly outnumbered, Learmonth was not in a mood to surrender. At times, the Delaware troops halted the British advance by a devastating volley from their muskets. At other times, the little man from Lewes led the Delaware troops in a bayonet charge against the redcoats. Eventually, the numbers were too great, and the Delaware troops were forced back. Some of the men were able to make their way to safety, but Learmonth was surrounded and forced to surrender.

After the Revolution, Learmonth returned to Lewes, where his reputation proceeded him. One day, he saw an old man parading around town blasting away on an ox-horn. The old man challenged anyone who did not like his obnoxious behavior to shoot him. Little John Learmonth heard the old man's challenge and went to fetch his musket. When the old man saw the little veteran, he ran away. Some say the man vaulted several fences in his frantic effort to avoid the tenacious John Learmonth.

JOSEPH VAUGHAN, MAN OF IRON

1752

Joseph Vaughan arrived in Delaware around the middle of the 18th century. At that time, nearly all of the colonists lived close to Delaware Bay. Most of Sussex County was still covered with thick forests; and the settlers shunned the marshy areas of the western reaches of the county.

For many centuries, ferrous material had been precipitating from the water of the Nanticoke and its slow-moving tributaries. The iron-laden matter settled to the bottom of the waterways to form a boggy iron ore. In the 18th century, the Vaughan family believed that Sussex County contained enough bog iron and a ready supply of timber to be exploited; and they decided to establish the Deep Creek Iron Works.

Iron-making was backbreaking business. After the ore was wrestled from the marshy ground and carted to the ironworks, a fire hot enough to melt the ore *Iron making* had to be created. Natural charcoal was the best fuel available and the Vaughans saw that the forests of southern Delaware as a seemingly inexhaustible source supply of timber to make charcoal. The process of turning raw timber into charcoal was nearly as laborious as mining the bog iron. Trees were felled, trimmed of their branches and piled into a conical stack, and covered with a *charcoal* layer of mud. Then the stack was ignited. The wood would burn slowly for several days; and during this time, a collier kept careful watch. If a hot spot burned through the mud covering, the entire stack would go up in a flash and the timber would be reduced to useless ashes. On the other hand, if the fire was not hot enough, too much moisture would remain in the timber; and the charcoal would be useless.

In addition to the technical difficulties of mining bog iron and processing timber into charcoal, the operators of the Deep Creek Iron Works had to contend with the British mercantile system. When the American colonies were established, the British Parliament passed a series of laws that restricted the settlers from producing manufactured goods. Parliament envisioned a system in which the colonies would supply England with raw materials and provide a market for finished products in return. British law restricted the manufacture of nails, hinges, and other iron implements. The Vaughans were only allowed to produce pig iron; they may have skirted the law to produce some finished goods.

In 1775, the outbreak of the American Revolution brought Joseph Vaughan's iron-making efforts to an end. The British Royal Navy controlled the waters around the Delmarva Peninsula. Without access to the water, the Sussex County ironworks were unable to ship their iron to markets. In addition, many of the workers left to enlist in the Continental Army. In 1776, Joseph Vaughan himself received a commission as the captain of the 8th Company of the First Delaware Regiment. Later, he was promoted to Lieutenant Colonel.

For much of the early part of the war, Vaughn and the rest of the Delaware soldiers fought as part of George Washington's Continental Army. In 1780, the Delaware troops were dispatched to the South, where they were part of an army commanded by General Horatio Gates. On August 16, 1780, Vaughan assembled his Delaware troops in a line of battle near Camden, South Carolina. The American forces consisted of several veteran regiments and a large number of local militiamen. Many of the militia had never faced a British bayonet charge. In an era when battles were often decided by bloody hand-to-hand combat, it took enormous courage to stand against an advancing line of British troops with their razor-sharp bayonets poised to be driven through the heart of anyone in their path.

At the battle of Camden, the sight of the British bayonets was too much for the militia. Many fled the battlefield without firing a shot. General Gates was overcome by the precipitous retreat of so many of his troops and he, too, scampered from the battlefield. Although Gates would later claim that he was "swept away" by the retreating troops, he rode one of the fastest horses in the American army, and he did not stop until he was 60 miles away.

With men fleeing like "an undammed torrent," Vaughan and his Delaware troops continued to fire into the British line. The militia ran "raving along the roads and by-paths" to safety, but the Delaware troops remained in place. With few other targets left, the British concentrated their fire on Vaughan and his men. The action of the Delaware troops helped most of the Americans to reach safety; but Vaughan and a number of other soldiers were captured. Camden was a major defeat for the American army; but the battle demonstrated that the Delaware troops and Joseph Vaughan were true men of iron.

DEATH BEFORE CAPTURE

"After several difficulties we arrived at Rehoboth Bay, at the mouth of Indian River, and there to our extreme concern and mortification we were informed that the *Roebuck* had sailed from Delaware bay on the eighth instant, just a week before our arrival." John F. Smyth's disappointment when he arrived on the Delaware coast was heightened when he realized that his difficult journey across Sussex County might end in his capture by American patriots.

John F. Smyth was an American who remained loyal to Great Britain. In January, 1777, after he had been imprisoned by American patriots in Baltimore, Smyth had managed to escape. Smyth and a small group of other loyalists crossed Chesapeake Bay and journeyed across the Delmarva peninsula to Sussex County. Although many residents of Sussex County were American patriots, significant numbers of county residents were loyal to England. Smyth and his companions managed to contact these Delaware loyalists, who guided them to the Delaware coast.

The day after they reached the coast, Smyth and his party were encouraged that they had found rescue when they spotted the small British sloop-of-war, *Falcon*, anchored near Indian River Inlet. One of the loyalists was dispatched to make contact with the British ship. As Smyth later recalled: "But on the day following his Majesty's sloop of war the Falcon having landed some prisoners, and burnt a schooner at the mouth of Indian River, we sent Slater on board her, in a little canoe or punt that could carry but one person, to desire the Captain to send his boat for us." Unfortunately for Smyth, Slater was unable to convince the captain to send a boat ashore. The Falcon sailed away, and the loyalists had to find some other way to escape from Sussex County.

Since many of the locals were dead set against England and would capture the loyalists without hesitation, Smyth and the others could not seek shelter and were forced to stay on the move: "For my own part I went constantly well armed, having procured a firelock and bayonet, a pair of pistols, and sword, with plenty of ammunition made up into cartridges; and I never went to rest without all of these at my side, nor did I ever part with them for a moment."

After two months of hiding from the American patriots, Smyth, who "infinitely preferred death to captivity," was determined to reach one of the British ships that frequently sailed near Lewes: "At night on the twelfth of March, after taking a tender and affectionate farewell of these truly meritorious and inestimable friends, who at every possible risque had rendered us such great and essential services, we set out, in a canoe from the head of Rehoboth Bay, bound for the men of war at the cape."

Smyth had ten companions in his canoe, which "was formed out of the trunk of a single tree hollowed or dug out, and we depended solely upon oars, as these kinds of vessels are at best very dangerous and never carry a sail." The Loyalists rowed through Indian River Inlet into the dark Atlantic. The heavy swells of the open sea soon made most of the men seasick. After several hours, Smyth spotted the beacon of the Cape Henlopen lighthouse: "With amazing fatigue, and very great danger, we at length doubled Cape Henlopen, and rowed all over Whorekill Road, without hearing or seeing any appearance of a ship. The night was very dark, and it was one continued storm of thunder, lighting, wind, and hail, the violence of which forced us to this shore; glad to get to any of it within the Cape for shelter."

At three in the morning, the crowded Loyalist canoe reached land a short distance from an American guard. To avoid detection, Smyth and his party were forced to remain on the beach exposed "to the snow, wind, and rain." Two of the loyalists decided to go into Lewes. They returned with the news that the British ship *Preston* was anchored near Cape Henlopen.

Toward morning, the loyalists again launched their canoe in the hope that they could find a British ship near the entrance to Delaware Bay, but a heavy fog obscured the view. If any ship was there, they could not see it; some of the loyalists wanted to return to land: "They all began to murmur and despond; our hands likewise were so blistered with rowing, that the blood ran down, and we were quite exhausted with cold and fatigue."

Just as they were considering giving up, they heard the sounds of men working aboard a ship. Then they spotted some trash floating in the water. As Smyth and his party tried to see through the fog, the large black shape of a ship appeared before the exhausted men. At first, the Tories were afraid that the vessel might be an American ship, but Smyth spotted the name "Preston" on the ship's stern.

John F. Smyth's long and difficult journey was at last over; but other Tories remained in Sussex County. When these men plotted to overthrow the patriot government, they encountered the harsh tradition of coastal justice.

Sussex Justice

The guilty verdict was delivered and the court announced the awful details of their sentence. For their treason against Delaware, the eight leaders of the Black Camp Rebellion were to be hanged, "By the neck but not until dead, for then your bowels must be taken out and burnt before your face, then your head must be severed from your body, and your body divided into four quarters, these must be at the disposal of the supreme Authority in the State." Right up until 1780, when this sentence was announced, such brutality was an accepted part of the Sussex County justice system.

When the European colonists arrived in coastal Delaware, they brought with them traditions that originated during the Middle Ages and before. Criminal justice was based on the premise that effective punishment had to be immediate, painful, and public. Jails were only for holding people awaiting trial; penitentiaries and long-term incarceration did not become common until the late 19th century.

During colonial times, minor criminals were given public floggings. In 1679, a Delaware woman was sentenced to 21 lashes after she bore three illegitimate children. When this sentence failed to convince her to change her ways, she was given another 31 lashes and banished from Delaware. The whipping post remained a part of the Delaware criminal justice system well into the 20th century.

The public nature of colonial punishment was not confined to the immediate execution of the sentence. After the English gained possession of Delaware in the 17th century, Marcus Jacobson (who was known as Long Finn) was arrested and charged with inciting a rebellion against the English. Jacobson was convicted of spreading rumors that a Swedish naval expedition was about to attack Delaware. For his punishment, Jacobson was whipped, branded with an "R" (for rebel), and sold into slavery in the West Indies.

The scarlet letter worn by Nathaniel Hawthorne's Hester Prynne was a common punishment in Delaware, as well as in New England. In colonial Delaware, some criminals were required to wear cloth letters that were an inch wide and four inches high on their outer garments. Thieves wore a "T" and forgers were required to display an "F."

Another public punishment was the town stocks. At some historic sites, re-created stocks are popular with modern tourists; but a sentence to the stocks was no laughing matter. Not only did those convicted have to bear the insults and abuses of the townsfolk and the weather, but sometimes their ears were nailed to the stocks — or cut off. An early Delaware newspaper commented that after one criminal was released from the stocks, the man had his severed ears sewed back on, but "the right one only appeared to adhere."

During the American Revolution, harsh punishments were routinely handed down on both loyalists and patriots, but the severity of the sentence given to the leaders of the Black Camp Rebellion was unexpected. Although many coastal residents supported the American cause and called for independence, it was not unusual to remain loyal to the King; a significant number of county residents believed it was only right. At the same time, the years of strife had driven some people of Sussex County to seek an end to government of any kind.

The Black Camp Rebellion threatened to erupt into a major uprising in 1780 when some 400 men from Cedar Creek and Slaughter Neck gathered in the swampy area near the center of Sussex County. The men who joined the ranks of the Black Camp Rebellion were motivated by a variety of issues. A contemporary reported that, "Some of these ignorant people were for opposing all law;" others were in favor of re-establishing British royal law. Some were tax rebels who opposed all government taxes. All seemed to believe that most of the people south of Virginia had already submitted to the British army, and the rebels believed "that they should very easily make Sussex County do the same."

When news of the Black Camp Rebellion reached the patriot authorities, the militia from Kent County was dispatched to disperse the rebels. The leaders were captured, convicted of treason and sentenced to be drawn and quartered. Fortunately for the eight condemned men, the American Revolution was also a rebellion against "cruel and unusual punishments." In those days, the trend was away from torture. On November 4, 1780, the Delaware General Assembly pardoned all of the leaders of the Black Camp Rebellion; and the eight men were saved from literally being torn "limb from limb."

Chapter 3. Shipwrecks and Wars

The Wreck of the *Faithful Steward*

[handwritten margin note: voyage ...]

In 1785, the 48 members of the Lee family arrived in Londonderry, Ireland, where they boarded the *Faithful Steward* under the command of Captain Conolly M'Causland. The rigors of even a routine crossing the Atlantic Ocean were well known; and the Lees joined 200 other passengers crammed into the primitive quarters aboard the three-masted sailing ship. The four dozen members of the Lee family probably shared not more than a small cabin or two. Most of the passengers ate, slept, and whiled away the time crowded together in one area below the main deck. Some may have lounged in the hold, where the ship's cargo of new copper coins was stored. During pleasant weather, passengers could get a little fresh air on the top deck and watch the crew work the sails. *[handwritten margin note: ship conditions]*

Close quarters and boredom were the least of the problems for those aboard the *Faithful Steward*. The lack of fresh food and poor food preservation techniques exposed ocean travelers to a diet that could be deadly. In the late 18th century, shipboard fare included salted meat, potatoes, cheese, and dried peas. The salted meat was months old and the diet lacked important nutrients. The damp conditions at sea rotted the potatoes and made the cheese grow moldy. *[handwritten margin note: food ...]* The peas were sometimes so hard that hours of soaking would not soften them. The *Faithful Steward's* passengers may have also eaten ship's "bread" that was more like an oversized cracker, known as "sea biscuit" and later by the descriptive name "hardtack."

Scurvy

Most passengers could tolerate a month or two at sea before the poor diet began to erode their health; but once the decline began, the effects of scurvy were rapid, debilitating, and often fatal. The skin dried, cracked and bled; teeth loosened and fell out. Victims of scurvy became lethargic and they had difficulty seeing. Left untreated, a scurvy-stricken traveler quickly died. In the early 17th century, Thomas West, Lord de la Warr, for whom Samuel Argall had named Delaware, was stricken with scurvy during one voyage to America. When he stopped in the West Indies he enjoyed a diet rich in citrus fruits, and he quickly recovered. West's experience was not unique, and the British Royal Navy ordered its sailors to partake of a daily ration of limes to prevent the disease. The incidence of scurvy among British sailors declined precipitously, and the tars earned the nickname, "Limey."

1785

The use of limes to prevent scurvy was not universal, and it is not known if they were part of the diet aboard the *Faithful Steward*. Captain Conolly M'Causland was an experienced commander; and he may have included limes in the ship's larder. However, he may have been more concerned with the cargo of coins that were intended to help relieve a currency shortage that had plagued America throughout most of the 18th century. The American Revolution had ended three years earlier, and the new coins would play a small role in invigorating American commerce. With the passengers safely aboard, and the coins stored securely in the ship's hold, M'Causland weighed anchor on July 9, 1785.

After eight weeks at sea, land was sighted. A generation earlier, a young Benjamin Franklin had described the thrill of seeing Cape Henlopen after crossing the Atlantic: "After dinner one of our mess went up aloft to look out, and presently pronounced the long wished-for sound, Land! Land! In less than an hour we could decry it from the deck, appearing like tufts of trees. I could not discern it as soon as the rest; my eyes were dimmed with suffusion of two small drops of joy."

Captain M'Causland made landfall somewhere south of Cape Henlopen; and he turned north toward the entrance to Delaware Bay. M'Causland was eager to reach Philadelphia and land his cargo of coins. The Lee family and the passengers yearned to escape the cramped sailing ship; and some of the passengers' eyes may have been "dimmed with suffusion of two small drops of joy."

In the late 18th century, captains navigated the oceans using simple instruments such as compass, quadrants and lead lines that had not changed in centuries. M'Causland had to determine his position without the aid of radar, geopositioning satellites or other electronic equipment. Charts lacked precision and often contained significant errors; sailors had to rely on experience and a little luck.

M'Causland needed to sail the *Faithful Steward* close to shore so that he would be able to spot the Cape Henlopen Lighthouse that marked the southern tip of Delaware Bay. At the same time, he had to stay far enough off the beach to avoid the shallows. Shortly after the ship reached the coast, on September 2, the weather turned bad. When M'Causland encountered shoals near Fenwick Island, he attempted to steer the ship into deeper water; but the rising north-easterly wind drove the ship back toward the beach. With a shudder that sent shivers through everyone aboard, the *Faithful Steward* struck bottom.

The vessel was now in a precarious situation, but Captain M'Causland did not panic. If he could reduce the weight of the ship, its natural buoyancy would lift it from the shoal. M'Causland ordered the mainmast cut and sent over the side. As if they were felling a giant tree, the sailors attacked the mast with axes. Soon the great wooden pole, with all its rigging spars and sails, splashed into the sea. Lighter now, the *Faithful Steward* began to bounce upward. In moments, the *Faithful Steward* rose from the shoal and floated free.

M'Causland knew that he was not far from Lewes, and safety. Making his way slowly with what sails were left, he edged the crippled ship northward along the coast. Just after passing the Indian River Inlet, the *Faithful Steward* ran aground again, and this time it was held fast in the Delaware sands.

As the waves relentlessly pounded the hull, locals began to gather on the beach. During stormy weather, coastal residents kept a sharp eye on the ocean for any sign of a ship in distress. (Ten years earlier, the *Three Brothers* had run aground along this same stretch of Delaware Beach. That ship also carried a cargo of coins that sharp-eyed coastal residents had been able to snatch from the beach.) *Faithful Steward* might prove to be another lucrative wreck; but the sight of the helpless ship crowded with passengers was disturbing. The people on shore could hear cries for help, but there was no way to reach the stranded vessel a hundred yards out in the rough surf. Unable to help, the horrified coastal residents stood on the sand for hours and watched while the waves continued to batter the ship.

After the ship's crew had intentionally jettisoned the mainmast of the *Faithful Steward*, the wind and the seas carried away the two remaining masts. With the ship hard aground, the pounding waves would soon make matchsticks of the vessel's hull. In a desperate attempt to reach shore, the ship's crew worked frantically to launch the ship's boats. There was not room for everyone, but the beach was not far away. Maybe the passengers could be ferried ashore. Unfortunately, they were unable to keep the boats from capsizing. With the boats gone, the people aboard the foundering ship could only hope that the storm would abate.

But it did not, and the *Faithful Steward* began to break apart. The crew and passengers plunged into the water and desperately struggled to reach the beach. Most slid beneath the waves. Only 68 people (including just six members of the Lee family) survived. The copper coins meant to start the new republic settled to the ocean floor with the timbers of the *Faithful Steward*.

THE WRECK OF THE *DE BRAAK*

The tragedy of the *Faithful Steward* resulted from an unfortunate combination of dangerous shoals, rudimentary navigation tools, and relentless onshore wind. Good weather and deep water, however, did not guarantee safety along the Delaware coast.

On May 25, 1798, Andrew Allen left the Lewes pilot boat, *Friendship*, and scrambled up the side of the British brig *De Braak*. Drifting quietly off Cape Henlopen, Allen studied the British vessel's rigging and gauged its draft. As a Delaware Bay pilot, it would be Allen's task to guide the British vessel past the shoals and into the safe waters of Lewes harbor. The *De Braak* was a not a large ship, and on a normal day Allen would have little difficulty negotiating the waters at the mouth of Delaware Bay; but the 16 stubby carronades that lined the two sides of the *De Braak* served as a reminder that the war between England and France meant that there were few normal days along the Delaware coast.

During the last decade of the 18th century, the French Revolution spawned a series of wars that engulfed most European nations; and soon the conflict spread to American waters. England and France were locked in a death struggle, and the two countries sought to strangle each other by attacking merchant ships of neutral countries that they suspected of carrying goods to the enemy. Some American ships were attacked by French privateers as soon as they rounded Cape Henlopen and entered the Atlantic Ocean. By 1798, so many American ships had been captured that the United States had embarked on an undeclared naval war against the French. The British did all they could to keep the former colonies on their side, this time; and the British navy often organized protective convoys for ships sailing along America's Atlantic coast. The *De Braak*, under the command of Captain James Drew, was to be part of such a convoy.

When British captain James Drew guided the *De Braak* to its rendezvous with Andrew Allen's pilot boat, he was in a cheerful mood. Drew was a veteran, but undistinguished, officer when the war between England and France led to an expansion of the British navy. The larger navy needed more captains, and Drew had been given command of the small brig *De Braak* that had been captured from the Dutch in 1795. The *De Braak* had been built fourteen years earlier as a single-masted cutter; but after it was captured by the British, it was fitted with an additional mast and re-rigged as a brig. In addition, the *De Braak* was armed with 12 carronades. These short, squat weapons fired a 24-pound solid shot that, at short range, inflicted a devastating impact against enemy hulls. The carronades added tons of extra weight to the *De Braak*'s top deck. In addition, Captain Drew complained that the refitted brig was overmasted, making it unstable and liable to catch more wind in its sails than the boat could handle. Nonetheless, after the *De Braak*'s conversion had been completed, Drew took command of the vessel, and he set sail for America.

James Drew was born in 1751 in the village of Saltash near the seaport of Plymouth, England. He was the youngest of seven children, and at an early age James decided to seek his fortune at sea. When he was 13, Drew enlisted aboard the 70-gun warship *Burford* as a captain's servant. Aboard the *Burford*, Drew learned the realities of life on a British man-of-war. He discovered the harsh world of long voyages, the cramped life below decks, the constant diet of wretched food, and the harsh and often arbitrary discipline of the officers. Despite the difficulties, Drew began the long climb up the ratings from captain's servant to able-bodied seaman to commissioned officer. At the start of the American Revolution, Drew was a lieutenant assigned to the HMS *Preston*, the 74-gun flagship of Vice Admiral Samuel Graves, commander of the North American Station, which was blockading Boston harbor.

During the Battle of Bunker Hill, Drew was sent ashore to assist the British forces that were assaulting the American lines. After a savage struggle, the British were able to drive the Americans from the hill, but only after sustaining heavy casualties. The Americans had also lost a large number of men, including the respected patriot leader Doctor Joseph Warren. When they retreated, the Americans were forced to abandon many of their wounded, and after the battle, reports of British atrocities began to surface.

A committee led by John Adams investigated the reports of the British treatment of American dead and wounded. According to one account: "Drew went up upon the Hill again, opened the dirt that was thrown over Doctor Warren, spit in his face, jumped on his stomach and cut off his head and committed every act of violence upon his body."

There is no evidence that Drew was punished for these alleged atrocities, and the incident did not retard his advancement in the British Navy. By 1786, Drew commanded the HMS *Powerful*, a new, 74-gun ship-of-the-line; but after two years in this position, he was abruptly transferred to a small sloop. Drew would spend the rest of his naval career in mundane commands. By 1798, when James Drew set sail for America in the *De Braak*, he was a middle-aged captain stuck in a mediocre career.

It is not clear exactly what happened as the *De Braak* crossed the Atlantic, but when Drew arrived along the Delaware coast, he had every reason to celebrate his good fortune. In Dutch, "De Braak" meant "beagle," and on this voyage, the brig had proven to be a good hunting dog. On the way to America, Drew had captured a cargo-laden Spanish ship, the *Don Francisco Xavier*, which reportedly carried a rich cargo. The successful voyage must have been sweet for the veteran of the king's navy. Captured ships and their cargo were considered war booty that would be divided among Drew and the crew of the *De Braak*. As captain, Drew would receive the lion's share. Drew was not only lucky, but he might also be rich enough to buy a title and retire to the leisurely life of an English country squire. Drew's wife was waiting for him in New York, and the British captain was eager to get the *De Braak* and the captured vessel safely into Lewes.

When Andrew Allen climbed on board the *De Braak*, Drew gushed, "I've had good luck;" and suggested that Allen drink a toast to his health. The Lewes pilot, however, was concerned about the clouds that he saw brewing in the southwest. Drew nonetheless went to his cabin for a drink, while Allen began to look after the ship.

The *De Braak's* sails were still set, and Allen knew that a spring storm along the Delaware coast could generate dangerous winds. He ordered the crew to take in the sails. At this point, Captain Drew returned to the deck and countermanded the order, calling for the sails to be reset. He swore at Allen and spat, "You look out for the bottom and I'll look out for the spars."

As Allen had feared, a violent squall soon struck. The winds caught the brig's mainsail and drove the *De Braak* over on its side. As the ship heeled over, the carronades on the high side of the deck began to break loose. Tons of weapons and their carriages rolled to the low side and smashed into the side wall, driving the vessel further over. Water began to flood in through the *De Braak's* gunports and down the hatches. The men struggled to abandon the ship; some sailors were trapped below decks, others were snared by the ship's rigging. A small group of men managed to get into a small boat that was next to the brig, and a few swam clear of the sinking brig. Just a few minutes after the spring squall struck, the *De Braak's* hull disappeared.

After the *De Braak* sank, the surface of the ocean was covered with debris; some sailors managed to improvise rafts. Standing amid the flotsam, the upper ends of the *De Braak's* masts rose silently above the waves. As the survivors from the De Braak struggled to reach the beach, people from on shore hurried to help. Among them was Gilbert McCracken, a Lewes bay pilot. As McCracken ran to the surf, he spotted three men clinging to a chest. When they reached the beach, McCracken helped them to dry land.

The three men were Spanish prisoners who had been captured aboard the *Don Francisco Xavier.* Fortunately, prisoners on naval vessels were seldom confined or put into chains. Most prisoners on ships were allowed to roam free, provided they assisted in the working of the vessel and pledged not to attempt an escape. These three prisoners had ridden ashore on a sea chest owned by Captain James Drew. McCracken led them across the sand to his home. Apparently, as they hiked across the dunes to Lewes, the sailors carried the chest that had saved them.

That night, the Delaware pilot dined with the three survivors. As they ate, they told McCracken of the rich cargo that the *De Braak* had taken to the bottom of the ocean. This conversation soon became well-known in Lewes. As it was told and retold, fabulous details were added. Over a century later, it was reported that: "By the glimmer of a tallow candle, with the gale still raging without, the Spaniard told of a fortune in coins and gold bullion about the sloop. It was the booty from two captured Spanish ships home-bound from South America. The man had held some gold bars in his own hands."

While the three lucky Spaniards were regaling McCracken with tales of treasures, other survivors were taken to Lewes. More than half of those aboard the *De Braak* were lost in the disaster. Pilot Andrew Allen suffered a broken leg in the sudden lurching of the British brig, but he managed to reach shore. Captain James Drew did not. His body was found in the surf a few days later. Drew was buried in a vault under St. Peter's Church at Second and Market Streets near the center of Lewes. Many years later, a monument was erected in the churchyard by

Drew's widow. It bears the inscription: "He was beloved for his virtues and admired for his bravery."

Seven years after the disaster, Gilbert McCracken and his 14-year-old son, Henry, went for a walk on the Delaware Beach. McCracken had something very important to show his son. In the years after the *De Braak* sank, many residents of Lewes speculated on the amount of gold, silver and other treasure aboard the ship. Some whispered that the Spanish sailors whom McCracken had rescued had given the Lewes pilot detailed information about the valuable cargo. If the *De Braak* carried such wealth, it is not surprising that McCracken wanted to keep track of the exact location of the sunken ship; but there was no immediate need to mark where the *De Braak* had gone down. For a few years after the brig had settled on the ocean floor, its upper rigging extended above the waves. Shortly after the disaster, a British salvage team had arrived at Cape Henlopen and they had no difficulty locating the ship as they attempted to remove valuables from the sunken vessel.

In 1805, when Gilbert McCracken and his son Henry trudged across the soft sands of Cape Henlopen, the masts of the *De Braak* were no longer visible. As he made his way across the dunes, Gilbert kept his eyes on the Cape Henlopen lighthouse. Finally, the pilot reached a point on the sand that gave him a clear view of the ocean just south of the cape. When he was satisfied that the location was right, Gilbert indicated to his attentive son the exact spot where the De Braak had sunk seven years earlier. As recounted by Donald Shomette in *The Hunt for HMS De Braak, Legend and Legacy*, McCracken told his son that the *De Braak* slipped beneath the wave at a point "From the Cape Henlopen Lighthouse, East Northeast by North one half East, a mile and half to sea."

After the bearings were scratched out on a piece of paper, the McCrackens went home where they carefully slipped the note into the family bible. For many years, McCracken's possession of Caption Drew's sea chest and the bearings in the family Bible caused many to wonder how much treasure lay just off the Delaware coast.

Neither Gilbert nor Henry McCracken recovered any treasure from the *De Braak*. Henry followed in his father's footsteps and became a Delaware Bay pilot. His devotion to the sea was such that, before he died, Henry requested that an anchor be buried with him. Henry McCracken was laid to rest in St. Peter's churchyard where the iron fluke of an anchor protrudes above the ground over his grave. A short distance away stands the stone pillar that marks the grave of Captain Drew.

Gilbert McCracken's rescue of the three Spanish sailors and their tales of golden treasure lured fortune hunters to Cape Henlopen for over a century and a half. Unfortunately, the shifting Delaware shoreline rendered McCracken's notations nearly useless. After many vain attempts to locate the remains of the British brig, the timbers of the *De Braak* were finally recovered in 1986. Despite a diligent search, the salvagers did not find any gold or silver; but thousands of bottles, barrel staves, and other everyday objects were recovered. A study of these artifacts indicates that life in the Royal Navy may not have been as bleak as once thought. The wreck of the *De Braak* contained a large number of ceramic cups, tea bowls, and saucers that were so fine that archaeologists at first assumed that they belonged to the officers. However, since no common tin or wooden mugs were recovered, the suggestion has been raised that the crew of the brig used the fine dishes as well — but, despite the failure to recover drinking mugs associated with the average sailor, it is difficult to accept the notion that the hardened British tars aboard the *De Braak* sipped grog from a delicate china cup.

In addition to the ceramics, many glass bottles were found. British warships were usually well-stocked with wine, port, sherry, brandy, beer and ale. More surprising was the discovery of a wine bottle embossed with the words "Marine Mess" on a glass seal. The *De Braak* was a small ship that contained no Marine officers, but there was a contingent of fourteen enlisted men aboard the ship. This bottle is the only one of its kind, and it has added to the understanding of the sharp distinctions among naval personnel at that time. Numerous glasses, tumblers, and decanters were also recovered with the timbers of the *De Braak;* they were used by the entire crew and not just the officers. One of the containers was a cylinder-shaped bottle marked "KETCHUP." The recipes for ketchup used by British sailors in 1798 were much different from the tomato-based sauce that is popular today. Some seamen used a condiment that contained mushrooms, spices, and beer.

The discovery of the ceramics and glassware on the *De Braak* softens the picture of shipboard life in the 18th century. Did the average British seaman dine in style, eating off ceramic plates, drinking beer out of delicate cups, and using "ketchup" on his salt pork?

War Returns to the Cape

On July 7, 1798, Stephen Decatur, Sr. sailed down the bay coast of Sussex County toward Cape Henlopen. Decatur may have felt a touch of nostalgia as he guided the 20-gun warship *Delaware* past Lewes and into the Atlantic. Twenty years earlier, during the Revolution, the sea captain had been living in Philadelphia and the Decatur family had to flee as the British captured the city.

We do not know what route the Decaturs took from Philadelphia, but a British squadron led by the frigate *Roebuck* had a firm grip on the mouth of the Delaware Bay and to escape by sea would have been exceptionally dangerous. Decatur and his wife probably traveled overland down the length of Delaware and through Sussex County to Maryland, where their son Stephen, Jr. was born.

By 1798, Stephen, Jr. was a midshipman in the new United States Navy; and his father was a veteran captain in command of the warship *Delaware*. In future years, the country would hear much of Stephen Decatur, but for the next few days it would be his father's name that would be on people's lips.

As Decatur guided the *Delaware* past Cape Henlopen, he spotted the merchant ship *Alexander Hamilton* and approached the ship. The captain informed him that they had been plundered by a French privateer named *La Croyable*. Attacks on American ships off Cape Henlopen had been occurring for over a century and a half. Pirates, privateers, and other marauders attacked vessels near the cape with little fear of retaliation. In the late 17th century, pirates ransacked Lewes; in 1747, French privateers captured two ships within sight of the cape; and during the American Revolution, the British navy had attacked any American ship that dared to sail the waters of coastal Delaware. Before the Revolution, the Three Counties on the Delaware had been owned by the family of William Penn, who were far more interested in Pennsylvanian affairs. Delaware had a separate legislature during the colonial period, but many residents of the Lewes area were convinced that the Quakers' pacifist beliefs restrained them from mounting a sufficient defense at the entrance to Delaware Bay.

When the American Revolution freed Delaware from the domination of the Quakers of Pennsylvania, the waters around Cape Henlopen remained as defenseless as ever. Peace had come, but not safety. The leaders of the new United States had no resources to spare, and the Atlantic Ocean would have to provide the primary defense against attacks from foreign nations.

The Continental navy that had served during the Revolution was disbanded, the captains were paid off, and the ships were sold. Without a navy to protect them, American merchant ships were easy prey for the pirates of the seven seas. And, the United States was caught up in the endless wars between Great Britain and France. During the 1790s, America's traditional trade relations with Great Britain remained strong, and the French, who were at war with the English, considered that American trade aided the British. France was determined to cut the flow of American goods to England. Captains of French warships were ordered across the Atlantic, and they began to capture American merchant ships.

Although the new American government lodged numerous protests with the French, attacks on unarmed American merchant ships had been taking place in the West Indies for several years. In 1798, the French grew bolder, and their cruisers appeared off the mid-Atlantic coast. The American government scrambled to establish a new navy to protect their merchant ships. In May, the *Hamburgh Packet* was purchased in Philadelphia, armed with 20 guns, and renamed the *Delaware*. Stephen Decatur, Sr. was given command of the *Delaware* and he was dispatched to the Cape Henlopen with orders to "Afford all possible protection to the vessels of the United States, coming on, or going off the coast against the depredations of the French cruisers." When Decatur learned of the attack on the *Alexander Hamilton*, he steered north to intercept the French privateer.

Crossing the mouth of Delaware Bay, he spotted a small cluster of sails in the distance; there was no way to determine which ship was the armed cruiser that had attacked the *Alexander Hamilton*. Decatur was afraid that if he continued to sail toward the four ships, they would scatter and he might pick the wrong vessel to chase. In order to draw out his target, Decatur decided to approach them slowly. When he was confident that all four had spotted the *Delaware*, Decatur changed course.

Decatur later wrote that he "Thought it best to stand off as if he were a merchantman, and alarmed at what might be armed vessels." The maneuver had the desired effect. As Decatur made his way back toward Delaware Bay, one of the ships began to chase him. As *La Croyable* approached the *Delaware*, the men aboard the French vessel saw that Decatur's ship was heavily armed. Now, the Frenchmen thought that they had stumbled upon an English warship, and they did not want to tangle with a vessel of the British Royal Navy.

The French captain set sail for Delaware Bay, neutral waters where *La Croyable* would be immune to attack from the English. But a short time later, they were shocked by cannon fire from the *Delaware*. The shots from Decatur's ship fell dangerously close to the French vessel; and a few moments later, *La Croyable's* captain lowered his flag in surrender.

When the captain of *La Croyable* came aboard the Delaware, he said to Decatur: "I am astonished that an American vessel would fire upon me. I know of no war between the United States and France." To this, Decatur replied, "The French have been making war on American ships for a long time, and it is now necessary for us to take care of ourselves."

The French captain had surrendered without firing a shot, and he appeared overwhelmed with embarrassment at having surrendered to an American. He told Decatur, "I wish I had been sunk." Decatur snapped, "I would have been gratified if you had stood on board your vessel and fought for her."

Shortly after this exchange, the Delaware and the captured French ship sailed past Cape Henlopen into Delaware Bay. As the *La Croyable* passed Lewes, the American flag flew from the vessel's rigging as a sign that it had been captured by the United States. The French ship was taken into the American Navy and renamed *Retaliation*.

Decatur's capture of *La Croyable* was the first capture of an enemy vessel by the new United States Navy. After enduring years of powerlessness America's merchant ships finally had a champion. Decatur's action demonstrated that the United States would, at last, act. During the next two years, vigorous action by the American navy would convince the French government to call off its attacks on American merchant ships. At the same time, Stephen Decatur, Jr. would begin his rapid rise to fame until he became one of America's greatest naval heroes; but in 1798, it was Stephen Decatur, Sr. who was toasted across the United States for his capture of *La Croyable* in the waters off Cape Henlopen, where the people of the coastal region had begun to "take care of ourselves."

The Luck of Jacob Jones

A dungeon in North Africa was not the best place to conduct class; but it was all Jacob Jones had. His pupils were a small group of naval officers who listened intently as Jones described the intricacies of mathematics, navigation and other topics. After Jones concluded the day's lessons, his pupils were free to relax; and the remainder of the day was often spent speculating about when the captive American officers would be rescued from their Algerian prison. As for

Jones, his capture by the Algerians was just another bump in a long road of bad luck.

Jacob Jones was born in 1768. His mother died when he was an infant, and Jacob's father married Penelope Holt, the granddaughter of Ryes Holt of Lewes. When Jacob's father died, Penelope raised Jacob in Lewes, where he was educated at the Academy. Following the American Revolution, Jacob studied medicine under Dr. James Sykes of Dover. After further study at the University of Pennsylvania, Jones began what he hoped would be a successful medical practice; but few patients appeared. Turning to politics, Jones became a clerk in the Delaware Supreme Court. At about this time, Jones inherited the Ryes Holt House, where he lived for a few years. When his wife died, Jones decided to begin a career at sea; and in 1799, he entered the new United States Navy as a 31-year-old midshipman.

Jones was soon promoted to lieutenant and assigned to the frigate *Philadelphia* under the command of Captain William Bainbridge. In 1803, the United States was fighting an undeclared war against the Algerian pirates, and Bainbridge boldly sailed the *Philadelphia* into Tripoli harbor. As the frigate cruised toward the fort that guarded the harbor, a violent shudder shook Jones and the other sailors. After a quick survey of the vessel, Jones and the other officers reported to Captain Bainbridge that the ship had run aground on a sandbar.

The Algerians, seeing that the American warship had run aground, launched a flotilla of small gunboats to attack the *Philadelphia*. Aboard the frigate, Bainbridge jettisoned the shop's anchors, cut away the foremast, and threw several of the ship's guns overboard in an effort to lighten the *Philadelphia*. All of these efforts to refloat the stranded warship failed, and they were soon surrounded by enemy gunboats. Bainbridge had no choice but to surrender; and the Americans found themselves locked in an Algerian prison. The Tripolitans dragged the warship off the shoals, and the *Philadelphia* was moored under the guns of the city's fort.

Fortunately for the captured crew, a friendly Danish diplomat gave Bainbridge a number of books. The captain ordered Lieutenants David Porter and Jacob Jones to set up a school for the younger officers. Most midshipmen in those days were still teenagers. Not only would the improvised school further their education, it would help maintain order and discipline while they were confined.

At this time, navigation required a detailed knowledge of mathematics to convert sightings of the sun and stars into a point on a chart. Jones drew upon his extensive background to conduct classes that helped the officers develop the navigation skills and other knowledge that they would need after their release.

On February 16, 1804, sounds of gunfire awakened Jones and the other Americans. Stephen Decatur, the son of the captain of the *Delaware* who had captured the *La Croyable* near Cape Henlopen, and a hand-picked crew of American sailors had entered Tripoli harbor on a small vessel appropriately named *Intrepid*, and they boarded the *Philadelphia*. After a sharp action, Decatur set fire to the captured American warship, reboarded the *Intrepid*, and sailed to safety. The destruction of the *Philadelphia* was hailed as the most daring exploit in the history of the young United States Navy.

Years later, Jones wrote to the wife of Stephen Decatur about the burning of the *Philadelphia*: "It was accordingly effected in the ketch *Intrepid*, by your husband and 70 volunteers from the schooner he commanded, at great hazard, not only of life or liberty, but that of reputation, and in the season most perilous in approaching that coast. The recollection of the difficulties and dangers he had to encounter in that expedition, of which I was an eyewitness, excites more and more admiration of his gallantry and enterprise — and although the results shed a lustre throughout Europe, over the American character, and excited an unparalleled emulation in the squadron, our county alone is where it has never been duly estimated, or properly understood."

The burning of the *Philadelphia* raised the morale of the captured Americans, but it would be over a year before they were released from their prison. Decatur's exploit inspired them to attempt escape several times; but each of these ended in failure. Jones continued to conduct classes for the young officers. In June, 1805, a treaty was signed with Tripoli, and the crew of the *Philadelphia* was released.

Despite the unfortunate tour of duty as a schoolteacher in Tripoli, Jones continued in the navy; and at the beginning of the War of 1812 he commanded the sloop-of-war *Wasp*. When Jones sailed the *Wasp* past Cape Henlopen on October 13, 1812, the United States and Great Britain had been at war for nearly four months. Jones had set a course to the southeast and headed for the busy Atlantic shipping lanes where he planned to attack British merchant ships.

A few days after leaving Delaware Bay, Jones spotted a disorganized convoy of British ships that were being escorted by the 18-gun sloop-of-war *Frolic* of the British Royal Navy. A storm the night before had scattered many of the ships; and the time was right to attack. While his crew prepared for battle,

Jones sailed the *Wasp* toward the *Frolic*. The two ships were evenly matched, and the outcome of the battle would turn on some small bit of luck.

The storm the day before had produced heavy swells, and both ships dipped wildly in the heavy sea. The *Wasp* and the *Frolic* were less than 60 yards apart when both vessels opened fire. Jones had his gunners fire as the *Wasp* rolled downward to direct the shot into the hull of the British ship. The captain of the *Frolic*, on the other hand, ordered his gunners to fire on the up roll. The British shot sailed high and ripped the *Wasp's* rigging and sails. Both crews were well-drilled, and the broadsides roared across the water as the Americans and British gunners blasted away at each other.

At first, the British strategy and Jones' luck seemed to be working against the Americans. One of the first English shots carried away the main topmast of the *Wasp*. As it fell, it brought other portions of the rigging down with it. But aboard the *Frolic*, the British sailors began to suffer frightful casualties as the American shot ripped through the men crowded around the cannons on the gun deck. In spite of the loss of so much sail, Jones was able to maneuver the *Wasp* ahead off the *Frolic*, and this enabled the American gunners to send cannon balls ricocheting down the length of the British ship.

The two warships maneuvered so close together that the gun crews could touch the other vessel with their rammers. When the English vessel lurched toward the *Wasp* in the heavy seas, the rigging of the two vessels snagged. With the two ships locked together, the American crew rushed aboard the *Frolic*, whose "deck was slippery with blood." The sailors from the *Wasp* took possession of the British warship, and the English surrendered. Out of a crew of 110 British sailors, 90 had been killed or seriously wounded. Minutes after the surrender, the *Frolic's* rigging collapsed. Theodore Roosevelt wrote of this battle: "The Americans had done their work with a coolness and skill that could not be surpassed."

The victory over the *Frolic* was nearly complete; and it appeared that the luck of Jacob Jones had finally changed.. The British strategy of firing into the rigging had taken only five American lives. Jones quickly went about the task of caring for the wounded and repairing the *Wasp* and the *Frolic* so that he could get both ships into an American port.

A few hours after the action, the HMS *Poictiers*, a 74-gun British ship-of-the-line commanded by Captain John Beresford appeared on the horizon. Under normal circumstances, the smaller *Wasp* could easily outsail the slower but more powerful *Poictiers*. Jones desperately attempted to escape, but the *Wasp's* damaged sails and rigging made it difficult to make much headway. Beresford fired shot the smaller American vessel, and Jones had to surrender.

Although the American crew was captured and the *Frolic* was retaken by the British, Congress voted the crew of the *Wasp* $25,000 in prize money. In addition, Jones was promoted to captain and given command of a frigate; but the war ended before he could see further action. Following the War of 1812, Jones continued in the navy for another three decades. Jacob Jones' death in 1850 ended a long, distinguished, and luckless naval career.

THE ROCKETS' RED GLARE

When the United States declared war on Great Britain in 1812, the citizens of Lewes knew that their exposed position on the doorstep of the Atlantic left them vulnerable to attack. Several months after Captain John Beresford of the *Poictiers* happened upon the *Wasp* and the *Frolic* after their deadly battle, the British commander led a squadron around Cape Henlopen. After dropping anchor not far from Lewes, Beresford demanded that the town provide his ships with "Twenty live bullocks, with a proportionate quantity of vegetables and hay," adding: "If you refuse to comply with this request, I shall be under the necessity of destroying your town."

Preparing for trouble, militiamen from Sussex County began to make their way toward Lewes, and the town prepared for the expected British bombardment. One observer compared the town's reaction to the scorched-earth policy that greeted Napoleon Bonaparte's invasion of Russia: "The enemy in our bay want bullocks; they should have them on terms which the Russians gave Bony Moscow."

As Beresford waited for a reply to his demand, the people of Lewes prepared to defend the town. They extinguished the lamps in the Cape Henlopen lighthouse and moved the buoys that marked the shoals in the bay. In addition, men from Sussex County continued to arrive to repulse the expected attack. One confident defender suggested: "We have about 1,000 citizens residing on the banks of our river and creeks who live by fishing, fowling and muskrat catching — put those useful men up, furnish them with suitable shot, embody them in classes of seven of every class, appoint a leader and rallying point, give them a handsome sum for every boat they destroy or capture belonging to the enemy, and good reward for every prisoner they take dead or alive."

As the militiamen assembled in Lewes, some of them were assigned to the high ground that overlooked the mouth of Lewes Creek. This was the bluff that had first been fortified by the ill-fated colonists of Zwaanendael in 1631. The native Americans had burned the original fort, but a new fort was built by the Dutch in the middle of the 17th century. With the arrival of Beresford's squadron, many citizens of Lewes gathered at the west end of Pilottown Road to help improve the old fortifications. Logs reinforced with earth, sand and gravel were used to assemble a rudimentary fort. A small watchtower added an impressive touch to the earthenworks. Near the center of town, the defenders built a second defensive work.

The militiamen did not lack for courage, but they could not match the fire-power of the British ships. Some of the guns of the British ships could fire solid shot weighing a staggering 32 pounds apiece. These iron cannon balls did not explode, but they could breach the walls of just about any building in Lewes. In addition, the British had mortars that could lob exploding shells into the Delaware town. These "bombs" were hollow iron shells which were about the size of a bowling ball. The inside of the shell was filled with gunpowder; and when the mortar was fired, the fuse to the shell was ignited. If the timing was right, the fuse reached the powder on the inside of the bomb just before the shell hit the ground. The resulting explosion could be deadly. A single well-placed shell could devastate the log-and-earth fortifications of Lewes.

Mortar bombs may have been the most destructive weapon in the British arsenal, but Congreve rockets were the most spectacular. These rockets were invented by a British artillery officer named William Congreve, who mounted a small explosive shell on the end of a sky rocket that was about ten feet long. If the rocket landed within the enemy's lines, the detonation of the shell could be deadly. The British also used Congreve rockets to illuminate targets at night; and the explosions of these rockets provided the people of Lewes with a spectacular fireworks show.

By April 6, Beresford's patience had expired and the British began a concentrated attack on Lewes. The movement of the buoys apparently did cause some confusion; none of the larger vessels was able to get close enough to do much damage with the heavy cannons. Some of the squadron's smaller vessels were able to negotiate the shallows and get close enough to shore to send smaller-caliber balls flying into town. One of the small balls lodged in the foundation of a house on Second Street; but most of them did little more than plow up the open land around Lewes. These cannon balls often landed in the soft soil, where they were retrieved by the defenders of Lewes who then fired them back at the British. One newspaper reported: "Our brave citizens being short of cannon-balls, the enemy was so accommodating as to fire eight hundred on shore, which on picking up and finding they suited the caliber of our cannon remarkably well, the loan was immediately returned with interest."

Another eyewitness commented on the effectiveness of the shot, shells and rockets: "About five hundred shots were fired. A collection was made of one hundred and fifty of small sizes and a few bombs. Houses were injured, chimneys cut almost in two, the corner-post, plates and studs cut in several houses. The foremast of a schooner was cut away, and another received a shot in her hull. Of two particular rockets thrown, one fell on a lot, another in a marsh."

Much of the British bombardment was directed at the battery near the center of Lewes; but even there, the damage was minimal. "Shot struck the battery and broke the pine logs. Two shots entered by the guns...The house of Peter Hall [a tavern on the bank] was demolished, and several others damaged; the bombs and rockets fell short of the town."

Beresford's ships spent 22 hours bombarding Lewes, but the town refused to surrender and the frustrated British sailed away. After the attack, it was reported that the British left "without bullocks, vegetables, hay, or so much as a cup of cold water." As one newspaper commented: "Commodore Beresford would seem to have suddenly altered his mind with respect to burning down Lewistown, to make a fire to roast the Delaware oxen by. It would be too offensive to suppose a British officer would threaten without meaning to make good his word...Delaware beef is highly seasoned, and if served up with forced meat balls, might prove as palatable to this nautical hero as the beef of old England."

Two weeks later, a newspaper summarized the results of the attack: "The people of Lewestown are making themselves quite merry for the late bombardment of that place. They enumerate their killed and wounded as follows: one chicken killed, one pig wounded — leg broken. It was a ridiculous affair on the part of the enemy. We have nothing new from this quarter except that Sir John Beresford has captured five oyster-boats, and, after a severe engagement, caused these whole cargoes to be devoured."

A year after the bombardment of Lewes, the British launched a similar attack on Baltimore, where the defenders of Fort McHenry braved the rocket's red glare and the bombs bursting in air. The attack on Baltimore inspired Francis Scott Key to write the words to the "Star Spangled Banner." At Lewes, a local poet was inspired to summarize the attack on the Delaware town in a simple ditty: "The commodore and his men, wounded a pig and killed a hen."

CHAPTER 4. DARK SECRETS AND DARK CORNERS

GUNS, CLUBS AND VOTES

Angry crowds swarmed through Lewes brandishing clubs, swords and guns, knocking down anyone who stood in their way; and some victims lay unconscious in the street. Many of the residents of Lewes retreated behind closed doors. Others scampered out of town. It was election day, 1787.

The American Revolution increased the deep divisions that existed between the coastal residents and those who lived in the interior of Sussex County. The natural differences between the older maritime settlements on the coast and the newer farming communities of the interior were intensified by the dominance of Lewes, which had served as the county seat for over a century. In addition, most residents of communities near the bay had supported independence from Great Britain; and many of the people from the settlements in the inland areas of the county had remained loyal to the king. In 1787, the lingering bitterness generated by the Revolution boiled over on election day.

At that time, voters were required to travel to the county seat to cast their ballots; and the wretched state of the roads in southern Delaware made this a dismal hardship for the people who lived in central and western Sussex County. Most of the early Delaware settlements were along the tributaries of the bay, and travel by water made it easy to reach Lewes. As more settlers moved inland, reaching Lewes to conduct county business required a daylong expedition. On election day, the extended trip was exacerbated by the hostile reception that voters from the interior were likely to receive in Lewes. Many voters traveled to the polls armed with pistols, cutlasses, and other weapons. In addition, the militias that sprang up during the Revolution gave some groups a quasi-military organization; and on election day in 1787, two of these groups marched into Lewes with colors flying and clubs at the ready. Most inhabitants of Lewes fled in terror, but the mob was able to beat and wound several people, including one of the election inspectors. The boisterous crowd challenged would-be voters to prevent those who opposed them from casting their ballots. Some were threatened with dismemberment, the traditional penalty for traitors.

When reports of the violence in Lewes reached the Delaware General Assembly, a new election was ordered; but the polling place was moved to Vaughan's Furnace in central Sussex County. The election was held a month later, with hundreds of men armed with muskets parading past the polls. Some intimidated voters by cocking their weapons and threatening to shoot anyone on the wrong side. After the voting was done, sheriff Peter Wright barricaded himself in the polling place and spent an anxious night waiting for a group of twenty armed men who were reported to be on their way to destroy the ballots. The mob failed to appear; and the election results were certified as official.

The election at Vaughn's Furnace was a victory for residents of interior Sussex County; and they clamored for a relocation of the county seat from Lewes to an inland location. The state legislature authorized the transfer In 1791. A group of commissioners was appointed to establish the new county seat and they selected a site in the center of the county. Land was bought, streets and lots were laid out, a new courthouse and other buildings were erected, and the new county seat was named Georgetown.

The creation of a new county seat, however, did not bring peaceful elections. To insure that the votes were counted with all due care, it became the practice to wait two days until the election returns were announced. Many residents remained in Georgetown and celebrated the completed election while they waited for the results to be proclaimed on what became known as "Return Day."

Although there was some jostling among political rivals, the votes already been cast; and there was no need to intimidate voters. After the legislature allowed polling places to be established outside the county seat, the votes were carried to Georgetown to be counted. Many Sussex residents continued to fill Georgetown on Return Day to hear the results. The Return Day celebrations shed the violence that had marred earlier elections; and the day became a carnival event. On Return Day, an ox was roasted; and Georgetown was crowded with vendors hawking biscuits, sweet potatoes, hot cornpone, roasted rabbits,

1791

64

(Above) Site of the 1631 settlement at Zwaanendael that was destroyed within a year of its establishment. (Below-left) Monument to the hapless settlement. (Below-right) The Zwaanendael Museum built to commemorate the 300th anniversary of the arrival of the first Dutch colonists.

(Above) Maull House where Betsey Patterson found the table service less than satisfactorily

(Left) The grave of Captain Drew of the De Braak.

(Above) Memorial Park with the Cannonball house in the background. This building withstood the attack by the British during the War of 1812. (Below) Cannonball embedded in the foundation of the Cannonball House.

(Above) Monument to General John Dagworthy at St. George's Chapel in Dagsboro. (Below) Patty Cannon's House on the Delaware-Maryland border

(Above) The Fenwick Island Lighthouse. (below) Two views of the stone that stands near the base of the lighthouse and marks the boundary between Delaware and Maryland. On the north side of the stone (Below-right) the stone has been incised with the symbol of the Penns. On the south side (Below-left), the stone has been cut with the symbol of the Calverts, Proprietors of Maryland.

(Above) Indian River Inlet Life Saving Station as it appears today. The station is north of the Indian River Inlet (Below) near where the Faithful Steward foundered.

(Above) Nanticoke Indian Museum that once served as a school
(Below) The Du Pont nylon plant near Seaford

(Above) Cape Henlopen in the 1950's. Fort Miles in the upper background, menhaden fish pro-
cessing plants in the center; and the Delaware Pilot station at the bottom. *Photo courtesy of the Lewes
Historical Society.*
(Below) The Delaware Breakwater

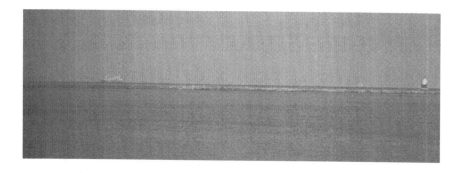

(Left) Michael Morgan in front of one of the spotting towers from Fort Miles.
(Below) The Delaware Pilots Station

fired chicken, fish, oysters, and clams, all accompanied by liberal helpings of beer, cider and other beverages.

The combination of strong politics and strong drinks sometimes led to minor hostilities, but there was nothing compared to the violence that had occurred in Lewes. Before the Civil War, a man was killed on Return Day as the festivities evolved into a boisterous celebration of the election results. The tradition went on, undeterred, and in 1882, a parade was held that featured an elaborate float of the sailing ship *Constitution*. The fully-rigged vessel carried Governor-elect Charles Stockley; and it was accompanied by more than a hundred horsemen as the ship was pulled through the streets of Georgetown. When the float reached the courthouse, the enthusiastic crowd surrounded the sailing ship to shake hands with the new governor. As the crowd cheered, several brawny men lifted the governor-elect and carried him on their shoulders into the courthouse. More recent observances of Return Day feature a parade of antique cars and carriages, blaring bands, fair food, and a ceremonial burying of the political hatchet.

KNIFE FIGHTS AND LOVERS

Stephen Girard was a merchant, financier and philanthropist. Born in France in 1750, Girard moved to Philadelphia during the American Revolution. After the war, he established a shipping business serving markets in the West Indies, Europe and the Orient. Girard's mercantile enterprises earned him enormous wealth that he funneled into several banking ventures. Always looking ahead to his next business move, Girard personified his favorite axiom: "To rest is to rust."

Girard's enthusiasm for his private business was matched by his devotion to civic projects. When a yellow fever epidemic struck Philadelphia, Girard personally supervised the workings of a hospital. Not content to run the facility from the security of an office, Girard became personally involved in the care of the patients. One commentator wrote that, "For sixty days, Stephen Girard performed both day and night the duty of receiving, nursing, and caring for those stricken with the fever."

Stephen Girard was an outstanding businessman and apparently, a model citizen; but when he came to Lewes in 1793, Girard ended up in a knife fight with the sheriff of Sussex County.

Following the American Revolution, the merchants of the United States found themselves in a precarious position. The trading advantages that America had enjoyed with Great Britain during the colonial period were now gone. In addition, the Founding Fathers disbanded the Continental Navy shortly after the peace treaty was signed. American merchant ships sailed at their own peril. Successful merchants could reap enormous profits, but only merchants with vision, daring and persistence could be successful. Such a man was Stephen Girard.

Although Girard's ventures had been highly profitable, in the early 1790s he suffered several financial reverses. He was having trouble with his creditors when a slave revolt began in Haiti; and Girard sensed an opportunity to turn a handsome profit. He set sail for the West Indies — but right at the mouth of the Delaware Bay, his ship was delayed by contrary winds. When it appeared that the weather would remain bad for several days, Girard came ashore and booked a room in a Lewes inn. It was there that he would encounter Sheriff Thomas Fisher.

Thomas Fisher came from one of the most prominent families in Sussex County. Some of Fisher's ancestors had accompanied William Penn to America in 1682. Thomas was born on a farm near Lewes in 1763. During the American Revolution, he had been seized by a British press gang from the frigate *Roebuck*, and only his father's quick action saved the teenager from a harsh life in the British navy. Thomas was a man of commanding presence whose affable manners earned him great popularity among residents of Sussex County. Fisher served in several public offices.

When some of Girard's creditors learned that he had sailed from Philadelphia, they were aghast. They suspected that he was attempting to flee the country. Immediately, they procured a writ for Girard's arrest and dispatched a rider to Lewes, in the hope that Girard could be intercepted before he sailed into the Atlantic. When the rider arrived in Lewes, he delivered the writ to Sheriff Fisher.

Fisher was not deterred by Girard's reputation as one of the leading merchants of Philadelphia. Having found out in which inn Girard was staying, Fisher marched over to serve the writ. Girard flew into a rage and drew a knife, but his hand was not as quick as his temper. Fisher deflected the blow with one hand and with the other he hit the Philadelphia entrepreneur so hard that Girard fell to the floor. After a brief struggle, the sheriff hustled Girard out of the inn and through the streets of Lewes to jail.

When things cooled down, Girard convinced Fisher that he had no intention of leaving the country permanently, and he was allowed to post bail. Only by completing a successful trip could he settle his debts. After catching a favorable wind, Girard went on to Santo Domingo, where he found many plantation owners who were terrified that the slave rebellion would be successful. The plantation owners were willing to pay anything for safe passage to America. Girard happily complied, and he earned enough money to satisfy his creditors and add to his financial empire. When he died in 1831, Stephen Girard left much of his money to charities. None of these, apparently, was located in Lewes.

Stephen Girard demonstrated quickness of mind and action. James Wiley was a little slower. In the late 18th century, Dr. Matthew Wilson of Lewes was one of the most prominent men in Sussex County. A devoted Presbyterian preacher, he was also a medical doctor and an ardent American patriot. During the Revolution, Sussex County was home to so many Tories that Dr. Wilson determined that everyone, even strangers, should know that he supported independence from England. Even though he risked ridicule or worse from the hot-blooded Tories, Dr. Wilson stitched the word "Patriot" on his hat. In addition, Wilson named his first son James "Patriot" Wilson.

James Wilson was a lawyer and a theologian of some note. Theodore Wilson, Matthew's second son, was trained as a doctor who established a practice in Lewes. When he died in 1790, Matthew's two sons were well on their way to becoming as well known as their father. Fortunately for Matthew, he did not live to see how his sons would become famous.

In 1792, Theodore Wilson was called to Broadkiln to treat James Wiley for a fever. Wiley was apparently a pleasant, but not a particularly observant, fellow. While treating Wiley for his fever, Wilson met his wife, Nancy. Wilson began to show as much interest in Nancy as he did in his patient. Even after James recovered, Wilson and Nancy continued to see each other. This long-range liaison was made easier two years later when Wiley moved to Lewes, where he opened a tavern. Wilson continued his affair with Nancy for several years, and it became a public scandal. Even Wilson's marriage in 1794 failed to cool the romance between the good doctor and the tavern-keeper's wife.

By 1799, nearly seven years after it began, Wiley learned of the affair between his wife and Theodore Wilson. At this time, it also dawned on Wiley that his wife had been overly friendly with quite a few other men. Still, Wiley did nothing. There was so much public comment on his wife's behavior that he agreed to meet with Wilson to discuss the situation. It was suggested that a duel would settle the issue honorably; Wiley declined on the grounds that he would have to extend that invitation to all of Nancy's lovers.

The meeting between Wilson and Wiley failed to resolve the situation, and matters continued as before. Within several months, the public outcry over the sordid affair had grown so loud that various groups tried to intervene. The local Masonic lodge called a meeting on December 6, 1799 at Elliott's Tavern. Wilson sat in front of the fire and listened as others discussed his affair with Nancy Wiley. As the men talked, James Wiley entered the room, walked up to Wilson, put a gun to his head, and blew the doctor's brains out.

Wiley was arrested and held in the county jail until he could be tried for murder. While he was confined, Wiley's business failed; his assets were seized and sold off. During a two-day trial, the details of entire affair were made public. The humiliated Wiley was found guilty and sentenced to death.

An appeal was dispatched to Governor Richard Bassett, who decided that Wiley had been grossly provoked, and he granted the tavern-keeper a full pardon. But the story did not end there.

James Patriot Wilson could not accept the fact that his brother's killer had been let go. He tracked down Wiley and put his own pistol to the tavern keeper's head. But when Wilson pulled the trigger, the weapon failed to discharge. Wiley took off, and Wilson decided that his honor at least had been served. He laconically remarked, "I tried, anyway!"

After his own brush with death, Wiley tried to win back Nancy's affections; but she rebuffed him. James Wiley, who had lost his business and his wife, died a short time later.

BETSY TAKES OFFENSE

By the beginning of the 19th century, Lewes had developed into a substantial little town that was a welcome stop for travelers. Contrary winds often forced ships to anchor near Cape Henlopen, while passengers enjoyed the hospitality of Lewes. In 1804, one such ship was detained near the cape, but not all the passengers were pleased at what awaited them along the Delaware coast.

At the dawn of the 19th century, Napoleon Bonaparte was busy conquering most of Europe. As the countries fell to his armies one by one, Napoleon installed his many brothers on thrones across the continent; but Jerome, Napoleon's youngest brother, was denied the honor. Not only was Jerome young (he was just 20 years old in 1804), he was immature, dull, and a lecherous wolf. To keep Jerome from causing problems in Europe, Napoleon dispatched him to America.

Jerome's American tour brought him to Baltimore, where he met the beguiling Betsy Patterson. Betsy, as the people of Lewes would one day learn, was beautiful, rich, and extremely ambitious. She also detested Baltimore, which was a town of several thousand inhabitants, a few substantial buildings, and many muddy streets. Years later she remarked that she "would have married the devil to get out of Baltimore."

Betsy and Jerome deserved each other, and when they met, they both heard wedding bells ringing. Despite the strenuous objections from the frantic French diplomats who had been assigned to keep Jerome out of mischief, and dire predictions of what would happen when Napoleon found out, Jerome and Betsy were married in Baltimore on Christmas Eve, 1803. After a year-long honeymoon in America, the young couple set sail to meet the groom's family in Europe. A storm at the mouth of the Delaware Bay forced the Bonapartes to land at Lewes.

That night in Lewes was not a pleasant one. Betsy found the Delaware town somewhat below her standards. Although a sumptuous dinner was prepared for the young couple at the Maull House, Betsy was appalled at what she considered the primitive table setting. She simple refused to be seated until more appropriate tableware was produced. While all the other diners cooled their heels, servants were dispatched to the Bonapartes' ship, where Betsy's silver candlesticks were procured and brought to the table.

A few days later, Jerome and Betsy set sail for Europe. They left behind a town deeply chagrined. Word of Betsy's actions spread quickly, and the story has been repeated so often that it is now an accepted part of the folklore of Lewes.

Betsy and Jerome did not live happily ever after. Napoleon was never reconciled to his brother's impertinence in marrying without permission. Napoleon ordered the ports of Europe closed to Betsy, and only Jerome was allowed to return to France. The marriage was eventually annulled, and Jerome married Princess Catherine of Wurtemberg to become king of Westphalia. Betsy spent the rest of her life in Europe, seeking the imperial title that had just barely eluded her.

In Baltimore, Betsy Patterson is remembered as one of the town's most beautiful belles who married into Europe's most important family. In Lewes, she is remembered for her boorish behavior during dinner. Elsewhere, she is not remembered at all.

A FRIGHTFUL LABYRINTH

In 1809, Thomas Nuttall, a young English immigrant who had a keen interest in the natural wonders of America, arrived at the house of a Sussex County resident known for guiding visitors through some of southern Delaware's darkest corners. The two set off from the man's house near Dagsboro, and they soon plunged into an immense, dark swamp where enormous trees and other vegetation formed such a tight canopy that it was often difficult to see the sky. Nuttall later wrote: "About a mile from this house we began to enter one of the most frightful labyrinths you can imagine. It was filled with tall tangling shrubs thickly matted together almost impervious to the light."

As Nuttall worked his way through the swamp, he was impressed with the variety of the plants and animals that he observed — but distressed to hear that bears frequented the area. After their tour of the swamp, Nuttall left Delaware to explore other parts of America; when he returned to the East, Nuttall became the curator for the Harvard Botanical Gardens and he wrote several pioneering books on the natural wonders of America.

When Thomas Nuttall visited Sussex County, the Great Cypress Swamp was already well known. In 1797, a resident of Delaware noted, "The Indian River Swamps, otherwise called the Cypress Swamps, are situated in Delaware and Maryland States, a little to the Southward of the True Cape Henlopen and distant from the sea about ten miles. They are full seven miles from East to West and ten or twelve from North to South, so that they must contain near fifty thousand acres of land. Several rivers are traced to this great source, such as the Pocomoke, the Indian River and the St. Martins. The whole of this immense swamp is a high and level basin and consequently very wet; tho' undoubtedly the highest land between the sea and the bay, the waters descending from it in all directions."

During the 17th century, the swamp was avoided by most people, and colonists preferred to settle on the thickly wooded land near the coastal bays. In the middle of the 18th century, however, Colonel John Dagworthy (whose role in the Revolution was discussed above) was given title to a large portion of the Great

Swamp. When Dagworthy arrived in Sussex County, he began to drain the land on the edge of the swamp to create more farmland.

Dagworthy also discovered that logs made from downed cypress trees made particularly high-quality shingles. Over the centuries, as the swamp's trees were toppled by windstorms, the cypress trunks often sank into the spongy mass of soft peat that covered the floor of the forest. The mossy mass had a curing effect on the submerged timber and shingles made from this wood were nearly impervious to rot. Dagworthy's workers established camps in the swamp where they cut the cypress logs, and his shingles were sold throughout the mid-Atlantic region.

Farmers on the perimeter of the swamp also began to fill in the marshland to extend their fields. By the middle of the 19th century, much of the southern end of the swamp had been drained and filled, but the Delaware portion of the marshland continued to be mined for shingles.

The shingle workers established a network of trails so they could reach their camps without danger. Although many areas of the forest bed looked firm, there were deep, soft spots that could swallow a person in seconds. The shingle workers used hollow logs that contained little usable timber to create pathways through the treacherous spots. These wooden walkways provided firm footing, but they created another hazard. Before stepping on a log, experienced men would tap the timber with their boots to scare off the water moccasins and other snakes that may have taken up residence in the wood.

The shingle cutters established camps on high spots in the swamp that gave them firm land on which to work. Heading out from these base camps, workers located buried cypress trunks by using a long iron rod to poke along the swamp floor. By carefully probing through the soft mossy ground, they could determine the location and the shape of logs that lay just under the surface. After a suitable trunk was located, a gang of a half-dozen men used wooden poles to pry it out of the muck. When enough of the trunk was exposed, they would cut logs of a convenient length and drag them to the camp. After the log was sliced into foot-log sections, a worker used a long blade and a wooden mallet to spit the sections into rough shingles. Another worker would taper one end of the shingle so that it would fit properly on a roof. Finished singles were stacked into bundles so that they could be carried out of the swamp. Shingles from the Great Cypress Swamp were so long lasting that some that were cut two centuries ago are believed to still be in place on homes today.

During prolonged droughts, the top layer of the Great Cypress Swamp would become unusually dry. After a long dry spell in the later 18th century, a fire began, and the dry peat burned for several weeks. Wind-blown embers from the fire drifted across southern Sussex County to the Delaware beaches. From this and other fires, the area was sometimes referred to as the "Burnt Swamp."

Once Dagworthy had demonstrated the value of the swamp, others began to copy his methods. By the time Nuttall arrived to explore the swamp, it had already begun to shrink; but the swamp retained much of its majesty. Near the end of the 18th century, it was noted: "About one fifteenth part of this vast tract was once covered with the beautiful green cypress...whose regular and majestic height cast such a venerable shade that it kept every other tree of the forest at an awful distance and impressed the beholder with a religious solemnity."

Some visitors to the swamp were less impressed with the "religious solemnity" of the area, but they appreciated its isolation. For many years, the dark and foreboding recesses of the Great Cypress Swamp provided hiding places for outlaws and other fugitives and gave rise to many legends.

During the early 18th century, when the swamp and the thick forests that surrounded it were at their height, John Fontaine, an officer in the British army, traveled arrived in southern Sussex County. After stopping at an inn north of the swamp, Fontaine wrote in his journal: "There were about eight rogues that were drinking there, being resolved to fall upon us and rob us. My comrade, going out, not expecting any thing was knocked down. He endeavored to defend himself with his sword, but with their stakes they broke it to pieces. They endeavored to serve me after the same manner, but I defended myself and my friend until we got to our horses and with a great deal of trouble got away from them, and put on forward on the road about six miles to avoid them, and put up, it being dark, in a poor man's house. About ten o'clock at night they came to steal our horses, and endeavor to surprise us, but when they see we were prepared for them, after some few injurious words and threats they made off. This is Sussex County."

It took two more days for Fontaine to get out of Delaware, and he observed: "This part of the country is hardly inhabited, and what people are here make it their business to rob all passengers."

Veteran travelers learned to be wary when venturing in the vicinity of the Great Cypress Swamp. In particular, they were leery of the heavily-forested area on the western side of the swamp near Woodland Ferry on the Nanticoke River. Not far from the ferry, Joe Johnson and Patty Cannon operated Johnson's Tavern. Patty Cannon was a striking woman with flowing locks of coal-black hair.

When her husband, Jesse Cannon, died, she took up with Ebenezer Johnson, who had an unsavory reputation and was known as the "Pirate of Broad Creek." After Patty had thrown in with Ebenezer, he was killed in fight; and Cannon joined with his son Joe to open Johnson's Tavern.

In 1822, Joe Johnson and Patty Cannon were accused of kidnapping free African-Americans, whom they sold to slave traders in the South. The charges against Cannon were dropped, but Johnson was convicted and sentenced to 39 lashes. In addition, Johnson was locked in the pillory with his ears nailed to the stocks. Johnson was also sentenced to have his ears cut off, but the governor rescinded that part of the sentence.

After his release, Johnson rejoined Cannon and the two continued to operate their tavern. Neighbors reported unusual noises at night, and wagons slipped away from the inn at odd hours. Travelers who were foolish enough to carry large sums of money through this part of Delaware and stopped at the tavern were never seen again. Many people were convinced that Johnson and Cannon were engaged in dangerous and illegal activity, and dark stories about the tavern owners circulated throughout southern Delaware.

In 1829, a farmer was working in his orchard when he noticed an odd, weed-covered depression in the ground near the house where Johnson and Cannon lived. He began to poke through the brush and uncovered a wooden box. Roused by visions of gold purloined from the missing travelers, the farmer pried open the chest. No shining gold coins rewarded his work, but an appalling pile of putrefied human remains.

Horrified, the farmer called for help; and soon a small posse was plowing up the ground around the house. The searchers uncovered four more sets of bones, and the crowd turned their attention to the house itself. Cyrus James, who had joined the growing mob, volunteered that he once lived in the house and offered to lead a search. The crowd broke into the building, and James led them upstairs to a closet that concealed a trapdoor in the ceiling. Slithering through the opening into the attic, they discovered that part of the garret had been converted into a cell. Thick planks had been used to create a strong, windowless chamber; a set of leg irons was bolted to the wall. It was here, the crowd concluded, that Johnson and Cannon had held the African-Americans that they kidnapped and sold to the slave catchers.

James led the mob to another hidden room that was entered through the false floor of a downstairs closet. The crowd concluded that the dark rumors were true; and they set out to seize Joe Johnson and Patty Cannon. Johnson apparently heard they were coming, and he disappeared; but on April 13, 1829, Patty Cannon was arrested as a serial killer.

Patty admitted to having personally killed eleven people, and she claimed to have helped in the murder of a dozen others. Most of her victims had been travelers who stopped at Johnson's Tavern, where they were robbed, killed, and buried in the backyard. Cannon was taken to the Georgetown jail to await her trial and probable execution; but on May 11, 1829, she was found dead in her cell, an apparent suicide.

Joe Johnson had used the dark trails of southern Delaware to make his escape. The son of the "Pirate of Broad Creek" headed for the western frontier. Reaching the Arkansas territory, he reportedly changed his name and lived out the rest of his life — as a probate judge.

THE MILFORD MASSACRE

The area west of the Great Swamp was noted for its thick forest and unsavory inhabitants. The area to the east was largely open country that settlers and their ubiquitous companions, pigs, found attractive. Early Delaware residents would have been unable to survive without their pigs. But the swine that the settlers introduced to the coastal region were not the chubby pink pigs found on modern hog farms. The colonial pig was a tough, smart animal with a ridge of bristles running down its back, and a pair of tusks protruding from its long snout. These hardy animals foraged for their own food, and they reproduced often. A few pigs left to wander the area around the early settlements could be counted on to multiply and provide a steady supply of food.

Colonial swine were allowed to roam free, but they seldom strayed far. Typically, the excess pigs were slaughtered in the fall, and the meat was preserved by smoking or salting. In colonial times, the settlers often used the terms "bacon" and "ham" interchangeably. A 1775 inventory of the John Waller's estate lists the Lewes farmer and shipwright as owning 150 pounds of bacon, but much of this may have been ham. Waller's supply of bacon was typical for a person of the middle class. Inventories of the estates of tenant farmers often indicated an ample amount of bacon.

Coastal farmers had to lay in stores to prepare for the rigors of winter. They filled their larders with as much food as possible, and they hoped that winter would end before their food ran out. Pigs were slaughtered in the fall, when they were the fattest. Animals judged to be too old or weak and not likely to survive the cold weather were the first to be slaughtered. Younger, stronger animals that would reproduce and provide a future supply of food were spared.

After the pig was slaughtered, the meat could be cured and smoked. In her essay on food practices published in *After Ratification, Material Life in Delaware, 1789-1820*, Judith Quinn cites a 19th century recipe for curing ham: "For 24 hams, take 6 pounds of fine salt, two pints of Molasses, and 1 pint of saltpeter, pounded fine. Mix all these together, rub every ham with the mixture, and pack them down in your cask, let them remain five or six days, then unpack them and put those at the bottom which were at the top, and sprinkle a little salt over them, let them remain so for five or six days, and then make a pickle which will bear an egg and pour it over them. Let the whole remain one month, and they will be fit to smoke."

Quinn says the amount of time that the ham was smoked varied widely. Some Delaware farmers smoked their ham for just six hours; others for as long as six months. She also found that smokehouses were very common in Delaware; and some farmers smoked beef and mutton in addition to ham.

The colonists also roasted, broiled and boiled their pork; and they consumed every part of the animal. In addition to the usual cuts of meat, the head, liver, tongue and ears graced the tables of the well-to-do; and the chitterlings were given to the servants. Scraps were turned into sausage that was considered a dinner dish. An 18th century visitor to the mid-Atlantic region commented: "Have had either Bacon or Chickens every meal since I came in to the Country. If I still continue in this way, I shall be grown over with Bristles or Feathers."

In the 18th century, there were so many pigs running loose in coastal Delaware that legislation was passed requiring farmers to protect the cultivated areas from the free-roaming pigs. Fields were to "be fenced with a post and rail-fence, or worm-fence, well staked and ridered, at least four feet and a half high from the top of the upper-most rail or rider to the ground; and all worm-fences not stacked ridered shall be at least five feet from the top of the upper-rail to the ground."

Around the time of the American Revolution, the human and swine population of Delaware reached a crossroads. There no longer seemed to be enough room to allow the pigs to roam free; and laws were passed that required the animals to be confined behind fences. When swine were allowed to roam free, Delaware's poorer residents were able to maintain a few without much difficulty. The care and feeding of the animals involved little or no cost, and a poor family could depend upon natural increase to provide a steady supply of pork. During the colonial period, there were two areas near Lewes where livestock was allowed to roam free. The Beach Marsh, which sat between Lewes Creek and the bay, had been set aside as a common area soon after William Penn took over the colony in the late 17th century, and people could pasture their livestock in the Great Marsh west of Lewes.

The new laws requiring pigs to be fenced meant that anyone owning a pig had to own enough land to raise it. In addition, he had to have sufficient resources to build a fence. At this time, the western part of Sussex County was still heavily forested, but the coastal area had been occupied for so long that most of the available timber was gone. Wood for fences was expensive and material had to be imported from New Jersey. Despite these difficulties, the supporters of the new fencing laws were determined to put an end to the free-roaming pigs. In 1809, the citizens of Milford hunted down the remaining swine that regularly wandered the town's streets. By the time the shooting stopped, so many pigs had been killed that the incident became known as the "Milford Massacre."

RESOURCEFUL RESIDENTS OF SUSSEX

Jeremiah Cole is not mentioned in any history books; and little is known of the Sussex County native, who apparently led a markedly ordinary life. When Cole died in 1863, he was living on farm that was not much different from the one on which he was born 57 years earlier. In those days, most residents of southern Delaware lived on small farms that produced corn, wheat and other crops. A European traveler remarked in 1800 that the "farms are in general small and ill-cultivated; they receive little or no manure and are in every respect badly managed."

Sussex County farmers used rudimentary equipment to manage their fields. Using a small, single plow pulled by a team of horses or oxen, a farmer could plow an acre or two of fallow land in a day. Most Sussex county farmers who planted corn plowed their fields twice so that the furrows met at right angles. The hills of corn were planted at the intersections of the furrows. Since all of this work was done by hand, the result was an uneven scattering of the hills. One commentator observed: "The usual mode, without any gauge but the ploughman's eye, is for each laborer to take his hoe and crossing the furrow, dig a hole for the corn at what he guesses to be about six feet having no guide but his eye, and his imagination both of which are often dwelling on other objects — so that nothing can be more irregular and unseemly, than a field of young corn so planted. One might suppose to look at that it had been done by a blind or drunken man."

Not only did the farmers plant their fields by hand, they also had to do all of the work necessary to maintain the growing stalks by hand. The six-foot spacing between the plants allowed the sun to reach the developing corn stalks and helped to insure that healthy ears would be produced. On the other hand, the wide spaces between corn stalks allowed weeds to sprout; and these intruders had to be kept in check by regular hoeing.

At harvest time, the ears were sliced by hand from the stalks and stored so that they could dry. The corn stalks and leaves, which would be used for animal fodder, were stacked in large round or square piles which came to a point so that they would easily shed the rain. Once the ears had dried, they would be husked and shelled. The corn could be shelled by rubbing the ears together, scraping the ears over a rod or flailing ears spread on the ground. The grain was then sold or taken to a miller to be ground into meal.

The farmhouses that dotted the Sussex County countryside were surprisingly small structures that often contained only four to five hundred square feet of living space. One house was described as a "good framed house eighteen feet long and sixteen feet wide, with two good floors, and to be covered with shingles and a good brick chimney."

In some homes, the second floor consisted of a single room that was accessible by a narrow staircase or ladder. Most rooms served as sleeping areas as well as day rooms. At night, furniture was merely shifted to the side. The walls of most homes were plastered, but the ceiling beams were left exposed. These beams were trimmed to give a more finished appearance and to help prevent checking or splitting of the wood. Houses were heated by a single fireplace situated in a wall on the first floor.

Surrounding the small house, most Sussex County farms had a number of outbuildings. Kitchens were separate buildings and sometimes were as large as the main house. The kitchen fireplace dominated the structure, but early kitchens were not only used for cooking. Spinning and weaving were commonly done in the same place. In addition to kitchens, many early Delaware farms had smokehouses where meat was cured; coops for chickens; and corncribs and barns.

On the farm where Jeremiah Cole was born, the family raised hogs, grew corn, and cut timber from the forests. Very little money passed through the hands of these isolated farmers, who were nearly self-sufficient and seldom needed to buy anything. When Cole was 32 years old, he posted a bond of $200 when he promised to marry Elizabeth Millin. After marriage, the couple began a family of their own on a farm in North West Fork Hundred. The couple had five children who survived infancy, but these were not the only members in the Cole household. According to the 1850 census, 10 people lived on the Coles' farm. This extended family ranged in age from Cole's 5-year-old son, Samuel, to 79-year-old Mary Dunn, who may have been one of Elizabeth's aunts.

Jeremiah Cole died in 1863 of unknown causes, and an inventory was made of his possessions. Most of these simple items were described as "old," "inferior," or "burnt out." To work his fields, Cole had a plow, a harrow, and two grubbing hoes. His furniture included an old table, a half dozen chairs, a bureau, a couple of beds, and a few chests. The small number of beds indicates that the children may have slept on pallets or mattresses placed directly on the floor.

Kitchen equipment included several iron pots and a pot trammel, which was a device that hung over the fire and could be adjusted according to the height of the fire. Cole also owned a "spider," which was a frying pan on legs which allowed the pan to be placed directly over the glowing coals. There were three water buckets to carry all the water needed for cooking and cleaning. All of Cole's possessions were sold for $222.45.

SLAVERY DIVIDES SUSSEX

Jeremiah Cole may have enjoyed few advantages during his life, but he did hold a significant advantage over many southern Delaware residents. He was white. It is impossible to document when the first slave arrived in Sussex County, but both the early Dutch and the English colonists brought slaves in. When the first European colonists settled near Cape Henlopen in the 17th century, the difference between slave and free was not as sharply defined as it later was. Although Europeans were not considered slaves, many were not completely free. Apprentices were bound to their masters for many years; and during this time they could not move, marry, or leave their apprenticeship without their master's permission. Apprentices were provided room, board, and instruction in a trade, but they were not paid for their labor. Indentured servants were likewise not paid wages. Such servants had mortgaged their labor for a set number of years; and they also could not move on without their master's permission.

Some of the Africans who arrived in Sussex County during the 17th century may have been indentured servants; others were free; and many were slaves. On June 13, 1682, William Clark bought a servant named Black Will, and the bill of sale indicated the ambiguous nature of Will's status: "Where as William Clark did buy of Captain John Osborne of Somerset County in the province of Maryland, a Negro man called or known by the name of Black Will for and during his natural life. Nevertheless, the said William Clark do for the encouragement of the said Negro servant hereby promise, covenant, and agree that if the said Black Will do and shall well and truly serve the said William Clark, his executors, administrators and assignees (for) five years from the twentieth day of May last past, the said Black Will shall be clear and free of and from any further or longer servitude or slavery."

It is not known if Will gained his freedom, but it has been established that during the early 18th century, the number of slaves imported into Sussex County rose dramatically. In 1738, Richard Ellis of Philadelphia directed a typical shipment of slaves to land at Lewes. The ship carried sixteen captive Africans, which Jacob Kollock sold to residents of Sussex County. At that time, many Philadelphia merchants preferred to send captured Africans directly to Delaware which, unlike Pennsylvania, did not have a tariff on slaves.

During the 18th century, slaves in Sussex County were most often used as field hands or house servants, but slaves performed many other tasks. In *Slavery and Freedom in Delaware*, historian William H. Williams described the many tasks performed by the slaves owned by Nehemiah Draper of Cedar Creek Hundred: "In addition to clearing, plowing, planting, cultivating, and harvesting corn and wheat, his thirty slaves looked after 105 cattle, 76 sheep, 54 pigs, 20 oxen, 8 horses, and 55 geese."

Draper, like many of the era's gentry, was a merchant; and his slaves helped in his store and sailed his shallop — a simple two-masted boat — up and down the inland waterways and the Delaware Bay. In addition, several of his slaves played essential roles in his extensive timbering activities. A slave owned by Thomas Robinson was "by trade a blacksmith." Another Sussex County slave was "a miller, and understands how to manufacture flour, can invoice the same." This talented slave also said to "understand the carpenter's and millwright's business middling well."

During the American Revolution, the lofty principles of the Declaration of Independence declared that "all men are created equal;" and the beginning of abolitionist movement led to an increase in the number of free African-Americans in southern Delaware. One, Levin Thompson, is documented as having moved to Sussex County from Maryland, though it is not known why he did so. The legal status of free Blacks was not significantly better in Delaware than it was in Maryland; neither were the economic conditions. Thompson, however, may have seen an opportunity that was missed by others; and in 1794, he purchased 200 acres of land near Trussom Pond in western Sussex County. Levin optimistically named his new farm, "Thompson's Beginning."

Levin Thompson was free; but he did not have legal equality with his white neighbors. Delaware had passed a number of laws that limited the rights of free Blacks. They faced restrictions when testifying against Whites; and Black debtors could be sold into servitude. Despite these legal hazards, Thompson's small farm was a success and he was able to use the profits to buy additional land. According to William H. Williams' *Slavery and Freedom in Delaware, 1639-1865*, Thompson eventually owned more than 500 acres of farmland in Little Creek Hundred and 135 acres of cypress timberland in Dagsboro Hundred. In addition to working the land, Thompson operated a gristmill and a sawmill near Trussom Pond. He also owned several spinning wheels and a loom that produced 2,000 yards of cloth a year.

To operate his extensive holdings, Levin Thompson employed numerous free African-Americans. At that time, free Blacks and skilled slaves who were allowed to take in outside work used their savings to purchase freedom for their relatives. By the time Levin Thompson died in 1816, he was one of the wealthiest residents of Little Creek Hundred.

Like Thompson, Noah Burton was a "free Negro"; but Burton made his mark through the justice system, rather than farming. The day he entered the Sussex County courtroom, with his small, notched stick, he had little inkling of the impact he was about to make. For three years, Burton had done odd jobs for James Rowland. When the work was finished, Rowland refused to pay and in 1837, Burton took Rowland to court. Rowland, who was White, was confident of victory. Burton was illiterate, and could have no written records to document the work that he had done. Burton, however, had a surprise for Rowland; and the repercussion of the proceedings would reverberate around the world and into the 21st century.

/

In the early 19th century, many free African-Americans in rural Sussex Count worked for a single farmer for an extended period of time; others worked for several different employers for a few days at a time. Free Blacks were struggling with the lack of an education system that left many rural residents of southern Delaware (both Black and White) illiterate. The inability to read and write left African-Americans particularly vulnerable. Without a written record of the work that they had done, workers were at the mercy of the goodwill of their employers to pay their obligations. Apparently James Rowland lacked that goodwill.

But Burton brought with him an ancient and nearly-forgotten form of recordkeeping. Burton took the stand to explain what Rowland owed him, and he produced his stick as evidence. Burton had cut the stick with notches to indicate the jobs that he had performed and the money that he was owed. The use of such tally sticks was common during the Middle Ages; they could be split down the middle so that both parties could have a record of the debt. In some areas, creditors took tally sticks to tax collectors and exchanged them for cash.

The court listened as Burton used the stick to describe each of the thirteen occasions when he had worked for Rowland. He also used the stick to recall the wages that he and Burton had agreed upon. The Sussex County judge decided that Noah Burton's stick provided sufficient verification to rule in Burton's favor. The decision demonstrated that free African-Americans had a chance of winning in the Delaware courts; and it also set a precedent for unconventional proofs. Noah Burton's notched stick is still cited in cases today, for it contained "regular entries made in the routine of business at or near the time of a transaction" and thus was admissible as evidence.

Tally sticks may have been somewhat more common when the first colonists arrived in America. Such a tally stick was uncovered at the site of the failed colony of Avalon, in Newfoundland. (Avalon was established by Lord Baltimore; but when the weather proved too harsh, he abandoned the settlement and turned his interested to the Chesapeake Bay.)

Slavery came into Delaware with tobacco, but it did not exit the state when farmers switched to other crops. Many slaves were retained as field hands, others as house servants, and in Sussex County, many worked at the ironworks. The Unity Forge near the Nanticoke River used slave labor to perform a number of tasks, from the hauling and lifting jobs to the skilled fork at the forge. The abilities that these slaves acquired made them especially valuable to their masters, who granted them important concessions. Skilled slaves were allowed

90

to take in extra work, and to keep the money they earned in this fashion. Many ironworking slaves used these funds to purchase their freedom.

Slaves with marketable skills had another advantage over the unskilled, field-working slaves. Studies have shown that skilled slaves who ran away to a large town where they could use their skills to support themselves were usually safe from recapture. One of the reasons for the decline of slavery during the 19th century was that many slaves, including those in Delaware, acquired skills that became their gateway to freedom.

By the beginning of the 19th century, the 4,000 slaves who lived in southern Delaware comprised about of a fourth of Sussex County's population; but the slave population was declining. White residents of Sussex pondered a dilemma. As long as they kept their slaves in bondage, White masters had to be on constant guard against a slave rebellion. On the other hand, many Whites believed that freed slaves would use their liberty to organize and avenge themselves on their former masters. Their fears were confirmed in August, 1831, when Nat Turner led a bloody insurrection in Virginia that left more than 50 White people dead.

Nat Turner's rebellion had been over for several months when rumors began to circulate that something sinister was happening in the trackless wastes of the Great Swamp. In October 1831, anxious White residents of Sussex began to repeat accounts of bands of runaway slaves gathering in the swamps. One report asserted that more than 3,000 armed Blacks had assembled and were preparing an attack on Seaford.

With most of the Whites already on edge, some of the men got the bright idea of tying black handkerchiefs around their faces and pretending to shoot at one another on the banks of the Nanticoke River. The incident was exposed as a prank, but many Seaford residents remained thoroughly convinced that a slave rebellion was imminent. So many people believed that an uprising was certain that half of the electorate remained home on election day.

No slave rebellion materialized in Sussex County; the rumors of armed bands planning to attack Seaford had no basis in fact. Unfortunately, the fears generated by this incident led to serious repercussions for the state's black population. Many locals were particularly nervous about the nighttime prayer sessions held by out-of-state Black preachers. Slave owners suspected that these meetings, which were one of the few occasions that Blacks could assemble without White supervision, were being used to plot rebellions. The Delaware legislature banned religious meetings after 10 p.m. In addition, Black ministers from outside the state were required to have a license to hold services. The fears sparked by Nat Turner's rebellion would not abate until slavery was permanently outlawed.

As the years passed, the number of slaves in Sussex County continued to decline; and a few Delaware slaves were able to use the legal system to gain their freedom. In April 1846, Ann Elliott took part in what would become a three-year struggle. As a slave, Ann knew that her decision was fraught with risk. Her action would place her at odds with much of the legal establishment of Sussex County. Ann also knew that if she failed, there would be severe physical consequences for her and her children. But after careful consideration, Ann filed a petition for her freedom in the Superior Court for Sussex County in Georgetown.

Ann Elliott was born a slave in 1807. Her mother was owned by George Moore, who farmed a small tract of land in Little Creek Hundred, tucked away in the southwestern corner of Delaware. The Great Cypress Swamp stood between Little Creek Hundred and the older Delaware towns along the coast. The farmers of this corner of Delaware looked across the Mason-Dixon Line to Maryland for their sullies and for markets. Moore and the other farmers in Little Creek Hundred shipped their crops down the Nanticoke River across Maryland to the Chesapeake Bay. In addition, many of the farmers of Little Creek Hundred agreed with their Maryland neighbors that the institution of slavery was a necessary evil.

At the time when Ann Elliott was born, the anti-slavery movement was taking root in Delaware. Although Little Creek Hundred was a traditional slave area, there were farmers who had come to the conclusion that hiring seasonal labor was cheaper than purchasing a slave. In addition, Moore and many of his neighbors had converted to Methodism, which was strongly opposed to slavery.

Other slave owners became convinced that the institution should be ended; but they were also fearful that a free Black population would have difficulty finding work and would become a drain on the community. It was a situation that Thomas Jefferson described as having a "Wolf by the ears." It was dangerous to hold on, and dangerous to let go. Many slave owners skirted the issue by freeing their slaves — in their wills. When George Moore died in 1805, he left a will that declared that all his slaves were free except Ann's mother and one other slave, who were to be given their freedom when Moore's widow, Sarah, died.

Sarah Moore died in 1828, and Ann's mother was given her freedom. But Ann was sold to another Sussex County farmer, named Robert Twilley. Under Delaware law, children of freed slaves were to become free when they reached adulthood, but Ann waited nearly two decades to claim her freedom. During that time, Ann married and had several children.

By 1846, Ann's children were nearing adulthood and reaching their greatest value as slaves. Apparently, Ann was worried that her children would be sold to a distant owner, and she decided to claim her freedom. If Ann could establish that she was free when her children were born, under Delaware law they would also be free. On the other hand, if Ann's status as a slave was confirmed, she would be in trouble. Her suit would outrage her owner, and if she failed he would make sure they were all separated and sold to oppressive owners as an example to keep other slaves from using the courts to gain their freedom.

In the 19th century, slaves were prohibited from testifying in court. Ann found an ally in Georgetown lawyer and slave owner, Caleb S. Layton, who was a veteran of the Sussex County legal system. Layton owned slaves, but he believed that there were important limits on what slave owners could do. Layton agreed to take Ann Elliott's case.

Since Ann could not testify directly, Layton took depositions from her and her relatives. He was able to establish that Ann should have been free when Sarah Moore died, but the court denied the freedom of Ann's children on a technicality. Layton appealed to the Court of Errors in Dover. When the appeal was heard, Layton argued that slave ownership was a property right that had certain limits. In addition, Layton contended that slaves also possessed certain moral rights that had to be upheld by the Delaware courts. On October 24, 1849, the court handed down its decision. Ann Elliott's long struggle was, at last, over. The court declared Ann and her children free.

Ann Elliott had used the courts to gain her freedom, but others held in bondage were forced to take extra-legal measures to escape from slavery. The ideals of the American Revolution challenged the institution of slavery. Many people who had fought for their freedom from England questioned whether the same freedoms should not be extended to slaves. Following the Revolution, several abolitionist societies were formed in Delaware; but some slaves could not wait a lifetime to receive their liberty. Advertisements for fugitive slaves began to appear in the newspapers: "Ten Pounds Reward. Ran away from the subscriber, living on Broad Creek, Sussex County, and the state of Delaware, on 6th

Sept. last, a NEGRO MAN, named CAESAR, nearly 6 feet high, stout and well made, he has a scar on one of his wrists..."

Charles L. Blockson (whose great-grandfather was a fugitive slave from Seaford) has studied numerous accounts of runaway slaves. In his book, *The Underground Railroad*, Blockson reported that runaway slaves made use of safe houses at Seaford, Laurel, Concord, Georgetown, Millsboro, Lewes, Milford, and other towns as they fled northward. At these stops, sympathetic residents provided them with food, shelter, and directions to the next stop.

Blockson offers an account of one of his ancestors, Jacob Blockson, who lived in western Sussex County near Seaford. Blockson, his wife and young son were owned by Jesse Layton, a "man of no business, except drinking whiskey and farming." When Blockson learned that his master had decided to sell the farm, Blockson decided to run away. Although he would be unable to take his wife and son with him, Blockson could no longer live as a slave. As he later recalled: "I left because I didn't want to stay with him any longer. My master was about to be sold out this fall, and I made up my mind that I did not want to be sold like a horse."

When he slipped away from the Layton farm, Blockson knew that if he were recaptured he could end up on a Southern plantation, where he would spend the rest of his life at hard labor and never see his family again. Blockson, however was determined: "When I started, I resolved to die sooner than I would be taken back."

Blockson made his way out of Sussex County and he did not stop until he reached Canada. At the town of St. Catherines, Blockson went to work for a butcher and received the first regular wages in his life. Although he only made $2.50 a week, Blockson was able to put together enough money to arrange for his family to join him in Canada.

Not all Delaware slaves used the "Underground Railroad" to reach freedom; William Cope, John Grey, Henry Boice, and Isaac White took a more direct route. Cope, Grey, and Boice were slaves of Sussex County farmer Shepherd P. Houston. According to John Grey: "Houston is a very small man; for some time his affairs had been in a bad way; he had been broke, some say he had bad luck for killing my brother. My brother was sick, but master said he wasn't sick, and he took a chunk, and beat him, and he died a few days after."

Houston also sold some of his slaves out of Delaware, and this helped convince the young men to form a daring plan. They had some experience with small boats; and on a cold January evening, they slipped away from Houston's farm.

The fugitives made their way to the beach near Lewes, where a fierce gale was driving high waves across the bay. Later they reported: "With simple faith they entered the skiff; two of them took the oars, manfully to face uncertain dangers from the waves. But they remained steadfast, oft as they felt that they were making the last stroke with the oars, on the verge of being overwhelmed with the waves. At every new stage of danger they summoned courage by remembering that they were escaping for their lives."

By the next morning, the four fugitives were in sight of the New Jersey shore. They were uncertain where to land, when the captain of an oyster boat spotted them. The oysterman guided them up the bay to Philadelphia, where abolitionists took them in.

THE RAILROAD ARRIVES IN SUSSEX

The fugitives who fled to freedom via the Underground Railroad may never have seen a real railroad. In 1832, the state's first regular railroad line began operating across northern Delaware between New Castle and Frenchtown, Maryland. Four years after the opening of the Frenchtown and New Castle Railroad, plans were made to run track southward down the length of Delaware. In 1836, the Delaware Railroad was granted a charter to build a line "From any point on or near the Wilmington and Susquehanna Railroad, or the New Castle and Frenchtown Railroad, to the southern line of the State, in a direction toward Cape Charles, with full power to construct lateral branches to Lewes, Seaford, or any other points or places within the limits of the State of Delaware."

Although the plans for the Delaware Railroad were received with enthusiasm by investors, a downturn in the American economy delayed the construction for several years. As the climate improved, investors warmed to the idea of a rail line running down the length of the Delmarva Peninsula. When plans for the Eastern Shore Rail Road were announced, residents of Sussex County were surprised to discover that the line would skirt the western edge of Delaware and remain entirely within Maryland. The route was selected to avoid crossing rivers that were wider on the eastern side of the state. The western route shifted the railroad away from the older towns close to Delaware Bay. The path of the tracks would lead directly into the western side of Sussex County that had always been the most isolated area of Delaware. Another reversal in the economy put the Eastern Shore Rail Road on hold, but in 1849 plans for the Delaware Railroad were resurrected and crews began to lay track in the direction of Sussex County.

In 1856, the Delaware Railroad was completed to Seaford, and three years later, the line reached Laurel. The first train slipped into town unnoticed on a Saturday, but two days later a large crowd turned out to celebrate: "On Monday,... the vicinity of the depot was crowded with people of all ages, sexes, colors and conditions to witness the approach of the 'iron horse,' which came in, snorting and puffing, to the wonder and amazement of a great many."

A few months later, the line reached Delmar on the southern border of Sussex County. For first time, residents of southwestern Delaware could reach Wilmington, Philadelphia and other major cities faster than people living on the coast. The Delaware Railroad carried passengers from Wilmington to Delmar in ten hours. Seaford, Laurel and other communities along the train line were now favored, whereas travelers from the coastal communities had to bump along the roads of Sussex County for many miles before they could begin their train ride.

The arrival of the train in western Sussex County also altered some of the economic patterns of southern Delaware. Traditionally, the Nanticoke River had carried part of Delaware's trade; and the river ran southwesterly to the Chesapeake Bay. The Nanticoke River tied western Sussex County to Maryland, Virginia and the South. The completion of the railroad promised to turn business away from the South toward Wilmington, Philadelphia, and other large Northern cities. By connecting different regions, the railroad had the potential to unify Delaware as never before; and construction began on tracks to connect Lewes and the coastal region with the mainline. As 1860 dawned, the growing train network drew southern Delaware closer to the industrial North; at the same time, the Underground Railroad was a link to the South, straining to meet the needs of fugitives traveling to escape the last days of slavery.

CHAPTER 5. CIVIL WAR DIVIDES SUSSEX

NORTH OR SOUTH?

"The Union is Dissolved!" Abraham Lincoln's election to the presidency in 1860 cracked wide the deep fissures that had divided the Union since the American Revolution. A 19th-century writer described the crisis in Delaware: "The questions of slavery, the rock on which our ship of state had struck, was, however, one of too great magnitude, and was too deeply rooted in its principles, not to affect very seriously the feelings and interests of the people of Delaware. Its citizens were closely united in habits, sympathies, and interests with that portion of our people dwelling in the gulf and cotton-raising states."

Delaware was as divided as the nation. The state had been the first to ratify the Federal Constitution and the people of Delaware proudly wore the nickname "First Staters," and many citizens of Sussex County recognized "the horrors and suffering that would over take the citizens of Delaware if the state should attempt to leave the Union." In addition, Delaware troops had been among the finest fighters during the war for Independence. Memories of the exploits of Caesar Rodney, Samuel Lockwood, Henry Fisher, John Dagworthy, John Learmonth and others who fought during the American Revolution still resonated in the minds of Delaware residents.

In spite of its traditions of fighting for liberty and a deep respect for the Union, Delaware remained a slave state. Sussex County, where slavery was strongest in the state, had considerable sympathy for the South. In 1859, the abolitionist John Brown and a contingent of his followers captured the Federal armory at Harper's Ferry. Brown's intentions were not entirely clear; but many believed that this was the first step in a general slave revolt. A militia unit led by Colonel Robert E. Lee stormed the armory, killed some of the insurgents, captured Brown, and prevented the spread of the insurrection. Brown was tried and found guilty of treason. At his trial, Brown declared: "Now, if it is deemed necessary that I shall forfeit my life for the furtherance of the needs of justice, and mingle my blood further with the blood of my children and with the blood of millions in this slave country whose rights are disregarded by wicked, cruel, and unjust enactments, I say let it be done."

On December 2, 1859, John Brown was executed, but many were convinced that his raid would be repeated elsewhere and that a widespread slave revolt would turn the horrors of Nat Turner's rebellion onto every slave-holder. Alarmed by the specter of violence the incident raised, communities in slave states began to organize militia groups. In Georgetown, Caleb R. Layton organized and armed the "Sussex Guards." But, Layton's company failed to drill regularly, and the unit was disbanded. Layton organized a second militia company and armed them with up-to-date rifled muskets, which gave the unit considerable firepower. In addition, Caleb R. Paynter formed a company and issued his troops weapons from the Georgetown armory.

After the Confederates fired on Fort Sumter in April, 1861, President Abraham Lincoln called for volunteers to put down the rebellion. On April 19, a regiment of Massachusetts troops attempted to march through Baltimore on their way to Washington and ignited a riot that left more than three dozen civilians and soldiers dead or wounded.. That night, several of the railroad bridges in Maryland that connected Washington with the North were burned by Southern sympathizers. Like Delaware, Maryland was a slave state teetering on secession. If either state joined the Confederacy, the viability of Washington as the Union capital would be in doubt. In May, 1861, the unexpected occupation of Baltimore by Union troops secured Northern control over Maryland, but the loyalty of Delaware remained questionable.

Shortly after the firing on Fort Sumter, Charles du Pont Bird wrote to General Robert E. Lee: "A strong feeling in the two lower counties of Delaware is aroused in favor of Delaware joining the southern Confederacy." Bird went on to outline a plan to tighten the stranglehold on Washington. During colonial times, north-to-south travelers often made an overland trip down the Delmarva Peninsula until they reached the Nanticoke River, where they boarded boats to continue their journey. In the 1850s, the completion of the railroad to Seaford made the land segment of this trip easy, and Bird warned Lee that Union forces could use these rail connections to shore up Washington's defenses.

Bird, however, had a plan that would disrupt this important link to the North. He wrote to Lee, "With a man or two from you to give directions and a hint that arms and men would come if necessary, the people of Sussex themselves would destroy the Delaware railroad terminating at Seaford, on the Nanticoke. This railroad, I am confident, the General Government of Lincoln wish to secure, that they may transport troops by the Nanticoke River to the Chesapeake, and thence to Washington by the Potomac River. A vessel or two sunk in the Nanticoke will hinder this design. There is considerable trestling work on the Delaware railroad near Dover, which would retard the road if it were broken."

Although there was considerable sentiment in Delaware in favor of the Union, Bird believed that: "The arms that Delaware owns are in the hands of the secessionists. The powder mills on the Brandywine (owned by relations of mine) should be secured at all hazards. With not a very large force, if we cannot hold them, they should be destroyed. Some of the du Ponts are friendly to the South. If it is possible to guard these works for a few weeks, the stock of powder for the Southern Confederacy would be largely increased."

Bird implored Lee to act at once to "stop the hordes of the North," but there was little that Lee could do. A number of men from prominent Sussex County families did head south to join the Confederate forces at about this time. Among those who are known to have gone "South" were Charles Rust, Thomas Horsey, and Edward Jacobs, all from Seaford. In addition, Caleb Ross (the son of former Delaware governor William Ross, whose sympathies for the South were well known) left Delaware to assist the rebellion.

In order to obtain sorely needed supplies, Southern sympathizers established a clandestine trade route that ran from New York City down the coast to Delaware and from Sussex County southward. So many Confederate agents were observed buying war material in New York that in August 1861, Hiram Barney, Customs Collector for New York City, wrote an urgent letter to Gideon Welles, the Union Secretary of the Navy: "It is a matter of notoriety that articles of all kinds are constantly transmitted by way of Delaware and Maryland into eastern Virginia. While it might be difficult to indicate particular instances in which this has been done, general report and numerous suspicious circumstances satisfy me that it is of the most frequent occurrence."

The ships engaged in this trade were small vessels that re-traced the routes that had been established in colonial times. According to Barney: "Vessels clearing from this port sail direct to Chincoteague and Sinepuxent bays, as well as to the inlets upon the Delaware coast, loaded with provisions and general stores, which are thence sent across the country to unguarded points and thence delivered into the hands of the rebels."

The Southern agents in New York City had no difficulty circumventing the wartime regulations that limited trade with the rebelling states. The needed goods were bought and loaded on a ship, and the brokers would merely declare that they were bound for a Northern port. The Union authorities had no grounds for detaining these vessels. Once they were at sea, the captains turned south and set a course for Indian River Inlet. In his letter to Secretary Wells, Barney complained: "To such an extent is this course pursued that Southern merchants come continually to this city, make purchases of goods, and prepare for their being forwarded to their homes with contemptuous disregard of the restrictions sought to be imposed upon them. Our coasters are leaving daily for the Delaware and Maryland ports, loaded with general merchandise designed undoubtedly for the use of parties on the Virginia side, but, of course, affording no such evidence of that purpose as to warrant me in detaining them."

The New York Customs Collector believed that any attempt to require captains to file affidavits as to their destinations would be circumvented by the Southern sympathizers. Barney suggested using small armed vessels that could negotiate the shallow water of the coastal inlets to intercept the clandestine trade. He advised the Secretary of the Navy: "The most obvious remedy for this state of things is evidently to be found in an increased watchfulness — upon the land and water boundaries of disloyal States. A few light-draft vessels, to run into the inlets and watch the coast from the Delaware Bay to the South, would be of great service. And I do not doubt that a regulation which would require all shippers, owners, or consignees of goods by vessels asking permits for a coastwise voyage to file a sworn manifest of their shipments would do very much to check the violations of the blockade. Such a regulation, however, it may not be possible to enforce."

In addition to Barney's letter to Secretary Welles, the existence of militia companies that were filled with men who favored the South, and the reports of men leaving Sussex County to join the Confederacy, President Lincoln was further alarmed when he learned that another plot was hatching in southern Delaware.

In 1861, the use of gas-filled balloons was one of the most advanced methods for observing enemy forces. The Union's capacity for aerial observation was far superior to that of the Confederates. Lincoln and other Union leaders were thunderstruck when they learned that four men from southern Delaware were part of a plot to steal a Union balloon and deliver it to the Confederates.

Lincoln's attention was drawn to Delaware on the issue of slavery, too. Lincoln had an idea that might help to end the war without additional bloodshed, and he decided to discuss it with Benjamin Burton. The Burton family was one of the oldest in the coastal region. The progenitor of the family had arrived during the 17th century, when Lewes was a village of a few dozen residents struggling to hang on in the face of attacks by pirates, privateers, and other marauders. The first Burtons emigrated from Accomack County, Virginia, sailed though the Indian River Inlet, and settled on Long Neck, where they established a thriving plantation.

In the early years, the Burtons and those who followed them to the western shore of the coastal bays planted tobacco, which they raised with the help of slave labor. By the time Benjamin Burton arrived at the White House, the Burton family had spread throughout the coastal region. Corn had replaced tobacco as the primary crop; and many slaves in southern Delaware had been freed. By the beginning of the Civil War, there were only 1,341 slaves in Sussex County; and at the same time, there were 4,370 free African-Americans living in the coastal region. Benjamin Burton had only 28 slaves, few compared to the hundreds owned by some in the Deep South; but Burton owned more slaves than anyone else in Delaware. Coming from a prominent family of long tradition, and finding himself the state's largest slave owner, Burton was the ideal candidate for a plan that Lincoln believed might end the Civil War.

The president proposed a system of compensated emancipation: the Federal Government would compensate slave owners for their economic loss when they set their slaves free. The president suggested the plan to Delaware Congressman George P. Fisher, who arranged for Benjamin Burton to come to the White House to discuss it. If Lincoln could convince the Delaware slave owners to accept his plan, he might be able to convince the other slave states that remained loyal to the Union (Maryland, Kentucky and Missouri) to go along as well. If it worked in those states, it could be extended to states throughout the South.

Delaware was pivotal to Lincoln's plan, and Benjamin Burton was pivotal to Delaware's agreement to the plan. Lincoln explained the details to Burton: all slaves over 35 years old would be freed at once; younger slaves would be freed in ten years. Congress would establish a fund of $900,000 that would be used to compensate slave masters, who would receive a generous payment of around $500 per slave. The cost for freeing the slaves of Delaware would be less than the government spent on a single day of fighting the Confederacy. "This," Lincoln explained, was "the cheapest and most humane way of ending this war."

Burton agreed; he was convinced that the slave owners of Delaware would react enthusiastically. But he was out of step with many of his neighbors. When he returned home to Millsboro and explained Lincoln's proposal of compensated emancipation to the coastal region's slave owners, they rejected the idea out-right. Slave owners of southern Delaware considered the plan an unwarranted interference in their affairs, and they resented Lincoln's attempt to buy his way out of the Civil War.

Lincoln could not wait long for Delaware to embrace the plan for compensated emancipation. Sussex County's activities in support of the South forced the president to act. Union troops stationed in Baltimore were ordered to make a quick raid. After crossing the Chesapeake Bay, the troops moved into southern Delaware and arrested Thomas B. Giles, Joseph Bacon, John S. Bacon, and S. B. Frost, all of whom had been implicated in the plot to steal the military balloon. Next, the Union soldiers marched into Georgetown, where they arrested Caleb Paynter and disarmed his militia company. The troops returned to Baltimore with two cannons that they had captured at Georgetown and the four balloon conspirators, who were confined at Fort McHenry. Although some residents of Sussex County continued to support the Confederacy, from this point on Delaware would remain firmly in the Union.

THIS IS A BAD WAR

Delaware may have continued loyal to the Union; but there were many people who questioned how soldiers from this slave state would act on the bat-tlefield. Shortly after Lincoln's call for volunteers to suppress the rebellion, the First Delaware Regiment began to recruit volunteers in Wilmington. William Swiggett of Georgetown was one of several Union supporters to join the First Delaware Regiment. He was elected a 2nd Lieutenant in Company G; and by the beginning of May, 1861, Swiggett and the rest of the Delaware troops were immersed in their training: "The task of drilling, pitching tents, military arrangement of camp, and instruction in guard duty was immediately begun, and the men, profoundly impressed with the novelty of their new life and the difficulties of studying an entirely new profession, took an ardent interest in their duties and made rapid progress in the school of the soldier."

The troops of the 1st Delaware were eager to fight the Confederates; but they soon learned that Delaware's position as a slave state made the Union high command uneasy. The men of the 1st Delaware had enlisted for 90 days, and they spent all of that time guarding bridges and railroad tracks far from the front lines. Swiggett was not dissuaded by the monotonous duty, and he remained determined to fight for the Union. At the initial re-enlistment period, the First Delaware was reorganized as a three-year unit, and Swiggett continued to serve.

While President Lincoln was fretting over reports of the strength of the Southern sympathizers in Sussex County, recruiters for the 1st Delaware combed the state for men. On September 13, dozens of volunteers joined the regiment at Georgetown. Among those who stepped forward were the four Carey brothers, John, Burton, Robert, and Thomas. During their first year of service, they were all restricted to guarding railroad bridges and performing other duties behind the line. They spent endless hours drilling in the intricacies of 19th-century warfare. During the Civil War, ranks of standing soldiers formed the basis of the most victorious armies. The Carey brothers and the other enlistees had to learn to charge their muskets with powder and a bullet, use a ramrod to drive the charge home, fix a percussion cap in place, cock the weapon, aim and fire. They had to be able to perform all of these movements in less than fifteen seconds, and they had to be able to load muskets while standing in a closely-packed rank of soldiers. The best-trained regiments were able to fire a volley of several hundred shots that ripped into the enemy lines with deadly effect.

After guarding railroad lines in Maryland, the 1st Delaware was shifted to Camp Hamilton near Fort Monroe, Virginia, by the mouth of the Chesapeake Bay. While the rest of the Union forces prepared for an advance toward Richmond, the Delaware troops were again relegated to guard duty. The endless hours spent in drilling instilled in the troops paid off, at least in terms of show. According to one of the regiment's officers: "Our dress-parades had become a fine military pageant to the other regiments of the brigade, some of which changed the time for their own evening parade to a later hour that they might have the opportunity to witness ours."

By early 1862, Lieutenants James Oates and James Rickards of Company B (which included several men from Sussex County) concluded that the tedium of drill and guard duty had taken a toll on the men. Oats and Rickards thought that a bit of theater would help revive the morale of the Delaware troops and other members of the Northern forces. Most of the troops had little experience with theatrical presentations, of course. On top of the isolation of rural life, they came from a tradition that suspected such cultural diversions of fostering immorality. In England, this attitude had contributed to the banning of theatrical performances and the closing of William Shakespeare's Globe Theatre. By the beginning of the 19th century, the attitude toward theatrical performances had begun to soften, but the population of southern Delaware was too sparse to support a resident theater.

Nonetheless, led by Oats and Rickards, the troops from Sussex County and other soldiers of the 1st Delaware Regiment spent several weeks constructing an elaborate theater with seats for 400 people. The auditorium contained a large stage that was lit by footlights, an enclosure for an orchestra, and chandeliers with tin sconces to hold candles. The building also had dressing rooms for the soldier-actors. To give their performances a professional setting, some backdrops were sent down the Delmarva Peninsula from the Boothenian Dramatic Association of Wilmington.

The Delaware troops named their theater "Hopkinson Hall" in honor of the popular Lt. Colonel Oliver P. Hopkinson; and the first event in the new theater was a ball hosted by the regiment's officers. Invitations were sent to officers in the Union army and to the officers of a French war-vessel that was anchored near Fort Monroe. In addition, some of the mischievous Delaware troops decided to extend an invitation to Confederate General John Magruder, whose Southern troops were camped nearby. According to William Seville, the Delaware regiment's historian, "Some of the wags amused themselves by nailing to a tree outside the picket-line a paper containing an invitation to General Magruder and staff to attend this ball, which, they said, was a polite recognition of General Magruder's attentions to us, by sending a flag of truce regularly once a week summing us to surrender Fort Monroe forthwith or remain in it at our peril."

On February 17, 1862, the Delaware troops presented their first entertainment, and according to Seville: "The audience which assembled to honor this first representation was, to use the well-worn phraseology of the newspapers, a large, fashionable, and intelligent one, embracing as it did all the officers of the fort and camp not on duty, with many ladies; and loud and earnest were the plaudits bestowed on the enterprising members of the Delaware Regiment for such a valuable contribution to the amusements of camp-life." They put on "La Tour De Nesle," a popular play written by Alexandre Dumas in 1832. Then Sgt. Charles Schaffer and Sgt. Allen Tatem stepped in front of the curtain and sang "Eighty Years Ago," which was followed by a farce entitled "B.B., or the Benecia Boy in England," having to do with an international boxing spectacle between the supposed American champion and the English champion in 1860.

Three weeks after their initial theatrical production, the 1st Delaware had front-row seats for the epic naval encounter of the Civil War. On March 8, the troops crowded onto rooftops and watched as the Rebel ironclad *Virginia* steamed into Hampton Roads. The *Virginia* had begun life as the steam frigate *Merrimack*, scuttled by the Union forces when they abandoned Norfolk early in the war. The resourceful Confederates had salvaged the hull, patched up the engines, and built a barn-like structure of iron on the rejuvenated frigate, which they christened "*Virginia*." Despite the name change, many in the North continued to refer to the Southern ironclad as the *Merrimack*.

The *Virginia* entered Hampton Roads to engage the entire Union fleet, and to lift the Union stranglehold on the Chesapeake Bay. The *Virginia* sank one Northern warship, set another afire, and forced the rest of the Union fleet to seek shallow waters where the heavily-laden *Virginia* could not go. At sundown, the Confederate ironclad withdrew from action, but it promised to return the next day. As the glow of the burning ship lit their camp, the troops of the 1st Delaware speculated about their own fate.

News of the Confederate ironclad's victory threw Washington into frenzy. Secretary of War Edwin Stanton stated that, "The *Merrimack*...would destroy every vessel in the service, could lay every city on the coast under contribution, could take Fortress Monroe; McClellan's mistaken purpose to advance by the Peninsula must be abandoned." Lincoln and his advisors were afraid that the Confederate war ship would sail up the Potomac, disperse Congress, destroy the Capitol and continue up the coast to destroy the other Northern cities. The only hope for the North was the recently-launched *Monitor*, which was making its way south from New York; but it was struck by a storm off the Delaware coast.

The new Yankee warship was radically different from any other ship afloat. Built of iron from the keel up, the *Monitor* rode so low in the water that small waves broke over the ship's deck. A single rotating turret carried the two cannons that were its only armament. The *Monitor*'s low freeboard and round turret earned it the apt description of "Cheese box on a raft." Shipyard workers were putting the finishing touches on the *Monitor* when it was towed out of New York harbor for the voyage to Hampton Roads. In an account written after the war, Rear Admiral Daniel Ammen described the *Monitor's* encounter with a winter storm: "The wind was moderate during Thursday night and Friday morning; but about noon, off the Delaware, it freshened to a strong breeze from the northwest, and caused a rough sea, which broke over the vessel's deck, forcing the water in floods through the hawse-pipes and under the turret. In the afternoon the sea increased, and breaking over the smoke-pipe and blower-pipe, caused the blower-bands to slip and break."

All power was lost aboard the *Monitor*, and, "As the engines were now useless either for propulsion or pumping, the water gained rapidly. The hand-pump was used and the men set to bailing, but with little effect, as the water could only be carried off over the wall of the turret. At last, the tug was headed for the shore. After five hours' steaming, the vessels came into smoother water; the engine-room was cleared of gas, the blower-bands were repaired, and the engine once more moved slowly."

After the storm slackened for a short time, the ironclad was again battered by high waves: "But the sea now broke violently over the deck, and again entered the blower-pipes. Another disaster seemed imminent...After five critical hours, daylight broke, and the tug was ordered to go nearer the shore. By eight o'clock the danger was over." The *Monitor* had weathered the storm, and it was able to continue past the Delaware coast.

On the morning of March 9th, the troops of the 1st Delaware searched the waters of Hampton Roads; but they could not find anything that looked like a warship. Again the menacing Confederate ironclad *Virginia* steamed toward the Union fleet. Adjutant William Seville recalled, "Then we heard a muffled report, and observed a puff of white smoke afar off in the direction of Pig Point, and, on leveling our glasses upon the spot, we could make out a dark streak on the water surmounted by what seemed to be a black bandbox."

During the first encounter between two ironclads, neither ship damaged the other; but the balance of power had shifted back to the North. The threat of the *Merrimack* terrorizing Washington and other Northern cities was over. The *Monitor* had arrived late the night before, and as the small warship battled the *Virginia*, the Delaware troops "laughed and shouted to see the thing fight."

The victory of the *Monitor* insured that the Northern advance toward Richmond could continue; but the 1st Delaware was again assigned a post far from the front lines. The regiment's reputation as a well-drilled unit, however, earned it a visit from President Lincoln. When Delaware troops learned that Lincoln would inspect them during a dress parade, the soldiers were determined to "make as imposing a martial appearance as possible."

During the inspection, Drum-Major Patrick Dooley, who wore "the tallest and most gorgeous of shakoes," led the regimental band across the front of the regiment. Lincoln quietly observed the Delaware troops as he rode behind the band. When the first members of the band reached the end of the regiment, the musicians turned about smartly. "Drum-Major Dooley, with his glittering staff presented at an angle of forty-five degrees from his manly breast, had advanced with martial stride through the midst of the musicians, [when] he suddenly came face to face with the President, and all were brought to a dead halt. The situation was growing serious. There sat the President, looking somewhat embarrassed, and there stood Dooley, firm as the rock of Gibraltar; the equestrian brigade supporting the President, and the band resolutely backing up the drum-major, 'marking time' and playing away with their best energy. After a few moments of hesitation, which provoked a hearty peal of laughter from all, the President...opened the road for Dooley and the band out of their dilemma."

After a year of service, the 1st Delaware had not fired a shot in anger; and several of the unit's officers petitioned the Union high command for the regiment to be assigned to front line duty. On September 5, 1862, General Joseph Mansfield summed up the 1st Delaware's service to that point: "Well drilled, and been in service for about fourteen months and have never fired a gun at the enemy."

Shortly after Mansfield made his comment, Robert E. Lee led the Army of Northern Virginia across the Potomac into Maryland. The Union authorities needed all available troops to repel the Confederate forces. The desire to stop Lee's advance overcame the reluctance to use troops from a slave state; and concerns about the loyalty of the troops of the First Delaware were cast aside. Although they had not yet fired a shot in combat, the year of drilling had turned the men from Delaware into excellent soldiers. When Major General John Dix detached the 1st Delaware from his command and sent them to join the troops massing to meet the Confederates in Maryland, he wrote to his superior in Washington, "You are perhaps not aware that these regiments are the flower of [my] command."

Two weeks later, Swiggett, the Georgetown volunteers and the other men of the 1st Delaware found themselves near Sharpsburg, Maryland, where they were part of the Union forces that met Lee's army at the battle of Antietam. On

September 17, 1862, the 1st Delaware led the regiment across a stream and over a mile of low rolling hills. The regiment halted and faced to the left. At the command, "Fix bayonets!" every man in the regiment understood that, at last, they faced a deadly encounter with the enemy.

The Carey brothers and the others snapped their bayonets into place and pressed forward through a cornfield. As they advanced, the Confederates opened fire; but the regiment maintained good order as it marched through the cornstalks. When they reached the edge of the field, the troops had to scale a post-and-rail fence. After they cleared the fence, the regiment reformed its lines, with each man touching the elbow of the soldier next to him. All eyes were to the front where the well-protected Confederate line awaited the Delaware troops.

A surviving member of the 1st Delaware recalled: "One line of rebels was posted in a sunken road, while across the road, on rising ground, was a second line and their batteries. The fire the enemy was thus able to bring to bear on our single line was so destructive that even veteran troops would have been repulsed. As it was, the right of the division, which approached nearest the sunken road, was staggered and recoiled, and the right of our regiment was forced back to the edge of the cornfield, while the remainder could make no farther advance."

Colonel John Andrews, the commander of the 1st Delaware, described the action: "The enemy's batteries now opened a severe fire. Having advanced steadily through woods and cornfields, driving all before us, we met the enemy in two lines of battle posted in road, or ravine, four feet below the surface of the adjoining field, with a third line in a cornfield in the rear, the ground gradually rising, so that they were able to fire over the heads of those in the ravine; our right was also exposed to the sudden and terrible fire from the troops who succeeded in breaking the center division of the line of battle. We were at this time about 20 paces off the enemy, and returned their fire for some time with much coolness and effect."

The men of the 1st Delaware hugged the ground, still firing away. When some of the men saw that the colonel's horse, "Spot" had been shot and killed, they used the horse's body as a breastwork. Swiggett was hit twice, and he very likely would have bled to death, but two men carried him to safety.

In the confusion of the battle, the Delaware troops discovered that two of their regimental flags lay in the open field between the Union and Confederate lines. A few men crept forward to retrieve the stranded colors, but the enemy fire quickly drove most of the them back. Finally, a sergeant was able to retrieve one of the banners and crawl back to the 1st Delaware.

While this was being done, a squad of sharpshooters was organized to provide covering fire for another attempt to recover the second flag. After the squad was assembled, a lieutenant slipped forward, snatched the flag and began a frantic dash back to the Union lines. Although he was wounded twice, the officer returned with the precious colors.

While this was going on, a wounded Southerner began to hobble across the field. One of the men of the 1st Delaware announced, "I'll drop that fellow," and took aim. Captain James Richards, who had led the regiment's efforts to build a theater, pushed the soldier's weapon down with the words, "You wouldn't shoot a wounded man!" An instant later, the Confederate swung his weapon up and shot Richards, who died almost instantly. The Delaware troops who witnessed the incident exploded with a volley of gunfire that killed the Confederate.

As men continued to be hit, Colonel Andrews attempted to extract the 1st Delaware from their deadly position. He reported: "A charge was then ordered and attempted; but our second line, composed of new levies, instead of supporting our advance, fired into our rear. We had now lost one-third of our men, and 8 officers commanding companies were either killed or wounded." Eventually, reinforcements arrived and drove the Southerners off.

The battle of Antietam took a high toll on the men of the 1st Delaware. At the beginning of the fighting, there were 650 men in the regiment; 286 of these were killed or wounded. Company B contained many men from Sussex County; and corporal Nelson Wood, Privates Samuel Laughlin, William Shaw and Bayard Wilson were among the dead. John Carey was hit; but it was a slight wound, and he was able to return to the ranks. Swiggett's wounds were so severe that he was not able to return to the regiment.

Following the battle of Antietam, the Union Army pursued the Southerners to Fredericksburg, Virginia. On December 13, 1862, the Union commander Ambrose Burnside ordered a frontal assault on the Confederates, who were entrenched near the top of a hill. The 1st Delaware was deployed as skirmishers, and they led the attack on the Southerner position: "The men bravely dashed up the hill through a perfect storm of bullets, shot, and shell, to the very rifle-pits of the enemy, where they were compelled to seek such shelter as they could find, since very few men of the several divisions that followed them up that awful slope reached as advanced a position on the field as did the skirmish-line." For several hours, the Union troops stormed up the hill, but they could do little to dislodge the Confederates. The attacks only added to the Union causality lists. At Fredericksburg, the 1st Delaware lost another 93 men. Burton Carey was among those wounded, and the injury to his side and arm would plague him for the rest of his life.

For the first year of the war, the men of the 1st Delaware had spent their time parading for the president, entertaining the troops, and watching a historic naval battle. After Antietam and Fredericksburg, they had tasted the reality of war in full, and John Carey wrote to his parents, "This is a bad war."

HOLDING THE LINE AT GETTYSBURG

On July 3, 1863, the men of the 1st Delaware Regiment looked over the low stone wall and across the gentle Pennsylvania field. Before them was a breathtaking sight. Twelve thousand enemy soldiers in full battle gear were aligned as if on parade. Guide flags were in place, and regimental colors were flying. The enemy line stepped off in good order, and marched steadily toward the line held by the Union troops and the 1st Delaware.

Their experience at Antietam and Fredericksburg made the men respected veterans of the Union army. No one questioned their loyalty, now, or their fighting ability. At Gettysburg, the troops of the first Delaware were part of Col. Thomas M. Smyth's Second Brigade that held a critical position on Cemetery Hill. To the right of the Carey brothers and the others from the coastal region, the line took a sharp turn to the front and a second turn to the south in what became known as the "Angle." A little to the left of the Angle, a small cluster of trees provided the Confederates a centering point for their attacking line. In the distance loomed Little and Big Roundtop. To their right, the line continued for a short way and turned at Culps Hill. Not far behind the Sussex County troops stood the headquarters of General George Meade, who directed the Union forces at Gettysburg. Behind that, there was nothing between the small Pennsylvanian town and the road to Baltimore, Washington, and complete Confederate victory.

As the Delaware troops maintained their position, across the valley, the Confederates were preparing to attack. Before they advanced, the Southerners bombarded the Union lines with a ferocious artillery barrage. The Sussex troops huddled behind a low wall of loosely-stacked stones. Most troops kept their heads down and the shells sailed a few feet above them. Thomas Carey, however, attempted to steal a glance over the wall; he was struck and killed.

For the moment, Thomas' brothers were unable to do anything with his body. When the shelling ceased, 10,000 Confederate soldiers appeared on the other side of the valley, and they began to march toward the Union lines. The advance of the Confederates on the third day of the battle of Gettysburg is known as "Pickett's Charge," but the Southerners did not rush across the green Pennsylvanian field. The rebel troops moved at a steady pace of 110 steps per minute. Each man was careful to maintain contact with the man next to him. An occasional glimpse at the regimental banners enabled the troops to maintain a steady front. At this rate, it would take them half an hour to cross the field. The Delaware troops had plenty of time to get ready for the Confederate attack; and they gathered extra weapons and ammunition.

As the men from Sussex County watched the enemy advance, the First State veterans knew that they were near the center of the Union line. If the Delaware troops could not hold their ground, the Confederates would come streaming through the opening and destroy the Union army. When the Southerners were within range, the Delaware troops opened fire. According to the regiment's historian, "Such an appalling sheet of flame burst from our line that the rebel ranks melted away like wax."

Despite their losses, the Confederates continued to advance. In some places, the Delaware men were standing four deep as they fired round after round at the approaching army. The rifles of the coastal troops were fired so often that they seared the hands of the men who fired them, but the troops could not slacken their fire in the face of the determined onslaught. For twenty minutes, the Southerners marched bravely toward the Union line. By the time the Southerners reached a position in front of the Delaware troops, their ranks had been considerably thinned, but there were enough men left for a final assault.

As the Confederates neared the Union Lines, they opened fire. Enlisted men and officers alike fell under the Confederate fire. So many officers were hit that the command of the 1st Delaware fell to a lieutenant. As the Confederates approached, Sergeant John Dunn leaped over the wall with the regimental colors. Other Delaware troops quickly followed him and the shock of the sudden action convinced many Confederates that their attack had failed. Many turned and went streaming back to the Confederate lines; others surrendered. After the

.war, some of these troops would boast that they had "gone farther at Gettysburg," only to be stopped by the men of the First State.

On January 1, 1863, six months before the battle of Gettysburg, the Emancipation Proclamation went into effect; and slaves across the South were declared free. Slaves in Sussex County, however, remained bound to their masters. Abraham Lincoln's proclamation applied only to the rebelling states, and it did not affect slaves in loyal Delaware. Still, the Emancipation Proclamation changed the nature of the Civil War from a conflict to preserve the Union to a crusade to end slavery. When the troops of the 1st Delaware first heard the news of the Emancipation Proclamation, some were upset; but they quickly returned to the business of fighting the war.

In addition to changing the nature of the war, the proclamation paved the way for African-Americans of the coastal region to join the fight for freedom. On January 26. 1863, Stanton ordered: "That Governor Andrew of Massachusetts is authorized, until further orders, to raise such numbers of volunteers, companies of artillery for duty in the forts of Massachusetts and elsewhere, and such corps of infantry for the volunteer military service as he may find convenient, such volunteers to be enlisted for three years, or until sooner discharged, and may include persons of African descent..."

Stanton's historic order led to the formation of the 54th Massachusetts Regiment of Infantry (whose heroic deeds were vividly portrayed in the movie *Glory*). When enlistments from Massachusetts proved insufficient to fill the ranks, recruiters were dispatched to other states, where they encouraged free Blacks to join the newly-formed regiment. On April 1, 1863, John H. Parker of Bridgeville accepted half of his $100 enlistment bounty and enlisted in the 54th Massachusetts. In addition to Parker, several other men from southern Delaware joined the new regiment.

After a few weeks of training, Parker and the rest of the regiment were dispatched to the South Carolina Sea Islands. At the time, many Whites had little confidence in the Black troops; and the 54th Massachusetts was quickly put to the test. Parker and the other members of the regiment were dispatched to Morris Island, where the Union Army was preparing an attack on Charleston. The guns of Fort Wagner commanded the sea-lanes to the Southern city, and this important battery would have to be captured before a direct attack on Charleston could be begun. It was going to be bloody; and the 54th was selected to lead the charge.

On July 18, 1863, two weeks after the battle of Gettysburg, an extensive naval bombardment the opened the attack on Fort Wagner. After the naval barrage was completed, the 54th led the advance across the open sand in front of the fort. A hail of shot and shell rained down on the 54th Regiment; but the troops did not falter. They scaled the walls of the fort, where they were met by the Confederates: "As the crest was gained, the crack of revolver-shots was heard, for the officers fired into the surging mass of upturned faces confronting them....Musket-butts and bayonets were freely used on the parapet, where the stormers were gallantly met. The garrison fought with muskets, hand-spikes, and gun rammers. the officers striking with their swords, so close were the combatants. Numbers soon told against the 54, for it was tens against hundreds." The attack on Fort Wagner ended in failure, and less than half of the soldiers from the 54th regiment were able to make it back to Union lines. Although John Parker survived the failed attack, he never returned to Delaware. He died in a military hospital on Hilton Head on February 8, 1864.

The valiant sacrifice of the 54th helped convince the Union high command to create regiments of United States Colored Troops and led to the widespread recruitment of African-Americans soldiers. Maryland and other states with significant African-American populations organized regiments of USCT's, although Delaware did not. The 8th Regiment USCT was organized in Philadelphia, but it established a recruitment center at Seaford, where a number of residents of southern Delaware enlisted.

After just a few weeks' training (which included little practice with live ammunition), the 8th Regiment joined the 54th Massachusetts and several white regiments under the command of Brigadier General Truman Seymour. On February 7, Seymour landed his troops at Jacksonville, Florida. At that time, President Lincoln and other Northern leaders thought that Florida residents would rally around a show of force by the Union army. Thus, after securing Jacksonville, the troops marched westward to slice Florida off from the rest of the South. The Union high command expected little opposition, but a large Confederate force had quietly assembled several miles west of Jacksonville.

As they pushed westward across northern Florida, on February 20 the Union troops were attacked by a Confederate force at what has become known as the battle of Olustee. When they heard the firing, the Black troops rushed forward — still encumbered with knapsacks and carrying unloaded weapons. After running half a mile, the 8th formed a line, in an open field, under heavy fire from the enemy concealed about two hundred yards away in rifle pits and behind trees.

At first the men of the 8th were stunned, but gradually they recovered their senses and commenced firing. In the face of mounting casualties, the commander of the 8th, Colonel Fribley, ordered the regiment to fall back slowly. Soon after he gave this order, Fribley was killed by an enemy shot. The soldiers of the 8th Regiment had begun to fall back when an artillery officer rode up, pointed out several abandoned guns, and called out: "Don't leave that battery; bring your flag, and rally the men around it."

An officer planted the regimental colors near the battery, and the troops desperately attempted to form a line of battle. The incoming fire became so destructive that the 8th regiment was again forced to fall back. The troops from southern Delaware gave ground grudgingly; and they gathered into small groups to fire at the Confederates. The exposed groups of Union soldiers made excellent targets for the Southerners; and casualties continued to mount.

After Colonel Fribley was killed, Captain R. C. Bailey took command of the regiment, and he reported: "Noticing that the color company was nearly annihilated, both officers being disabled also, I went with the few men that I had left (about 20) to its assistance, observing only the regimental color, which I ordered to fall back with my men...I will here state that of 43 men of the color company who went into the action 30 were killed, wounded, and missing."

After the 54th Massachusetts and the other Union regiments arrived on the battlefield, the situation was stabilized; but the Northern troops could not dislodge the Confederates, and the Union soldiers retreated eastward back to Jacksonville. In his report of the action, General Seymour commented: "A losing battle receives little praise but officers and men, nevertheless, often display soldierly qualities far beyond those that are brought out by successes." The battle of Olustee was not one of the great battles of the Civil War; but it was the first time that the African-American soldiers of the 8th USCTs came under fire. Before the war was over, 251 men of the 8th Regiment (USCT) would die in the fight.

By the time of the battle of Olustee, African-American regiments were becoming a regular part of the Union forces. When Joseph Berry of Milford joined the fight for freedom, he went to Maryland, where he enlisted in the 39th regiment of United States Colored Troops. The 39th was assigned to the Union forces that were pressuring the Confederacy army defending Petersburg, Virginia. The campaign had degenerated into trench warfare that presaged the fighting during World War I.

To break the stalemate of the trenches, one of the men from a Pennsylvania regiment (which was composed mostly of coal miners) suggested that a tunnel be dug under the Confederate lines, where several tons of gunpowder could be exploded. The blast would blow a gap into the Southerner's defenses and enable the Union troops to rush through the Confederate lines, capture Petersburg, ensure the fall of Richmond, and bring the war to a speedy conclusion.

Berry's 39th regiment was one of the units that was to make the initial charge after the mine was exploded. The troops that would lead the charge into the crater would be the key to the operation's success. For several weeks, the regiment practiced their attack. They were strictly enjoined not take prisoners or capture equipment. The Union troops charging into the crater needed to get past the destruction caused by the explosion and quickly gain secure positions behind the Confederate lines.

The objective of the 39th was to take the high ground beyond the Confederate lines, which would insure that the Confederate defenses would be broken irreparably. Although Berry and the other African-American troops were eager to make the attack, the Union commanders changed their minds at the last minute. They were afraid that if the attack failed, they would be criticized for using the Black soldiers in a repeat of the Fort Wagner-style attack. Twelve hours before the blast was to be detonated, Berry and the troops of the 39th were pulled from the line and replaced with White troops.

When the mine exploded, it did create a huge crater in the Confederate lines, but the Union troops hesitated. The Southerners were able to reestablish their lines, and the Union troops suffered heavy casualties. Berry, however, not only survived the debacle but he lived for another three-quarters of a century. When he died in December, 1941, he was one of Delaware's last Civil War veterans. He was just one of the nearly 1,000 Black troops from Delaware who, in the words of one of these soldiers, "came out to be true Union soldiers, and grandsons of Mother Africa, never to flinch from duty."

"DIXIE"

It is hard to say where John E. Harmon's sympathies lay before the Civil War began. A Frankford native, he could have been on either side. Although most men from southern Delaware who fought during the Civil War wore Union uniforms, some of the men from Sussex County quietly slipped south and joined the Confederate forces. Harmon may have shared the Southern inclinations of some of his neighbors, but he was a sea captain; and most sailors were loyal to the Union. When the Civil War started, Harmon apparently decided to ride out the conflict. He took his pet poodle and went to sea in the bark *Wave Crest*. In the fall of 1862, Harmon stopped in New York, where he took on a cargo of grain, and set sail for England.

Raphael Semmes was also a sea captain. Semmes was born in Maryland, and he was one of the few career naval officers to join the Confederacy. The Confederacy began the war without an organized navy, but the Southerners managed to have several vessels built in England. In August, 1862, Semmes was given the command of one such ship, the *Alabama*. From a distance, the *Alabama* looked like a merchant ship; but the Confederate vessel carried several guns that made it one of the most powerful commerce raiders on the high seas.

A week after leaving New York, Harmon spotted a distant sail that flew the American flag. Unconcerned, the Sussex County captain maintained his course. As the distance between the two ships lessened, the American flag aboard the other ship was lowered, and the Confederate flag fluttered aloft. Harmon had encountered Raphael Semmes and the rebel raider, *Alabama*.

There was little that Harmon could do. The *Wave Crest* was a sailing bark; it did not have an auxiliary engine. The *Alabama* carried sails and a strong steam engine, and Semmes could easily run down the *Wave Crest*. Harmon stopped and waited patiently as a small boat rowed over from the Confederate ship.

After the Southerners climbed aboard the *Wave Crest*, they directed Harmon to fetch the ship's papers. Harmon was then rowed over to the *Alabama*, where he was confronted by Semmes, who recorded the encounter in the ship's log: "Tuesday, October 7. — Weather moderate and became calm after 10 a.m. At 4 a.m. gave chase to a sail, and came up with and caused to be hove to an American bark. Sent on board for the master and his papers. She proved to be the *Wave Crest*, of and from New York, for Cardiff, laden with grain."

The *Wave Crest's* papers clearly indicated that Harmon's ship had sailed from a Union port. Semmes ordered his crew to strip the vessel of anything of value. Semmes also decided that he would be unable to get the *Wave Crest* to a Confederate port, and he ordered Harmon's ship destroyed. Although the loss of the *Wave Crest* was inevitable, Harmon pleaded with Semmes to allow him to bring his pet poodle aboard the *Alabama*. Semmes refused. Harmon may have argued for special consideration on the grounds that he was from a slave state. A few days later, Semmes commented about Delaware in his journal: "This little State, all of whose sympathies were with us, had been ridden over, rough-shod, by the Vandals north of her, as Maryland afterward was, and was arrayed on the side of the enemy. I was obliged, therefore, to treat her as such."

The Confederate commander ordered the crew of the *Alabama* to their guns, and he used the *Wave Crest* for target practice. After Harmon's vessel was riddled with shot, Semmes ordered the bark burned. Whatever mixed feelings Harmon may have had for the South were clarified when the *Wave Crest* wallowed beneath the surface with his dear poodle "Dixie" still aboard.

Harmon may have wished to sit on the fence as far as the Civil War, but there was no doubting where Russell Baker Hobbs stood when he boarded the *Alabama*. Hobbs was born in Georgetown in 1808; and at a young age, he was apprenticed to a cabinetmaker. Apprentices often had to work long hours in return for food, shelter and training; they could not marry, move away, or make any other important decisions without their master's approval. The Georgetown native could not tolerate these demanding conditions. Hobbs ran away from his master, jumped aboard a ship, and sailed to England. The fugitive apprentice did not come back until the cabinetmaker died.

Shortly after Hobbs returned to Delaware, he married Mary Paris. When she died eleven years later, Hobbs married Elizabeth Wilson, of Milton. The Wilson family were Southern sympathizers; and when the Civil War began, Hobbs supported the Confederacy from his home in Sussex County. Early in the war, Hobbs aided the Southern forces by shipping supplies through Seaford, down the Nanticoke River, and across Chesapeake Bay to Virginia. In 1862, the Federal authorities arrested Hobbs, but he was released on the condition that he would stop aiding the Confederacy.

After he was paroled, Hobbs seemed content to spend the rest of the war working on his farm near Milton. A year later, however, Hobbs was drafted by the Union army; and he again fled Delaware by going to sea. Hobbs showed up in Capetown, South Africa, where the Confederate raider *Alabama* lay at anchor.

Commanded by Captain Raphael Semmes, the *Alabama* had destroyed scores of Union merchant ships; and Semmes had so irritated the Union navy that some Northerners considered him a pirate. The chance meeting with the dynamic Confederate raider rekindled Hobbs' Southern sympathies, and he enlisted aboard the *Alabama*. In June, 1864, the *Alabama* stopped in Cherbourg, France, where it was discovered by the Union warship *Kearsarge*.

The two ships were equally matched; and Captain John A. Winslow, the commander of the *Kearsarge*, waited patiently for the *Alabama* to leave the harbor. While Winslow bided his time, crowds of spectators flooded into Cherbourg to witness the impending battle. On June 19, bands on shore played "Dixie," the crowd cheered, and the *Alabama* steamed out of Cherbourg to meet the *Kearsarge*. Captain Winslow of the *Kearsarge* described what happened next: "At 10:20 a.m. we discovered her steering toward us. Fearing the question of jurisdiction might arise, we steamed to sea until a distance of 6 or 7 miles was attained from the Cherbourg breakwater, when we rounded to and commenced steaming for the *Alabama*. As we approached her within about 1,200 yards she opened fire, we receiving two or three broadsides before a shot was returned. The action continued, the respective steamers making a circle round and round at a distance of about 900 yards from each other."

Aboard the *Alabama*, Hobbs felt the shock of the Union shells reverberate through the Confederate ship. After the battle, Winslow described the destruction wrought by the *Kearsarge*'s guns on the *Alabama*: "One shot alone had killed and wounded eighteen men and disabled the gun; another had entered the coal bunkers, exploding, and completely blocked up the engine room, and Captain Semmes states that shot and shell had taken effect in the sides of the vessel, tearing large holes by explosion, and his men were everywhere knocked down."

After an hour of fighting, the *Alabama* began to sink. With the Confederate raider settling quickly, Semmes, Hobbs and several other members of the *Alabama*'s crew scrambled into one of the ship's boats, from which they watched the *Alabama* go down. It appeared that Hobbs' flight from the Union forces was over; but before the *Kearsarge* could pluck the Southerners from their boat, another vessel appeared. This was the British steam yacht, *Deerhound*, and the men quickly scrambled aboard. Much to the consternation of Winslow, the *Deerhound* sped across the channel to England, where the Southerners were safe from capture.

APPOMATTOX

After Gettysburg, Sergeant John Carey had little time to mourn his brother Thomas's death. Thomas was buried in the Gettysburg cemetery a few hundred yards from where he fell. John and the rest of the Union forces left Gettysburg in slow pursuit of Lee's battered Army of Northern Virginia. As they forces moved south, Carey's size, strength and courage earned him the honor of serving as one of the flag bearers for the regiment. On May 5, 1864, the 1st Delaware was advancing though the thick Virginia forest as part of the Second Division of the northern Army of the Potomac, when they were attacked. The confusing encounter that followed became known as the "Battle of the Wilderness." Sergeant Carey and the other members of the color guard led the 1st Delaware down a gentle slope towards a swamp. The troops were surrounded by a dense thicket of scrub-oak and dwarf-pine that made it difficult to maneuver.

As the Delaware troops advanced, the Confederates, who were positioned on the opposite edge of the swamp, opened fire with several well-aimed volleys. Although the Union troops returned fire, the heavy vegetation made it difficult to see their targets. Musket fire ripped through their ranks; and the Delaware troops looked to the color guard for a glimpse of the flag that enabled them to maintain their line.

Thick forest and undergrowth prevented the Union forces from employing artillery or cavalry. According to the historian of the 1st Delaware: "A continuous fire, varied at intervals with volleys, was kept up until sunset, when the fire from the enemy slackened. An immediate forward movement was ordered, the rebels retreating before us, and night overtook us, closing the action, leaving us in possession of the field."

Seventeen men of the 1st Delaware were killed during the Battle of the Wilderness; and Joseph Carey sadly recorded in his diary: "On the 5th day of May, 1864, while going into battle, John Carey was shot through the head and died soon."

Following the Battle of Wilderness, the 1st Delaware and the rest of the Union army lay siege to Petersburg, which controlled the railroad lines to Richmond. During this siege, the 39th USCT participated in the battle of the Crater. After the battle of Olustee, the 8th Regiment had been ordered to Virginia, where it joined the 1st Delaware and other units of the Union army that were closing the grip on Confederate capital at Richmond.

When the Union army was able to break the lines at Petersburg, the Confederates retreated westward until they were stopped at Appomattox. After the surrender had been accepted, the troops were drawn up, and the commanding generals rode along the lines to congratulate the men on their success and the approach of a peace. As the generals passed by, the men of the 1st Delaware cheered and "general joy and jubilation reigned supreme, which was also shared in, to a great extent, by very many of the captured rebels."

After a few weeks of rest, the 1st Delaware participated in the grand review of troops held in Washington: "This was the grandest military pageant the civilized world ever witnessed; for nowhere in the annals of modern history can we find an instance where nearly two hundred thousand victorious veterans marched in review previous to disbanding to the occupations of civil life. The column was so long that two days were required for it to pass a given point, moving in quick time."

At the beginning of the war, there had been doubts whether the men of Delaware, and particularly Sussex County, would fight to defend the Union. As the regiment's historian wrote: "They sprang to the front, seized their weapons, fought the traitors to the death, aided in the delivery of their country, and when the enemy was stretched out exhausted and harmless, they laid down their arms and returned modestly to their former stations of industrious and law-abiding citizens."

Chapter 6. Vacationers and Beachcombers

The Father of the Nation's Summer Capital

In July, 1863, as Robert E. Lee led the Confederate Army of Northern Virginia into Pennsylvania, he ignited a storm of hysteria throughout Delaware. Many in Delaware had secretly supported the South, but they had remained quiet until Lee's army marched north. At that point in the Civil War, Lee seemed unstoppable; and the prospect that his army might attack Wilmington or Philadelphia caused some Southern sympathizers to speak up in support of the Confederate cause. The South had numerous supporters in Sussex County, but the man who caught the attention of several Union leaders was William Bright of Wilmington.

Bright had been born in Philadelphia in 1814; and when he was 16 years old his father apprenticed him to be a ship carpenter. When Bright reached the age of 21, he was freed of his obligations and he immediately moved to Delaware. The booming city of Wilmington presented many opportunities for a man with Bright's energy, ambition and skill.

Bright turned from ship carpentry to home construction, and he soon became a successful real estate developer. In addition, he started a grocery business; he also owned the "Beehive," which was one of Wilmington's largest industrial buildings. At the start of the Civil War, Bright was one of several prominent Delaware citizens who sided with the Confederacy. He believed that President Abraham Lincoln lacked the constitutional authority to force the

Southern states to remain in the Union. Although his sympathies would not have stood out in Sussex County, in Wilmington they did.

When Lee invaded Pennsylvania in 1863, some predicted that the Confederate army would next strike eastward and attack Wilmington. Residents of the city were thrown into a panic. Emergency meetings were held to organize the defenses of city; the mayor appealed to all male citizens to volunteer in some military capacity and the city was placed under martial law.

For Bright, the prospect of a Confederate army matching into northern Delaware was an occasion for rejoicing; and he was deeply disappointed when the news arrived that the Confederates had been defeated at Gettysburg. As Wilmington celebrated the Union victory by ringing church bells and holding a parade, people who knew Bright quietly advised the Union military officials of his pro-Southern actions. They claimed that Bright had written to the Confederates and encouraged them to attack Wilmington's shipyards, machine shops, and the du Pont powder works. It was also rumored that Bright had offered to open his industrial holdings to the advancing Southerners. Business rivals may have instigated some of the charges against Bright, but his southern sympathies were well known. Union authorities roused him out of bed, declared him under arrest and marched him off to Fort Delaware.

When William Bright entered Fort Delaware, a marshy island in the Delaware River, he joined thousands of captured Confederate soldiers. Unlike most of the inmates at Fort Delaware, Bright had not borne arms against the United States; but he was one of hundreds of what were unabashedly known as "political prisoners" arrested during the Civil War.

At Fort Delaware, the granite walls wet with moisture, the stone floors were damp, and the air was cold. The prisoners had no beds, and slept on the floor. There was little water for washing, and they were surrounded by filth and vermin. The descent into Fort Delaware brought an end to Bright's booming career as one of Delaware's leading industrialists. Shortly after his arrest, Brigadier General Daniel Tyler reported: "During the week, I have sent 2 men to Fort Delaware for treasonable language — one of them, William Bright, of Wilmington, a man of some position; and thus making him an example is undoubtedly doing good to the community. I think political asperity is wearing away here, and another victory will make Delaware a very loyal State."

After Lee's army retreated back to Virginia and the prospect of an attack on Wilmington dissipated, Bright was offered a chance to leave Fort Delaware. All he had to do was to take an oath of loyalty to the United States. He detested the growing influence of the burgeoning federal government in Washington, so Bright refused. He preferred to endure a dismal confinement at Fort Delaware rather than to change his political views. Only when the dreary conditions at the prison caused Bright's health to deteriorate did he reluctantly take the oath and gain his release.

By the end of the Civil War, Bright's health and his business ventures had been temporarily broken. Bright may have also found the political climate in Sussex County more in tune with his pro-Southern sympathies, for instead of returning to Wilmington he made Sussex County his next home.

In 1873, the Rehoboth Beach Camp Meeting Association of the Methodist Episcopal Church received approval from the Delaware legislature to establish a seaside Camp Meeting ground. For centuries, the towering dunes north of Cape Henlopen had stood as quiet sentinels over the entrance to Delaware Bay; but when William Bright arrived on the coast, the massive sand hills were undergoing a dramatic change. Early in the 19th century, a high dune formed a ridge that ran across the northern face of the cape. Thick stands of twisted pines and dense patches of coarse grass covered the top of the towering ridge of sand. Occasionally, strong nor'easters would drive the surf to the base of the dune, but there was minimal erosion of sand. In 1845, a government engineer surveyed the cape. He determined that the top of the dune was seventy-two feet above the sea, and the ridge was nearly two miles long. Behind the high ridge, a tidal swamp stood between the sands of Cape Henlopen and the solid ground of the mainland. A dense forest of towering pine trees stood on the landward edge of the swamp. A road that had been built during colonial times ran parallel to the beach to the Cape Henlopen Lighthouse.

In 1828, workers arrived at the mouth of the Delaware Bay to begin work on one of the largest construction projects ever attempted in the United States. Periodically during the 19th century, tons of stone would be piled on the floor of the bay to create the Delaware Breakwater. Over the years, the breakwater was modified and expanded so that the stone barrier was nearly a mile long. When it was completed, the breakwater provided sailing ships with the calm waters of a harbor refuge during severe storms.

When work began on the Delaware Breakwater in the early 19th century, residents of Lewes noticed a change in the large dune on Cape Henlopen. Northerly winds began creating dense storms that sent clouds of coarse sand whipping across the cape. The sand that had been lifted from the northern face of the ridge was carried up and over the crest. The lighthouse keeper, beachcombers, and others who ventured onto the dune during one of these gales covered their faces with handkerchiefs to avoid the choking sand. Wind drove the sand across the top of the ridge and deposited it in the lee of the dune. Slowly, the wind was moving the sand ridge inland. As the dune shifted, the trees that once stood on the crest of the ridge collapsed, and trees that had thrived in the low ground on the landward side of the ridge were inundated by a flood of wind-blown sand.

Some observers likened the moving sand to an ocean wave that "Towers aloft like a sea-wave, even curling over in places like a huge breaker, is rolling inland irresistibly, and lacking only the elements of speed in its career to carry such terror to the hearts of the inhabitants, as is inspired by the sea-waves that follow an earthquake, for the destructiveness of the sand-wave is limited only by its scope."

Eventually, the sand wave reached the marsh and filled the ditches that the tides had once kept clear. The walking dune piled sand on the tree-covered ridges on the edge of the marsh; and the flying sand invaded the forest. In some places, the sand flowed between the trees like lava from a volcano. Where there was thick underbrush, the sand was piled higher and higher until it toppled over the treetops. The great trees that had stood on the high dunes for decades slowly turned from green to yellow to black, and died. The "Walking Dune" of Cape Henlopen traveled as much as sixty feet a year as it shifted inland.

William Bright and the founders of Rehoboth Beach were making another fundamental change to the coast. Members of the Camp Meeting were attracted to the coast by the cooling sea breezes and quiet, woodland atmosphere that would provide a peaceful setting to pursue their religious goals. In addition, it was thought that the salt air of the ocean would restore a person's health; and some of these early summer visitors even boldly ventured into the surf.

When Rehoboth Beach was established, Europeans had long considered visits to the seashore beneficial to one's health. In 1702, John Floyer published *The History of Cold Bathing*, in which he advocated a dip in the ocean as a cure for a wide range of infirmities. According to Floyer: "Cold baths cause a sense of chillness, and that, as well as the terror and surprise, very much contracts the nervous membrane and tubes, in which the aerial spirits are contained, and they being kept tense and compressed, do most easily communicate, all external expressions to the sensitive soul. Not only the external senses are more lively in cold water, but all other animal actions and reasonings are then more vigorous by the external compressure of cold air." Floyer also believed: "To bathe in the seas is to have not only a cold bath, but a medicinal cold bath."

For the next hundred years, European physicians wrote glowingly of the benefits of ocean bathing. Doctors viewed seawater as an antidote to disease and a natural brake on aging. Some doctors also considered a plunge in the ocean to be an aphrodisiac. Belief in the health benefits of hydrotherapy was strong in Europe; but the practice of ocean bathing was slow to gain popularity in America, where diseases were still treated with purges, blisters, and blood-letting. Little was known about the actual causes of disease and ill health. One school of thought had it that certain illnesses were brought on by the bad air that emanated from swamps, marshes and other stagnant water. Under such circumstances, it is not surprising that American doctors failed to see a dip in the ocean as a healthy practice.

In the middle of the 19th century, American attitudes toward ocean bathing underwent a radical change. By the time William Bright was released from Fort Delaware, medical research had established the causes of several important diseases. In addition, doctors had learned that cleanliness played a major role in halting the spread of infection and certain illnesses; and the aversion to immersion in water was quickly overcome.

Of course, few people owned specialized clothing for a dip in the ocean. In Europe, the problem had been neatly sidestepped by the use of bathing machines, which resembled wooden outhouses on wheels. These contraptions were mobile dressing rooms. After the bather disrobed, the bathing machine was rolled into the surf, and the bather climbed down a ladder for a few minutes of splashing in the waves. Canvas awnings on the seaward side of the bathing machine preserved the modesty of the nude bathers as they descended into the sea. Bathing machines never caught on at Rehoboth Beach, and most early ocean bathers entered the water wearing garments adapted from their everyday clothes.

At the time that Bright and the founders of the Rehoboth Beach Camp Meeting Association were establishing their resort on the Delaware coast, the expansion of Washington produced a large number of government clerks, managers, and office workers who spent long hours toiling at their desks in hot and stuffy buildings. These folks had the time and money to spend on an annual vacation, and they sought to escape the oppressive heat of the cities to engage in a few days of invigorating activities.

In 1873, Bright built the "Bright House," which became one of the resort's leading hotels. Railroad service had been opened to Lewes in 1869, and Bright led the drive to have a rail line run into Rehoboth. In 1878, the first trainload of vacationers came chugging into the resort. From Washington, it was an easy trip up the western shore of the Chesapeake Bay and eastward across the Delmarva Peninsula. Many of the vacationers who rode the train to Rehoboth were government officials from Washington.

After the early vacationers at Rehoboth Beach spent a little time frolicking in the surf, many hiked northward to see the "walking" dunes of Cape Henlopen. Coastal residents entertained the vacationers with stories of treasures hidden by Captain Kidd, riches carried to the bottom by the sinking of the *De Braak*, and other tales. The combination of surf, sand and coastal lore helped make Rehoboth Beach extremely popular. William Bright, who had once been a guest of the Federal government in somewhat less luxurious accommodations at Fort Delaware, hosted at his hotel many of the bureaucrats that he had once detested.

MAKING COASTAL HISTORY

In 1865, Dr. Joseph Leidy decided to take an excursion boat from Philadelphia to Lewes. As the small vessel neared Cape Henlopen, it turned into the calm waters behind the Delaware Breakwater. At high tide, only the peak of the artificial stone ridge appeared above the surface of the water. Dr. Leidy had little interest in the unimpressive stone barrier, but he was intrigued by a series of mounds that dotted the shore.

Leidy looked like the college professor that he was. A large man with long shaggy hair and black beard, he was a professor of anatomy at the University of Pennsylvania and an expert on the parasites that infected livestock. Besides worms, Leidy was interested in zoology, botany, and mineralogy. As the excursion boat edged toward shore, the passengers gathered at the rail. Leidy and the others studied the piles of clam and oyster shells that nestled in the dunes. Some of the passengers speculated that the mounds were the remains of a natural clam bed or oyster bank that had been exposed by the shifting waters. Others believed that they were waste shells discarded by local oystermen. Leidy turned to the boat's captain, and asked, "Well, skipper, what's your guess about it?"

The captain replied, "Well, Doc, our folks always said they was Indian heaps, but we don't pay them no attention."

Leidy considered the captain's comments, and quietly replied, "My, my."

After the boat docked at Lewes, the professor hiked across the beach to the shell mounds, and poked at the piles with a stick. The mound contained mostly oysters shells, but he discovered pieces of pottery, a red clay pipe, a jasper arrowhead and other man-made objects. Sparked by this discovery, Leidy returned to Lewes the following year for a more thorough investigation. After several days' work, he concluded that the mounds were Native American refuse dumps. The news of Leidy's work inspired others to investigate the buried history of Delaware; and his pioneering discoveries made Leidy the "Father of Delaware Archaeology."

Although many of the methods and conclusions reached by early Delaware archaeologists have been called into question by 20th century historians, Leidy's exploration of the Lewes shell mounds came just in time. A spate of unbridled expansion engulfed the area after the railroad came to town in 1869. So many people were employed constructing new homes that one observer commented: "If you have a hatchet and a saw, you can go into the carpenter trade now."

The building boom destroyed some of the archaeological evidence of Lewes' long history and transformed the old town's rugged colonial appearance, as well. Home builders bought shingles, laths, scrollwork, and moldings from local suppliers, and they combined these elements with factory-built doors, sash blinds, shutters, and windows to create large homes with wide porches that were decorated with elaborate ginger-breading. The homes were painted with bright contrasting colors that gave the streets of Lewes a look far different from the simple boxy brick and dark-shingled homes of the past.

Lewes was in the middle of its Victorian building boom when the young artist, Howard Pyle, arrived in town for his annual vacation. Pyle spent his time observing the town's historic buildings and listening to residents spin yarns about swashbuckling pirates. Here was a deep well that Pyle would draw from for many years. Born in 1853, near Wilmington, where his Quaker ancestors had settled in the late 17th century, Pyle lacked the academic discipline to pursue higher education but he possessed a natural talent for art and writing. His formal art training consisted of three years of commuting from his Wilmington home to the studio of the Belgian artist Van der Weilen in Philadelphia.

In 1877, Pyle wrote and illustrated an article for *Scribner's Monthly* that described the annual penning of wild ponies in Chincoteague, Virginia.

Encouraged by this success, Pyle embarked on a more ambitious project, and in 1879, *Harper's New Monthly Magazine* published three installments of "A Peninsula Canaan," an illustrated exploration of the Delmarva Peninsula. In part three of "A Peninsula Canaan," Pyle provided a succinct description of Lewes in the 19th century: "The old town of Lewes lies on a cove, the coast of which juts into Cape Henlopen — a rambling old town standing back from the water's edge behind a stretch of white sand beach, the quiet houses imblossemed in trees. It possesses among many points of interest, an old fort built in 1812 for the defense of the town, which is still in a perfect state of preservation, with guns mounted precisely as they originally were."

Pyle was relatively unknown when he provided American readers with this glimpse of Lewes; but George Alfred Townsend was a well-known writer when he began to write about coastal history. Townsend was born in Georgetown, on January 30, 1841. His father was the Rev. Stephen Townsend, who served Sussex County as a Methodist clergyman for more than a half century. George completed his education in 1860, and he was still a teenager when the United States was less than a year away from the Civil War.

When the war began, Townsend became a correspondent for the *New York Herald*; and he wrote graphic dispatches that described the fighting in Virginia. In 1862, the Georgetown native began a lecture tour of Europe, where he found audiences eager to hear his eyewitness accounts of the American war. Townsend returned to America in time to cover Grant's final campaign against Robert E. Lee. The Georgetown author's Civil War reporting earned him a national following. After the war, Townsend's newspaper commentary on politics and other topics continued to attract a wide following. For these columns, Townsend adopted the *nom de plume* "Gath."

Townsend was a successful newspaperman and lecturer; but in 1880, he was stumped. He had been invited to make a speech in his native Georgetown on July 5; but Townsend did not know what to say. The newspaperman sat in his hotel room and thought about the coastal region's long history. He wanted to talk about Caesar Rodney and his famous ride to Philadelphia; and Townsend began to compose the speech that would change Delaware's history.

Rodney was in Lewes, Townsend told his enthralled Georgetown audience, when the vote on the Declaration of Independence drew near. Rodney needed to bet back to Philadelphia for the critical vote; but he was being entertained by the captivating widow Sarah Rowland. Sarah was charming, engaging, and a rank Tory who had intercepted the dispatches that urged Rodney to return to Philadelphia at once. Seeing a chance to thwart the colonial drive to independence, the delightful woman hosted Rodney as graciously as any belle could do.

The way Townsend told the tale, a maid upset Ms. Rowland's plot by showing Rodney the stolen dispatches. Aghast at the prospect of missing the decision the Declaration of Independence, Rodney hopped on his horse and began his long ride to Philadelphia. In 1880, the tale of Sarah Rowland's plot was a big hit in Georgetown; but as William Frank points out *Caesar Rodney, Patriot*, Townsend fabricated the story to please his audience.

With Townsend's reputation for historical accuracy, the tale of Sarah Rowland was commonly accepted as true. The story found its way into school-books and clouded the facts of Rodney's ride. Rodney's dash to Philadelphia was actually delayed by a thunderstorm and not by a flirtatious Tory widow.

While Townsend was mudding the waters of local history with the tale of Sarah Rowland, Howard Pyle was becoming increasingly popular. After the success of "A Peninsula Canaan," Pyle continued to vacation along the Delaware coast, where he continued to listen to tales of Captain Kidd and other bucca-neers. In addition to his paintings of pirates, with their gritty reality, Pyle was inspired to spin the fanciful story of "Blueskin." As told by Pyle, Levi West was the stepson of a Lewes miller, but Levi was bored with life in Lewes and left town for the sheltered waters of Rehoboth Bay. There, West established a base from which he was able to sail out through the Indian River Inlet into the Atlantic Ocean and attacked unarmed merchant ships. West's piratical career was so successful that he soon earned the colorful nickname, "Blueskin."

Despite his achievements as a buccaneer, Levi longed for the love his life, Sally Martin, the prettiest girl in Lewes. Sally was betrothed to Levi's half-brother Hiram, but Blueskin returned home to Lewes, captured Sally, and carried her off to his lair on Rehoboth Bay.

Hiram followed the pirate, captured Blueskin, and liberated Sally. After Levi West was hustled off to be tried as a pirate, Hiram and Sally were married, and they lived happily ever after. Like Townsend's story of Sarah Rowland, Pyle's tale of Blueskin is sometimes taken as fact. Yet, had these two authors looked to the south end of the Delaware coast, they would have discovered an authentic story of love on the beach.

LOVE ON THE BEACH

For the passengers of the *Virginia Merchant*, the barrier island was as desolate as an uncharted atoll in the middle of the Pacific Ocean. It was a blustery
January, 1650. The English ship had arrived off the Delaware coast after a fright-
fully long and difficult voyage from England. The vessel was bound for the
Jamestown colony, but a stormy ocean crossing had left many of the ship's passengers desperately ill.

While the ship anchored offshore, some of the colonists were ferried to the
beach by rowboat in hopes that a few days on *terra firma* would enable them to
regain their strength. They splashed through the surf and found themselves on
an empty beach with no sign of human habitation. They were more than twenty
miles south of the small settlement near Cape Henlopen.

Finally relieved from the constant motion of the ship, the colonists spent a
quiet night on the beach. When they awoke the next morning, they were shaken
by the sight of the crew raising the *Virginia Merchant*'s sails. As they watched in
horror, the ship sailed away.

Frightened, frozen and facing starvation, the nineteen marooned settlers
set off to explore, only to discover that they had been stranded on an island.
They managed to gather some oysters and kill a few wildfowl, but were soon
forced to the extreme. Colonel Norwood in his *Voyage to Virginia* described what
happened next: "Of the three weak women ..., one had the envied happiness to
die about this time; and it was my advice to the survivors, who were following
her apace, to endeavour their own preservation by converting her dead carcase
into food, as they did to good effect. The same counsel was embrac'd by those of
our sex: the living fed upon the dead; four of our company having the happiness
to end their miserable lives..."

Somehow the settlers missed the fact that the island was connected to the
mainland by a narrow, swampy neck of land. After several harsh weeks on the
island, they were rescued by Native Americans who transported them to the
mainland. The Native Americans fed them and helped them regain their
strength, and apparently pointed them in the right direction, for soon the
Englishmen were able to continue on their way to the Virginia settlements.

They had been marooned on a barrier island that was astride the disputed
land claimed by Lord Baltimore and William Penn. Lord Baltimore had granted
the Maryland colonist William Stevens a deed for the island, which Stevens
named "Fishing Harbor"; but he had little interest in the island and sold it to

Thomas Fenwick of Sussex County. Fenwick gave the island his name, and in 1706, he sold Fenwick Island to William Fasset of Somerset County, Maryland.

While Fenwick Island bounced back and forth between Delaware and Maryland owners, the leaders of the two colonies promoted rival claims to this part of the coast. After William Penn pirated the boundary southward, the line between the two colonies was held to begin at Fenwick Island, but few settlers moved to the area.

After the American Revolution, Fenwick Island was further isolated by a 4-foot by 3-foot trench that was dug across the swampy isthmus that connected the island with the mainland. The trench was quickly widened to a 40-foot by 20-foot channel called, "The Ditch." While humans were severing Fenwick Island from the mainland, nature was silting closed the inlets that once marked the northern and southern limits of the island. By the middle of the 19th century, Fenwick was part of the continuous ribbon of sand that ran from Indian River Inlet in Delaware to Chincoteague Inlet in Virginia. At this time, one of the few people who came to Fenwick Island was Zippy Lewes.

Zippira "Zippy" Lewis was born in 1825; and after she married Jonathan B. Lewis of Williamsville, the young couple settled near the Maryland-Delaware line. Zippy and Jonathan spent much of their time salvaging timbers from wrecked vessels and using the reclaimed lumber to build their house. Then, one day, Jonathan decided to go to sea, and he set sail on a vessel that glided out through the Indian River Inlet.

After her husband left, Zippy went down to the beach every day to watch for his return. Days turned into weeks, months into years. Eventually, she built a small shack on the beach so she could keep an eye on the sea. Wearing a long dress and sunbonnet, Zippy was an unmistakable figure as she hiked across the dunes. With no visible source of income, it was rumored that Zippy supported herself from a treasure trove of coins that she had collected on the beach.

For many years, Zippy maintained her solitary vigil on the beach; but prior to the Civil War, she was joined by several other permanent residents. Fenwick Island had posed a special problem to mariners. Viewed from the unsteady deck of a sailing ship, the high wooded ground between the Ditch and the ocean combined with the slight bulge to the south and could easily be mistaken for Cape Henlopen. Captains who sailed too close to the coast to get a better look risked running aground.

The construction of the Cape Henlopen Lighthouse in the 18th century helped alleviate some of the danger. Mariners looking for the entrance to Delaware Bay knew that if they could not see the bright beacon of the Cape Henlopen Lighthouse, they were not near the mouth of the bay. On the other hand, there were times when storms or fog could obscure the light; and some captains continued to mistake Fenwick Island for the entrance to Delaware Bay.

In 1856, the government decided to bestow upon desolate Fenwick Island its first man-made landmark when it authorized the construction of a lighthouse near the southern border of Delaware. Two years later, workers arrived to begin work on the second lighthouse on Delaware's short Atlantic coast. The new structure was a round tower, placed on a high point of land a quarter of a mile from the beach. When the Fenwick Island lighthouse began operations on August 1, 1859, the new beacon could be seen fifteen miles from shore. In addition to the lighthouse tower, a house for the keeper and his assistant was built next to the tower. The keeper and his family lived on the first floor of the house; the assistant and his family occupied the second floor. In 1878, a second house was built for the keeper and the original house became the home of the assistant.

After the Civil War, vacationers would occasionally visit Fenwick Island, where they would admire the lighthouse and make the acquaintance of the lonely beachcomber, known to youngsters as "Aunt Zippy." One resident of the coastal region remembered visiting her in 1872: "We found a widow, Zippy Lewis, her skin browned by the sun. We had dinner with her. It is reported that she has a lot of money buried on the island somewhere."

When Zippy Lewis died in 1884, coastal residents descended upon her beach shack in hopes of discovering her legendary hoard of coins. No such cache was ever found, and it remains a mystery how she sustained herself all those years. Apparently, Zippy Lewis, a regular country girl, was resourceful enough to survive on her own, a recluse on the beach, faithfully waiting for the love of her life who went to sea and never returned.

KEEP A HAT ON

Charles E. Garner was dressed in his vest, coat and stylish derby hat as he stood on the deck of the Charleston steamship *Champion* and watched the bow slide beneath the waves. A few minutes earlier, Garner, who was an advertising agent, had felt a slight thud as the steamer passed Cape Henlopen. Although he was not alarmed by the jolt, Garner had gone on deck to investigate. Curiosity was replaced with dismay when he saw that the bow go under; the ship could not survive.

On Friday morning, November 7, 1870, the *Champion* was making its way past the mouth of Delaware Bay. At the same time, the British sailing vessel *Lady Octavia* was working its way around Cape Henlopen. Around 3 a.m., lookouts on each ship spotted the other's running lights, and there appeared to be no danger. But as the distance between the two vessels shrank, neither ship changed course. Finally, the steamer shifted to avoid the British sailing ship. It was too late.

The two ships collided and the steamer began to fill with water. The bow of the *Lady Octavia* was badly damaged but a watertight bulkhead prevented the ship from sinking. On the *Champion*, the situation was desperate. As the bow of the *Champion* went down, the stern of the ship was lifted into the air. The angle of the ship made it impossible to launch the lifeboats, which were lashed into position. Passengers cried, "For God's sake, cut the boats loose!" and the crew scurried about looking for axes to cut the lines. As the ship tilted more and more, people and objects slid down the deck and began to fall into the sea.

Garner decided to abandon ship, and the sooner the better. Otherwise, the suction created by the sinking steamer would pull him so deeply underwater that he would drown. Garner picked up a chair that might give him a bit of added buoyancy, pulled his hat down firmly, and jumped into the ocean. Garner was hardly in the water with his improvised life-preserver when the steamship went down. The cries of the passengers were obscured by a great rush of water as the ship plunged toward the bottom. As Garner had feared, he was carried deep under the water.

Many of the fifty-five people aboard the steamer sank with it; but Garner's descent was slowed and while the suction of the sinking ship prevented most form making their way back to the surface, Garner's drift downward was slowly reversed. Nearly breathless, but alive, he finally got his head above the waves.

The top of a skylight was floating nearby; Garner joined other survivors who were clinging to the wooden frame. A rescue boat found them and hauled them out of the water. Once he was safely aboard, Garner removed his hat and discovered why he had not been pulled to his death by the suction of the sinking ship. The inside of his hat was still dry. When he pulled it down over his head before jumping into the Atlantic, Garner had created an air pocket that gave him just the necessary margin of buoyancy to make the difference.

CHAPTER 7. SHIPWRECKS AND SUN WORSHIPPERS

A DAB OF COLOR ON THE BEACH

In 1876, a construction crew arrived at a spot a short distance north of the Indian River Inlet. With no other structures in sight, the crew began to clear the grasses and shrubs on the west side of the dunes not far from the spot where the ship, *Faithful Steward*, had foundered nearly a century earlier. During the next two months, the workmen erected a wooden frame structure whose sloping red roof and pumpkin-colored walls were an unmistakable landmark to passing ships. When the building was completed, Keeper James Raymond welcomed a crew of surfmen to the Spartan life at the Indian River Life-Saving Station.

Before the Civil War, several seacoast communities had established volunteer life-saving stations to assist vessels in distress — but the organization and administration of these early stations was irregular and ineffective. With the return of peace after Lee's surrender at Appomattox, the number of ships cruising the Delaware coast increased dramatically; and so did the likelihood of disaster. The Federal government responded by establishing the Life-Saving Service, which would be manned by professional, trained surfmen, housed in a series of stations along the coast.

In 1876, Life-Saving Stations were constructed at Cape Henlopen and Indian River Inlet. Eventually, stations also would be established at Lewes, Rehoboth Beach, Bethany Beach and Fenwick Island. Architecturally, each of the six Delaware stations had distinctive features; but the crews followed the same organizational regimen (similar to the operation of a modern fire station). The station was manned by a keeper who commanded a crew of six men. The surfmen arrived at the station at the start of the active season, which for the Delaware coast extended from November through April. The duties of cooking, cleaning and other housekeeping chores were assigned on a rotating basis. The surfmen slept on simple cots arranged dormitory-style in a small room. A larger mess room served as a common area where they ate, relaxed, and read from a small library. Few decorations adorned the walls; these men had a serious mission. The keeper had his own room and office, but these areas too were far from luxurious.

On the first floor, the largest room in the station was reserved for the surfboat and other equipment. The surfboat, which sat on a light carriage with large wheels, was kept ready at all times to be rolled across the beach and launched into the pounding waves. After the surf men reached a point on the beach near a stranded ship, they would slide the boat off its wheels and launch it through the breakers. Each surf man manned an oar; and as they pulled together, the keeper steered directly toward the waves. According to an official of the Life-Saving Service: "Few sights are more impressive than the passage out through the flashing breakers of the frail red boat, lightly swimming on the vast swell of the surge, held in suspension before the roaring and tumultuous comber; or darting forward as the wall of water breaks and crumbles, obedient to the oars of the impassive crew."

The surfboat of even the most skilled crews occasionally capsized; and to prepare for this eventuality, the surfmen spent hours on capsize drills. At the command, "Go," the surfmen intentionally overturned the surfboat, righted it and regained their original seats.

In addition to being skilled with the surfboat, the crews of the Delaware Life-Saving Stations had to be proficient with the Lyle gun. In 1877, Major David A. Lyle of the US Army was asked to develop a line-throwing mortar that could be used by the Life-Saving Service. He soon perfected a short cannon that could carry a line several hundred yards. Part of the success of the cannon was the elongated projectile that resembled a sash-weight, with an eyebolt for the line at one end.

When a ship in distress was sighted, the surfmen rolled a small cart that contained the Lyle gun and several hundred feet of carefully-arranged line across the beach to a position opposite the endangered vessel. Working under the direction of the station keeper, the surfmen fired the projectile that carried a light shot line to the ship. After the shot line reached those aboard the stranded vessel, the crew used it to pull a heavier whip line from the beach to the ship. Attached to one end of the whip line was a pulley block and a small tally board. The board had instructions printed in French and English: "Make the tail of this block fast to the lower mast well up. If masts are gone, then to the best place you can find. Cast off shot line. See that the rope in the block runs free and show signal to shore."

Once the block had been fully rigged, breeches buoys and surf cars could be used to ferry ashore those aboard the stranded vessel. The breeches buoy was a life ring attached to a set of leather breeches. The person being rescued climbed into the breeches; and, with the ring around his or her waist, was pulled ashore. In cases where the breeches buoy was impractical, a surf car was employed. The surf car was a small boat fitted with a metal top that made it look like an over-sized football. After two or three people climbed in, the top was closed and they were pulled to the beach by lines that had been run from ship to shore.

Finally, each surfman carried a collection of Coston flares. These devices were developed by Martha Coston, of Baltimore, and they were vital to the success of the Life-Saving Service. The flares were activated by a plunger that stuck a charge, which, in turn, ignited the brightly-burning chemicals of the flare. Coston flares were simple to use, easy to carry, and could be used in all types of weather to signal vessels in distress and to summon aid from a Life-Saving Station.

The construction of the Rehoboth Beach Life-Saving Station provided protection for mariners along the coast, but the station provided entertainment, too, for vacationers at the resort. The drills of the surfmen working with the Lyle gun, breeches buoy, and other apparatus provided an amusing diversion for some beach visitors.

THE GREAT WHITE HURRICANE

The weather along the Delaware coast had been unseasonably mild during the first week of March, 1888, when the schooner *Allie H. Belden* set sail from Maine, bound for Lewes with a cargo sure to be needed during the summer. During the 19th century, the introduction of steam engines had driven most sailing ships from the seas; but some operators could still turn a profit with their schooner-rigged vessels. The *Allie H. Belden's* fore-and-aft sails could be managed by a small crew; it entailed no fuel costs; and most of the space below decks could be used to carry cargo.

As the *Allie H. Belden* pushed down the New Jersey coast, it encountered heavy rain. At Cape May, the schooner captain eagerly steered across the mouth of the bay, and with some relief, the crew soon dropped anchor behind the Delaware Breakwater which offered some protection against the growing waves. The heavy rain had driven many mariners to seek shelter behind the Delaware Breakwater; and the *Allie H. Belden* was joined by over four dozen other vessels. While the sailors waited for the storm to pass, a high-pressure system with subfreezing temperatures slid down from the north. The two systems collided to create high winds, low temperatures, and one of the worst storms ever to visit the Delaware coast.

The crews of the life-savings stations knew that winter storms brought rain, snow, and shipwrecks. Despite the blinding wind and numbing cold, they began their nightly patrols, trudging across the sand with their trusty Colson flares in hand. During the winter season, the men patrolled the beach every night; and most patrols ended with the surfmen returning to their station with nothing to report. On the night of March 11, the surf men discovered not one, or two, but dozens of vessels in distress.

The falling temperatures turned the rain to ice that coated the masts, spars, and hulls of the vessels behind the breakwater. Then the rain turned to snow, and the storm became a blizzard that dumped several feet of snow on the mid-Atlantic region. Ninety-miles-per-hour winds tore the ships from their anchors and slammed vessels together, littering the water with debris. Even those sailing vessels that managed to avoid colliding with other ships had their masts snapped by the high winds; and the crews struggled under a glazed canopy of canvas, tangled spars, rigging lines and snow to keep their ships afloat. Several vessels were driven into the long railroad pier that was shattered in three places.

On shore, the surfmen spotted several ships in distress but there was little that they could do. Their brightly-shining Coston flares were small comfort to the frozen sailors whose ships had begun to founder. The surfmen attempted to string lines from shore to the sinking ships, but they were frustrated by the howling winds and driving snow.

Unable to reach the stranded sailors, the surfmen retreated to their stations until morning. When March 12 dawned, the blizzard had eased; and the crews of the life-saving stations returned to the beach, where they were confronted with over 20 shipwrecks. Despite the heavy waves, a surfboat was launched; and after a Herculean effort, the men reached some of the damaged ships. Several sailors had already died from exposure; but nearly 200 crewmen from wrecked vessels were saved.

The *Allie H. Belden* had run aground several hundred yards from the beach, and most of the crew had taken refuge in the schooner's rigging. Two sailors died, but four men from the *Allie H. Belden* were rescued. The vessel had run aground just short of its destination of Lewes.

The Great White Hurricane, as the blizzard of 1888 was sometimes called, damaged or destroyed thirty-five vessels near Cape Henlopen. Telegraph and telephone lines were disrupted from Washington to Boston. Cities and towns were buried under mountains of snow. The blizzard paralyzed New York; and the storm helped convince some of that city's leaders of the need to build a subway system.

Near Cape Henlopen, the work of the crews of the Life-Saving Stations had saved many lives, but little could be done for many of the damaged vessels. As soon as the weather cleared, plans were made to salvage the *Allie H. Belden*; but there was little interest in saving the schooner's cargo — of *ice*.

QUARANTINE STATION

In a scene repeated countless times, immigrants strained for a glimpse of the white tower of the Cape Henlopen Lighthouse that indicated that they had, at last, reached America. The introduction of steam power had considerably reduced the time needed to cross the Atlantic, but on many ships immigrants spent most of the voyage crowded below decks, crammed into poorly-ventilated areas that lacked privacy and contained only the most rudimentary sanitation facilities. Robust individuals who boarded ships in Europe might be racked with illness by the time the ship rounded Cape Henlopen. And the diseased were not allowed to enter America. For some, the jubilation of arrival was short lived.

In the late 19th century, the causes of many illnesses were unknown; and residents of port cities like Philadelphia and New York were terrified that new-comers would bring in deadly diseases. Isolation was the only defense against smallpox, yellow fever, and other infectious illnesses.

Before the Civil War, a quarantine station for immigrants bound for Phila-delphia was established just south of the city, but growth required a site further down the bay. In 1880, the federal government established the National Quarantine System to provide a uniform defense against contagious diseases. Forty years later, a quarantine hospital was established on Cape Henlopen to examine people on ships entering the Delaware Bay. In 1885, the Delaware Breakwater Quarantine Hospital opened on 41 acres of land a short distance from Lewes. Dr. William P. Orr, a native of Lewes and assistant acting surgeon in the marine hospital service, served as the Quarantine Hospital's first director.

Orr was a direct descendent of William Orr, one of the three men from Lewes who had been dazzled by the treasure aboard Captain Kidd's ship two hundred years earlier. William Orr had ignored William Penn's command that the three collaborators should "not be endured to live near ye sea-coast nor trade, least they become receptacles and brokers for younger pirates."

Now, whenever a ship arrived at Cape Henlopen, Dr. Orr was ferried out to the waiting vessel, where he determined whether the crew and passengers were free of contagious diseases. Those who were deemed disease free were allowed to continue on to Philadelphia. Immigrants suspected of carrying contagious diseases were required to land at the hospital, where they were quarantined from ten days to two months. With the number of immigrants increasing yearly, the hospital was expanded. A series of barracks buildings were constructed that could sleep 1,500 steerage class passengers. A separate building was built for up to 150 cabin-class travelers. In addition to the accommodations for quarantined passengers, the station included a bathhouse, surgeons' quarters, a disinfecting house, and support buildings. Captains often gave Dr. Orr a gift for his work. The doctor refused gifts of alcohol, but he did accept a parrot from the commander of a three-masted schooner. When the bird repeated some of the colorful language that it had learned from the sailors, however, the parrot was summarily expelled from the Orr household.

In the first decades of the 20th century, the Breakwater Quarantine Station was a flourishing facility; but the outbreak of World War I put an end to the flow of immigrants from Europe. When the United States entered the war in 1917, the Navy took over the station. After the war ended, legislation was passed that restricted the number of immigrants allowed into the United States and the quarantine station was no long needed. A few years later, the station was abandoned and the buildings dismantled.

SHIPBUILDING TAKES A STEP BACKWARD

In the closing years of the 19th century, Bethel was a pleasant little town on the banks of Broad Creek, a tributary of the Nanticoke River. On some days, schools were closed, families packed picnic baskets, and celebrated a holiday at a local shipyard. Another sailing vessel was to be launched, and that was an event that was not to be missed. The hull that sat on the ways lacked many of the graceful curves that marked earlier sailing vessels. The new vessel had the lines of a barge, and its straight sides rode high in the water after it splashed into Broad Creek.

In the late 19th and early 20th centuries, shipbuilders in western Sussex County began constructing a vessel that became known as a sailing "ram." These long, narrow ships had squarish sides like a barge. Rams were intended for use on inland waters, principally the Delaware and Chesapeake Bays. The boxy shape was expected to enable the rams to navigate the narrow confines of the Chesapeake and Delaware Canal, which had been built in 1829 as a lock canal (it was widened and deepened to a sea-level canal in the 20th century). To reduce operating costs, a ram's sails were fore-and-aft rigged with the sails attached directly to the masts.

At the same time that rams were being developed in western Sussex County, shipbuilders in Milton, Milford and other towns close to the Delaware Bay began turning out more traditional schooners. These vessels were used in the coastal trade, and since they were expected to spend most of their time sailing the Atlantic Ocean, the Delaware schooners needed to be more seaworthy than the rams.

The *Albert S. Paul* was a four-masted schooner constructed in 1916 at Milford. In addition to trading along the Atlantic coast, the schooner made several voyages to South America. As a sail-powered vessel she was out of date, but with no steam engine and its bulk coal or wood fuel, she had more room for cargo. Her low operating coast enabled her to survive the economic hardships of the Great Depression. At the beginning of World War II, some of the old wooden sailing craft were pressed into anti-submarine duty, but the *Albert S. Paul* continued to operate as a merchant vessel.

On March 13, 1942, the *Albert S. Paul* was just over a hundred miles south of the Delaware Bay and heading for home. Captain Johannes Liebe, commander of the German submarine U-332, sighted her as she sailed silently through the night. The details of the encounter are not well documented, but in all likelihood the

German submarine was running on the surface when it spotted the Milford schooner. The small wooden sailing ship was not worth the expenditure of a torpedo, so Liebe ordered the crew to man the U-boat's deck gun. The *Albert S. Paul* was blown apart and was scattered, more than sunk, in the dark.

The sailing ram *Edwin and Maud* was more fortunate. Built at Bethel in 1900, the ram was named after her first captain's two children. The ram plied the waters of the American coast for a century. During the first half of the 20th century, *Edwin and Maud* carried lumber and fertilizer along the eastern seaboard. During World War II, she was pressed into service checking the antisubmarine mine fields in the Chesapeake Bay. (The vessel's wooden hull enabled her to approach magnetic mines without danger, and so she could investigate whether and where the mines were in place.) After World War II, *Edwin and Maud* was converted to the passenger trade, and for several years sailed out of Annapolis. In 1954, the ram was sold to new owners and taken to Maine, where it was recreated *Victory Chimes*. In 1997, *Victory Chimes* was designated an American National Historic Landmark. A century old, the Delaware ram sails out of Rockland, Maine as a reminder that the age of sail is still alive.

SCANDAL ON THE BEACH

When William Bright and the Rehoboth Beach Camp Meeting Association came to the Delaware coast, there was plenty of sand, surf, and sun; but they were not much interested in any of the three. The founders of Rehoboth Beach had religion in mind, and were attracted to the coast by the cool breezes and quiet woodland atmosphere. Most resorts on the Atlantic coast were built on barrier islands separated from the mainland by a coastal bay. Thus, most resorts developed parallel to the beach. The Rehoboth Beach Camp Meeting Association had selected one of the few spots on the coast where the mainland was washed by the surf, and pine forests abutted the beach.

The Camp Meeting Association laid out a town that was shaped roughly like a triangle with its base at the beach and its two longer sides extending inland. Rehoboth Avenue was the resort's widest street, and it ran from the inland tip of the triangle to the beach. The other principal streets radiated from the inland point of the triangle toward the beach. A few blocks north of Rehoboth Avenue, the irregular shape of Lake Gerar interrupted the geometric street design. Surf Avenue ran along the base of the triangle near the dunes. Near the inland point of the triangle, ground was reserved for the camp meetings, a tradition in the Methodist Church. At week-long camp meetings, people would preach, pray, and repent. When Rehoboth Beach was first established, the highlight of the day would be a visit to the camp meeting grounds that were nestled in the shade and cooled by the sea breezes.

The town offered few oceanfront lots. The early leaders of the resort did make one concession to the usual beach amenities when they built a short eight-foot-wide boardwalk near the dunes.

In the early 19th century, Brighton, England, was a popular port for travelers crossing the English channel. On pleasant days, people from the surrounding area came to Brighton to watch the steady stream of passengers on their way to and from France. In 1823, an enterprising businessman constructed a pier that was designed to serve both the travelers and those who came to watch. The new pier featured a number of refreshment stands; and it proved so popular that when Dover replaced Brighton as the major channel port, the pier went on serving vacationers who came to town to enjoy the sea air. The success of Brighton's pleasure pier led many other English seashore towns to build similar structures. By the time that Rehoboth Beach was established, no first-class resort was complete without a pleasure pier. Besides providing a fine promenade, these piers were used for fishing, band concerts, vaudeville shows, and a host of other activities. When the wooden walkways were built parallel to the ocean, the boardwalk was born.

At Rehoboth, vacationers did not venture onto the boardwalk unless they were fully attired: suits for men, and long dresses and high-heeled shoes for the ladies. As the resort and the boardwalk grew, several "roundhouses" were constructed along the wooden walkway. These covered pavilions were built on the seaward side of the boardwalk to give strollers a place to rest in the shade and watch the waves. Some of the larger roundhouses could accommodate several dozen people, and could also be used for church services.

From the northern end of the boardwalk strollers were rewarded with a glimpse of the Cape Henlopen Lighthouse silhouetted against the sky. At night, the lighthouse's beacon shined pleasantly in the distance. Although the lighthouse appeared rather close by, many who started out across the dunes to get a closer look at the tower discovered it took quite a hike to reach the lighthouse.

In the early years, Rehoboth's vacationers rarely ventured closer to the ocean than the boardwalk. A few made the arduous trip across the sand and stopped at the water's edge. Only the boldest actually ventured into the surf. At that time, bathing outfits were rare and so was the ability to swim. Men and women alike wore attire that covered the torso and extended to the elbows and knees. Women also wore bloomers, stockings, and hats. Besides the considerations of modesty, in the 19th century milk-white skin was a sign of beauty and a life of leisure; tanned skin was for field hands and other laborers. To avoid the tanning rays of the sun that would bring out freckles and other blemishes, early visitors to the Delaware beach carried parasols on sunny days.

The 19th century concept of beauty also considered slenderness a sign of want: underfed, unhealthy, and care worn. The plump, full-figured bodies depicted by the painter Peter Paul Ruebens in the 17th century were considered ideal. The beautiful people who walked Rehoboth's early boardwalk looked prosperous: well fed, fully-clothed, and untanned.

The cumbersome bathing suits made it nearly impossible to move about in the water. To protect the bathers in their water-logged suits from being swept away, a safety line was attached to a piling driven into the ocean floor several hundred feet from the beach. The line was attached to a second piling on shore, and bathers held tight as the waves washed over them.

Toward the end of the century, bathing costumes began to be modified so that people could let go of the safety line for a frolic in the waves. In 1890, Duffield Osborne wrote "Surf and Surf-Bathing" for *Scribner's Magazine*. Osborne offered advice on how to enter the surf without being tossed head over heels, how to avoid the undertow, and how a gentlemen should assist a lady to enter the surf. He advised the couple to stand facing each other as they awaited the arrival of the next wave. The man should place his hands on the lady's waist: "You thus stand with your left and her right side toward the ocean, and as the wave rises before you, your companion should, at the word, spring from the sand while at the same moment you swing her around with all of your force, and throw her backward into the advancing breaker." For those who objected that flinging a delicate female into a breaking wave may not be the best way to help her enjoy the surf, Osborne offered a second method: "Let her stand in front of and facing you. Standing thus, she springs and pushed backward through the wave somewhat as in the former instance."

It is hard to say how many ocean bathers followed Osborne's advice; but whatever method they chose, bathers were entering the water more and more. By this time, the resort was no longer dominated by those who came to the beach to attend a religious camp meeting, and ever-smaller swim suits began to appear. Promoters of the resort boasted: "Rehoboth is noted for its safe surf bathing; the beach is clean and free from stones, rough shells, etc., and has no dangerous undertow. Bathing hours are from 11 a.m. until 2 p.m." Vacationers were pushing the limits of modesty, and on August 3, 1905, the Rehoboth Beach city commissioners decreed that it was illegal "...for any person to bathe in the ocean unless clad in a bathing suit which shall cover the body from the shoulders to the knees."

That same year, a new boardwalk 16 feet wide and a mile long was constructed on pilings across the top of the dunes between Surf Avenue and the beach. The new walkway was lighted by gas at night; and during the day, beachgoers quickly discovered that the shady area under the new boardwalk was an excellent place to escape the broiling sun. A promotional brochure proclaimed that Rehoboth was "Queen of the Summer Seas" and declared: "Here during the season may be found representatives of the wealth, beauty and fashion of our large cities, and while the walk may be crowded, it is always a well-behaved crowd."

SHOTS ECHO ON THE COAST

In the waning years of the 19th century, the sound of gunfire sometimes echoed along the Delaware coast, and clouds of birds fluttered into the air; but few residents took note. From the time that the first settlers arrived in Delaware, Sussex County residents had supplemented their diet by hunting the ducks, geese, and other waterfowl that inhabited the coastal region. The sound of a hunter's gun attracted little attention. After Rehoboth beach was established as summer resort, vacationers came to the coast looking for a few quiet days at the beach; but during the winter months, other vacationers arrived, toting their hunting guns. Many of these bypassed Rehoboth Beach to check into the Douglass House south of town.

The Douglass House was a large, three-story structure that sat a scant hundred feet from the shore. Guests at the 60-room hotel enjoyed the wide porches with their excellent view of the ocean. Hunters, who paid $14 a week to stay at the Douglass House, were attracted by the number of birds that inhabited the nearby marshes. They were also attracted by the fact that the Douglass House was not governed by the social restrictions in force at Rehoboth Beach. They could stay up late, drink liquor and play cards.

The hunting season began in the fall and lasted through the winter. The weather was often damp and cold. Those who pursued coastal birds might dig a hole in the dune, and wait in their sandy burrows for hours until the quarry arrived. Others went after the birds gathering along the coastal bays. These hunters used blinds built on stilts in the tall marsh grasses. Some hunters had more luxurious quarters aboard floating "gunning shacks." These primitive houseboats were equipped with bunks, stoves, and other facilities so that small groups of hunters could spend several days on the bay waters. By 1898, small clusters of beach cottages had also sprung up around the Douglass House.

While residents of the growing beach community were looking forward to the summer season, the conflict between the United States and Spain continued to smolder. The battleship *Maine* exploded in Havana harbor on February 15; and for two months, American newspapers were filled with stories on Spanish atrocities in Cuba. On April 25, the United States formally declared war on Spain; and coastal residents again looked to the horizon for signs of an approaching enemy fleet. Most of America's Atlantic fleet was concentrated at Key West, south of the Florida peninsula, where they were preparing to attack the Spanish forces in Cuba. At the same time, a squadron of navy warships was stationed at Hampton Roads, Virginia. This squadron was assigned the daunting task of protecting the coast from any energetic Spanish captain who might attempt to bombard the beach communities.

On the other side of the world, Captain George Dewey's Pacific fleet was steaming toward the Philippine Islands. Dewey's destination was Manila Bay, where a Spanish fleet lay at anchor. Five days after war was declared, Dewey reached his objective. At dawn on May 1, Dewey sailed directly for the Spanish ships and drolly told his executive officer, Captain Charles V. Gridley, "You may fire when ready, Gridley."

Moments later, the American guns rocked the Spanish ships. Gaping holes were torn through the Spanish vessels and fires broke out. The Spanish gunners struggled to return fire, but the situation was hopeless. Dewey had won a resounding victory; the Spanish ships were destroyed, the American ships were relatively unscathed, and only six American sailors were wounded. George Dewey's victory at Manila Bay made him an instant hero. He was promoted to admiral and proclaimed to be the greatest American naval hero since John Paul Jones. Dewey wrote in his diary: "Towns, children, and articles of commerce were named after me. I was assured that nothing like the enthusiasm for man and deed had ever been known."

Along the Delaware coast, vacationers were not deterred by the prospect of Spanish warships appearing on the horizon; and the wartime summer of 1898 was another successful season for the ocean resorts. When the road ended at the sand south of Rehoboth Beach, the small collection of beach cottages near the Douglass House had begun to coalesce into a distinct community. Some residents were admirers of Admiral George Dewey, and they dubbed their cluster of cottages, "Dewey Beach" in his honor.

RAISING A TABERNACLE AT THE BEACH

On July 12, 1901, a new song sung to the tune of "Marching Through Georgia" echoed through the open walls of the Tabernacle that sat a short distance from of the Delaware sand dune. The Tabernacle was the crowning jewel of the new resort of Bethany Beach that was established a few miles south of the Indian River Inlet. At that time, this section of the Delaware beach was a long stretch of sandy dunes, and the nearest community was several miles inland at Ocean View. As the Rehoboth Beach Camp Meeting Association had done a quarter of a century earlier, F. D. Powers, minister at the Vermont Avenue Christian Church in Washington, DC intended to establish a meeting ground on the Atlantic coast, where church members could spend a few summer weeks enjoying the beach and sharing Christian fellowship.

A nationwide contest was held to select a name for the new meeting ground and "Bethany Beach" was selected. The meeting ground was divided into 40- by 125-foot lots, which were offered for sale at prices ranging from $75 to $200. Lots could be bought with $10 down and payments of only $1 a week.

The early directors of Bethany Beach put a distinctive stamp on the new resort when they erected an auditorium near the center of town in an area designated the Assembly Grounds. The auditorium was a large eight-sided structure dubbed the Tabernacle. The tall, brown-shingled auditorium was designed with sides that could be opened to allow the breeze to blow through. The Tabernacle was designed primarily for the two Sunday services that were held each week, but it was also used for lectures, political meetings and musical concerts. The sight of the Tabernacle surrounded by beach cottages gave the resort a distinctive look; but it was the trip to Bethany Beach that distinguished it most from other resorts on the Delaware coast.

The rail connections ended at Rehoboth Beach; so vacationers took the train to Rehoboth, then loaded their luggage onto horse-drawn buses that carried about two dozen passengers to a landing on the Lewes and Rehoboth Canal. Then they climbed aboard a steamboat for the trip down the canal and across Rehoboth and Indian River bays to Pennewell's Landing in Ocean View, where a second bus was boarded for the final ride into Bethany Beach.

Early in the 20th century, the Loop Canal was constructed from the bay waters to the center of the resort. The canal, which terminated at the foot of First Street at Pennsylvania Avenue, made it possible for small steamers to carry passengers from Rehoboth right to the center of Bethany Beach.

Despite the strenuous journey necessary to reach the resort, lots at Bethany Beach sold quickly, a post office was established, and a Life-Saving Station was built on the northern edge of town. The resort grew from a temporary summer camp into an incorporated town that boasted: "Ocean City has one railroad. Rehoboth two can claim; Bethany Beach has none at all, But we get there just the same." And none of the other resorts had a building anything like the Tabernacle.

Chapter 8. Into a New Century

Unlikely Savior

Black veterans of the Union Army returned to Sussex County following the Civil War to discover that Delaware had only grudgingly accepted the changes that the war had brought. Delaware was a slave state that had remained loyal to the Union. Sussex County slaves were not covered by the Emancipation Proclamation, and Delaware had steadfastly refused to ratify the 13th Amendment that outlawed slavery. In addition, Delaware was exempt from the reconstruction process that was imposed on the former Confederate states.

African-American veterans who had fought at Olustee, Petersburg and other battlefields to end slavery in the South returned home to find slavery was still legal in Delaware. It was not until six months after the end of the war that enough other states had ratified the 13th Amendment to end slavery throughout the United States and the last slaves were freed. Delaware laws, however, continued to restrict the rights of African-Americans, who could not vote or hold public office, own firearms or assemble in groups of more than a dozen after 10 p.m. Only under special circumstances could they testify in court; and African-American males were liable for imprisonment for non-payment of debts.

Not only were there many laws that restricted Delaware's African-American population, the state's government was firmly in the hands of the Democrats (the principles and priorities of the major parties were quite different from what we think of them today), who were in no mood to improve the situation. When Governor Gove Saulsbury was inaugurated in June, 1865, he proudly proclaimed the superiority of the white race and branded any attempts to legislate racial equality as "wicked and perverse."

The passage of the 15th Amendment in 1870 was supposed to guarantee the right of all African-American males to vote, but Delaware's Black residents soon discovered many obstacles to their participation in the political process. The names of some of Delaware's African-American citizens were mysteriously stricken from the tax rolls, and others were discouraged from voting by threats of violence. When Federal laws were passed to halt these practices, Delaware passed a poll tax to discourage Blacks from voting. Not only was the tax an economic hurdle for many of Delaware's African-American citizens, but the tax collector was often absent when Blacks attempted to pay their tax.

During the last quarter of the 19th century, when the growing power of the Republican Party challenged the Democratic control of the state legislature, John Edward Addicks bought a home north of Wilmington in Claymont, which was a train stop for Philadelphia commuters. Addicks was born in 1849 in Philadelphia, where his father was a minor Republican politician. Although he was a confirmed Republican, young Addicks was more interested in business schemes; and he thrived in the rough-and-tumble world of unrestricted capitalism. Using every device at his disposal (some of which may have included fraud), Addicks acquired a substantial fortune. Although he was active in the wheat market and in various railroad enterprises, Addicks was particularly adept in the natural gas business. He was so successful in organizing gas monopolies that the crafty businessman became known as "Gas Addicks" and the "Napoleon of Gas." Although he had never held elective office in his life, the gas magnate became enamored with Delaware politics, and he had the one attribute that instantly made him a political power: money. On New Year's Day, 1889, he proudly announced that he was a candidate for one of Delaware's two Senate seats. At that time, the state legislature, not the people, selected Delaware's US Senators; and for the next decade and a half, Addicks used every penny at his disposal to secure his election. He contributed mightily to candidates who would support him. In addition, there were innumerable back room meetings accompanied by rumors of large exchanges of cash. When Addicks learned that citizens who had a delinquent debt could be barred from voting, he began to pay the debts of voters, earning himself an immediate base of supporters. Addicks also paid the poll taxes for many African-Americans, thus enabling them to vote for the first time. To insure that he got what he paid for, Addicks sent workers to the polls to "assist" these supporters in the voting booth.

In 1894, many of his supporters had won election to the Delaware General Assembly, and Addicks celebrated at a victory dinner where he boasted, "Well boys, we've won...I've bought it, I've paid for it, and I'm going to have it."

Addicks had put a significant number of supporters in position, but he had so divided the Republican party that the Delaware legislature was deadlocked on the selection of a US Senator. As the years rolled by, Addicks never flagged in his determination to represent Delaware in the US Senate. At the same time, those who were appalled at his blatant attempt to buy a seat in the Senate never tired of opposing him. In 1906, a reform movement enabled the Republican party to unite and deny Addicks most of his tools for building that support. The poll tax was repealed, and the secret ballot was established to prevent another politician from buying his way into office. But in the intervening years, many of Delaware's African-Americans had learned how to use their new-found political power. In 1901, the first African-American was elected to the Wilmington City Council.

When Addicks' business ventures went into decline, the funds that financed his political career dried up and his supporters abandoned him. The deadlock in the Delaware legislature was broken, and the state was again fully represented in the Senate. The hard times for Addicks resulted in a court a judgment against him for four million dollars; and he was forced to go into hiding to avoid court subpoenas. Addicks was arrested several times, but jumped bail. Once he was found in a cheap Hoboken hotel room without light or heat. In 1919, the man who had once been worth millions and had sought to buy one of Delaware's seats in the Senate died, forgotten, in poverty.

OLD MEETS NEW

By January, 1915, the hazards of sailing along the Delaware coast had at last been conquered. Or, so it seemed. Over the years, the watermen of Lewes had gradually acquired a knowledge of the bay's shallows and they were experts at guiding ships from the mouth of the bay to Philadelphia. Some of the pilots were Native Americans who drew upon their forefathers' knowledge of the bay. Information on the underwater hazards was mostly passed down in foggy oral traditions, until 1756, when Joshua Fisher published "A Chart of Delaware Bay and River." Fisher's chart was so accurate that it became the basis for navigation in the bay for nearly a century.

By the beginning of the 20th century, buoys marked the bay channels; the Cape Henlopen Lighthouse stood at the entrance to the bay; the Fenwick Island Lighthouse warned mariners that they had approached a false cape; and lightships had been introduced to mark offshore hazards. In the late 19th century, lightships were anchored at the Overfalls shoals near the entrance to the bay and at the Fenwick shoals near the southern border of Delaware. These vessels were stubby craft built for stability, not grace. Each lightship had its name painted in large white letters on bright red sides that made the vessel a floating billboard, warning of danger.

By the time that the Delaware lightships had taken up position, most new ships were powered by steam engines. No longer at the mercy of the winds, steam ships could navigate around the coastal shallows more easily than sailing ships. In addition, the development of radio enabled ships to communicate with other vessels and stations on shore to report any unusual threats to navigation.

By 1915, the crews of the *Elizabeth Palmer* and the *Washingtonian* sailed along the coast, secure in the knowledge that technology had made them safe. The freighter *Washingtonian* was built of steel, powered by steam, and a little more than a year old. On January 26, 1915, she sailed northward along the Delmarva coast.

Although the sea was far from calm, the night was clear, and those aboard the *Washingtonian* should have had no problem seeing the beacons of Fenwick Island Lighthouse and the Fenwick Lightship. In addition, the clear weather should have enabled the crew of the *Washingtonian* to spot the large form of the schooner *Elizabeth Palmer*.

A five-masted schooner, the *Elizabeth Palmer* was one of the largest in the world, and it was a product of the 20th century. The *Elizabeth Palmer* was launched in 1901 and a small crew could easily handle the sails on the vessel's fore-and-aft rigged masts. With a favorable wind, she could make excellent time, without any fuel cost. On January 26, packed with a cargo of coal, she sliced through the waters off the Delaware coast.

As the two drew nearer, it became clear to Captain George A. Carlisle that the steamer had failed to see the *Elizabeth Palmer*'s lights. The steel freighter was headed directly across the wooden schooner's bows. Yet, Carlisle could do nothing. Under the international rules of navigation, it was the responsibility of the steam-powered freighter to change course to avoid collision with a sailing vessel; the steamer surely must have begun a last-minute maneuver to veer out of the way, and now any change of course on the part of the schooner would risk turning her into the path of the turning *Washingtonian*. The only thing that Carlisle could do was to maintain a steady course and hope the freighter was doing what it had to do.

The *Elizabeth Palmer* was as long as a football field and its masts towered over 200 feet above the sea; but the *Washingtonian* did not see her in time. In the fine sailing breeze the *Elizabeth Palmer* was knifing through the water at a speed of eight knots. Behind the schooner's sharp bow, a heavy cargo of coal turned the speeding wooden vessel into a battering ram. Thus, when the *Elizabeth Palmer* crashed into the midship section of the *Washingtonian* at around 3:30 a.m., the impact crushed the steel plates of the freighter's hull and the cold Atlantic cascaded into the hold. The freighter filled with water so quickly that the crew scrambled straight for the lifeboats; and ten minutes after being struck, the *Washingtonian* disappeared. The crew of the Fenwick Lightship spotted the collision and radioed for help. All but one of the freighter's sailors were rescued.

Conditions were only marginally better aboard the *Elizabeth Palmer*. The schooner's bow was crushed, and the vessel was slowly filling with water. Captain Carlisle ordered the ship abandoned. The crew boarded the schooner's motor-lifeboat, and Carlisle steered for the Fenwick Island Life-Saving Station, less than two miles away. Several centuries of improvements to navigation had reduced the hazards of sailing along the Delaware coast, but human error had not been conquered.

SUSSEX KEEPS ITS HEAD

The unthinkable had finally come; and in January, 1916, residents of Wilmington and Dover watched for enemy warplanes to appear in the night sky. Reports of aircraft bound for the Du Pont powder mills fueled speculation that bombs would be falling at any moment. Along the Delaware River, frightened residents reported seeing a veritable squadron of mysterious planes above the New Jersey shore and crossing the river into Delaware. They were convinced that World War I had reached America.

The United States was at peace in January, 1916, but war fever was rising. When the war began in Europe in 1914, President Woodrow Wilson attempted to keep the United States out of it. At first he was successful; but in May 1915, the passenger liner *Lusitania* was torpedoed off the Irish coast, and 124 Americans lost their lives. Public sentiment shifted in favor of entering the war against Germany.

The German use of submarines changed the nature of war on the high seas; and at the same time, the German used zeppelins to attack England by air. At a time when fixed-wing airplanes had difficulty flying long distances, the giant German airships were able to float effortlessly over the English Channel. Reports of nighttime zeppelin raids on England spooked some Delaware residents. Then, on November 30, an explosion at the Du Pont powder plant killed thirty-one workers, and some people thought it was sabotage. President Wilson asked Congress for an immense increase in the size of the army, and war fever became epidemic.

Soon, strange things were spotted in the Delaware sky. Beginning on January 31, mysterious aircraft were reported over northern and central Delaware. The planes were said to carry lights of red, white, and bluish-green; some people said they could hear the unmistakable rough hum of a gasoline engine. There was a fear that the great German zeppelins used to bomb England had crossed the ocean and were about to bomb the First State.

It soon became apparent that the Germans were not conducting flights over Delaware. Neither were the Americans. The mysterious lights were the result of the close conjunction of Venus and Jupiter in the early night sky, which created an unusually bright celestial object that the fearful imagination readily interpreted as the light of an aircraft. By the same token, the sight of several dark oval clouds convinced some in Kent and New Castle counties that German airships were hovering over Delaware.

While inland residents may have found these changes in the sky alarming, coastal residents were unmoved. That region was home to mariners who had spent their lives navigating by the stars. They knew that one day enemy warships might appear off the coast, but they were not likely to be frightened by a dark cloud and the light of two planets in the night sky.

A year after the strange night sightings were reported in northern Delaware, the United States entered World War I and now, for coastal residents, the prospect of enemy attack was real. Indeed, one German submarine did slip into Delaware Bay, where it planted several underwater mines. Other mines were planted in the shipping lanes along the coast.

After these explosives were discovered, the Navy commandeered several Lewes fishing boats as mine sweepers. Mines often had magnetic detonators; but the wooden fishing vessels were able to cruse through the minefield with relative safety. When a mine was spotted, a gunner on the fishing boat could detonate it from a safe distance. However, not all the mines were located. The American battleship *Minnesota* was damaged by a mine off Fenwick Island, but it was able to steam to Philadelphia for repairs; and near the end of the war, a freighter was sunk by a mine off Fenwick Island.

UNWANTED VISITORS TO THE BEACH

In April, 1918, Rehoboth Beach was preparing for its second wartime summer; and residents of the resort were keeping a careful eye on the Atlantic. Although an occasional sailing vessel still passed the Delaware coast, most ships were powered by steam. A few years before World War I, a postcard showing Rehoboth Beach was enhanced by the addition of several vessels; every one of the ships that was added to the scene was powered by steam. Ships in the coastal trade were joined by steam tugs that towed barges to Atlantic ports. Some of these tugs were powerful enough to tow several barges at once. In April, 1918, the steam-tug *Eastern* struggled through a storm with two barges, the *Merrimac* and the *Severn*, in tow.

As the *Eastern* struggled to maintain headway in the heavy ocean swells, the wind continued to blow the steam-tug and its two barges toward the Delaware beach. Wartime shipping practices may have encouraged the *Eastern* to sail closer to the coast than normal; but it soon became evident that the three vessels were dangerously close to the beach. Aboard the tug, the captain could see the oceanfront buildings at Rehoboth Beach looming closer and closer. As the three vessels were driven nearer the shore, his only recourse was to cut the lines that bound the tug to the *Merrimac* and the *Severn*. At least, the tug was able to power away from the beach. The 640-ton *Merrimac* came to rest in front of St. Agnes by the Sea, which was maintained by the Franciscan Sisters as a home for nuns who taught in the Delaware Catholic schools. The *Merrimac* had sustained significant damage and began to settle into the sand at the end of Brooklyn Avenue. The *Severn* appeared unscathed as it slid to a stop on the beach.

When the weather cleared, wreckers from Lewes arrived. The opening of the summer season was less than two months away, and the two beached barges were unsightly. Tugs were able to float the *Severn* off the beach; but the *Merrimac* was in such poor condition and so deeply mired in the sand that it could not be refloated. The wreckers salvaged what they could, and the remains of the barge were left to settle in the sand.

In 1887, a ship was slowly making its way across the Atlantic. Aboard the ship was Rudyard Kipling, the rising star of British literature. Also on board was John Hanna Mulholland. Kipling's stories earned him a generous income, and no doubt he traveled in comfortable quarters. Mulholland slept with the cows.

Mulholland was born in Ireland in 1865. When he was fifteen years old, he emigrated to Canada where he served on the frontier with the Northwest Mounted Police. In 1887, he decided to return to Ireland for a visit; but Mulholland did not have the ready cash to pay for his passage. Instead, he agreed to tend a small herd of cattle that was being shipped to England. Mulholland spent his time in the cattle pens deep within the darkest, nastiest part of the ship.

During the crossing, a storm came up which hammered the ship with high waves. The vessel shuddered with each blow, and some of the cattle pens broke open. The cattle were crazed with fear; and Mulholland had contracted to keep the beasts safe. As he dodged horns and hoofs, he worked to calm the animals and get them back into their pens.

After the storm passed, the news of the man who had refused to abandon his post in the face of great danger spread over the ship. Kipling took a special interest in what Mulholland had done, and he used it as the basis of the poem, "Mulholland's Contract." The poem began with: "The fear was on the cattle, for the gale was on the sea, An' the pens broke up on the lower deck an' let the creatures free — An' the lights went out on the lower deck, an' no one near but me." According to Kipling, Mulholland promised to become a minister if he were saved; and the poem ends with his preaching to sailors who sometimes threatened him with guns and knives.

After the voyage, Mulholland returned to America. He settled in Philadelphia, where he established a successful sign business. Some of his customers were the city's many ice cream parlors. Mulholland noticed that the small tin spoon that most parlors gave customers had sharp edges and tainted the taste of the ice cream. Mulholland began searching for a better spoon.

In southern Delaware, gum trees once had been considered worthless: the wood was too soft for to use for building or furniture and made poor firewood, as well. However, in the 19th century, peach orchards spread across southern Delaware and inexpensive, light containers were need to carry the fruit to market. The gum trees provided the ideal raw material to make peach baskets as their wood split easily into thin veneers; and several factories were established in Sussex County to produce the thin slats that were assembled by hand into baskets.

After the Civil War, more advanced equipment was developed that made it possible for a machine to produce a complete basket. After the gum logs were steamed and stripped of their bark, they were sliced by lathes into thin sheets. The sheets were then cut into strips which could be assembled into baskets, trays, plaques and other items. In the last quarter of the 19th century, Huxford and Co. operated veneer platens in Frankford and Georgetown that produced a variety of baskets and other wooden articles.

When Mulholland began looking for a replacement for metal ice cream spoons, the veneer industry had gone into a decline. Fruit blights had devastated many of southern Delaware's peach orchards, and the need for baskets had begun to diminish. John Mulholland found another used for the gum tree veneer. He spent several years developing a way to cut it into small spoons; and in 1918, he set up a stamping press at the Robinson Basket Company in Laurel. The early spoons were flat, but after Mulholland established his own plant in Milford, he used steam to bend the spoons, and this curve made them much easier to handle. After he was able to convince the Breyer's Ice Cream company of the advantages of his "Bentwood" spoon, Mulholland's Milford factory flourished for decades turning the gum trees of Sussex County into the ubiquitous wooden spoons. These were not replaced by plastic until after World War II; gradually, the demand for Bentwood spoons disappeared and the Mulholland Spoon Mill closed in 1973.

GIFTS OF THE DU PONTS

In the early years of the 20th century, the quiet of coastal Delaware was occasionally shattered by the clickety-clacky sound of a horseless carriage. As more and more cars tried to negotiate the dirt roads of Sussex County, road-side signs appeared to remind drivers that the speed limit was twelve miles per hour. Some of the early signs also admonished drivers to "Blow Horns at Crossings."

At Rehoboth Beach, which was connected to the mainland, drivers were able to motor directly into town and park a short distance from the surf. To reach the resort, however, drivers had to contend with Delaware's primitive roads, which had not changed much from colonial days. The King's Highway had been the principal route that connected Sussex County with northern Delaware. Another road ran across the county from Lewes to Dagsboro, where travelers could follow trails through the Great Cypress Swamp to reach the Sussex County's western communities. Nearly all the roads were unpaved, deeply-rutted and virtually impassable in rainy weather. Drivers of horse-drawn carriages had difficulty enough navigating, and drivers of the horseless variety had even more. The sad state of Delaware's highways made motoring an exercise in frustration. A decade later, cars had become common, and the demand for better roads was rising; but state and local governments had little inclination to spend tax dollars on hard-surfaced roads. Then T. Coleman du Pont stepped forward.

Eleuthere Irenee du Pont had fled to America during the French Revolution; and in 1802, he established a powder mill on the Brandywine River near Wilmington. The Du Pont mills earned a reputation for making the best gunpowder in America; and the family became one of the wealthiest in the United States. When the first horseless carriages began chugging their way across the Delaware countryside, T. Coleman du Pont was often at the wheel. Du Pont offered to build a modern highway from one end of the state to the other and donate it to the citizens of Delaware. The first twenty miles of the Du Pont Highway from Selbyville to Georgetown were completed in 1917, but the rest of the project was delayed by World War I. After the war, in 1923, the new road finally reached Wilmington. In 1925, a hard-surfaced road joined the Du Pont Highway to the coast; and each summer, thousands of vacationers drove their cars to Rehoboth. The resort's streets soon became crowded with vehicles. The number of vacationers using the train declined precipitously; and in 1928, railroad passenger service to the beach ended.

At the same time that Delaware was acquiring a modern highway system, car manufacturers were producing vehicles that were more dependable, more comfortable, and inexpensive enough to be purchased by a large segment of the population. In the 1920s, a roadster could be bought for under $50, and even a fancy coach cost only $100 or so more.

The noisy, open horseless carriages that had pioneered auto travel were quickly being replaced by enclosed vehicles that offered riders protection from rain, dust and other road irritants. The avalanche of automobiles that motored into Rehoboth Beach during the 1920s was a mixed blessing for the resort. The cars were jammed with happy vacationers who would spend hundreds of dollars before returning home; but the traffic choked the resort's streets and threatened to ruin Rehoboth's pleasant small-town atmosphere.

In June, 1928, an open meeting was held to discuss Rehoboth Beach's traffic difficulties. At least one local observer was hopeful that a solution could be found: "On Monday evening the meeting scheduled to take place in the Blue Hen Theatre should bring forth some solution to the transportation problem which now confronts Rehoboth Beach and adjoining towns. The present rails services given by the Delaware Division of the Pennsylvania Railroad is absolutely null and void in the estimation of the traveling public and businessmen of this community."

The people who gathered at the Blue Hen Theatre concluded that the best way to reduce the number of cars in the resort was to improve bus transportation to the coastal area. The proposed bus service would enable vacationers to travel from Wilmington to Rehoboth Beach in only two-and-a-half hours along the Du Pont Highway.

The Highway also had an enormous impact on farmers. For years, the railroad was the only practical way for Sussex County farmers to ship their goods to the big city markets. Tight railroad schedules left little room for innovation; but the new road enabled farmers to ship their apples, strawberries, watermelons, tomatoes and eggs by trucks to markets in Wilmington, Philadelphia and other major cities. T. Coleman du Pont is said to have commented, "I will build a monument a hundred miles high and lay it on the ground." Indeed, his highway is a monument to a man who helped shape the state.

Long before T. Coleman du Pont began to build his highway, three army officers assigned to the Freedman's Bureau made their way across Cedar Creek Hundred to Slaughter Neck. When the men reached the property owned by Charles Shockley in 1867, they started down a road that angled through the adjoining land. On the north side of the road, they reached their destination and stopped to examine the charred remains of the Slaughter Neck schoolhouse.

The Civil War had been over for two years; and the Freedmen's Bureau had been established to ease the transition from slavery to freedom. Nominally, Delaware had a public school system based upon the principle of free education for Delaware's children, but at the end of the Civil War, there were only seven schools open to Blacks, and none were in Sussex. At Slaughter's Neck, the new school had been constructed with lumber provided by the Freedmen's Bureau. The building was erected on land rented for $5 a year, and coastal residents volunteered their labor to finish the job. While the students waited for the new school to open, classes were held in a nearby Methodist Episcopal church.

The African-American residents of Slaughter Neck eagerly awaited the opening of their new school, but some of their White neighbors were not happy about it. A school for African-American students recently had been built in Georgetown, and classes were set to begin. On June 27, 1867, a White mob attacked the boarding house where the teacher for the new school was staying. The teacher escaped, but she was so badly shaken that she quit her job.

At Slaughter Neck, the inside of the new school had been nicely plastered, and as soon as the plaster dried classes were to begin. Perhaps emboldened by the apparent success of the Georgetown mob, disgruntled Whites in Slaughter Neck got together and vowed that it was, "No use to build a nigger school. It shall not stand. It shall be burned down." Shortly afterwards, the new school was reduced to ashes.

The Freedmen's Bureau dispatched the three army officers to Sussex to investigate the incident. According to Bradley Skelcher, in *African American Education in Delaware: A History through Photographs, 1865-1930*, they reported the threats that had been made against the school but concluded, "But the evident was not sufficient to warrant an arrest." A second school building was erected. After it opened, one of the army officers noted: "The scholars had not been frightened away but were in force over 40 in their old church one [of] the most interesting schools I have visited."

While African-Americans struggled to establish a rudimentary education system in Delaware, the state passed a law that recognized the Nanticoke Indian tribe as a separate entity. In the mistaken belief that many Native Americans had intermarried with African-Americans, members of the tribe were often referred to as the Delaware "Moors," a term that is now considered offensive. In the 19th century, the Nanticoke tribe established elementary schools. When it became apparent that such a basic education was not enough, students were sent to Haskell Indian Institute in Lawrence, Kansas to continue their education.

The education system for White students in Delaware was only marginally better than the schools provided for African-American and Native American children. The desire to keep taxes at a minimum had made many people complacent about the quality of Delaware schools, which had changed little in the last quarter of the 19th century. Delaware was divided into 424 independent school districts; and many of them operated a single school with only one classroom. In most small one-room schoolhouses, the teacher's desk sat at the end of the room in front of rows of fixed desks for the students. The teacher wrote assignments for the various grades on slate blackboards mounted at the front and one side of the room. Large windows that ran down the side opposite the blackboards flooded the room with light. During the winter, a wood stove provided heat.

In 1875, four school districts in and around Lewes were consolidated into a single district; and this enabled the Lewes Board of Public Education to issue bonds for $6,000 to build a secondary school. The Lewes Union School was constructed at Savannah Road and Vickers Avenue on what is now the grounds of Beebe Medical Center.

Although a two-story school building was opened in Rehoboth Beach in 1908, most school districts had not kept pace with the example set by Lewes. Before World War I, the schools had poorly-paid teachers in schools that held classes an average 164 days a year, and most students missed a third of those days. At that time, three out of four schools in Delaware were one-room buildings. Classrooms designed for 20 students sometimes held as many as three times that number. Most of the school buildings were poorly ventilated, dimly lit and lacked modern sanitation facilities. In addition, outside of Wilmington transportation to secondary schools was so poor that only half of Delaware's high school graduates came from outside that urban center.

In 1919, with cars rolling on the first sections Coleman du Pont's new highway, Coleman's cousin, Pierre du Pont, wrote to a friend: "The schools of Delaware are a state and national scandal." The deplorable condition of public education convinced du Pont to provide the money to construct a new elementary school in Lewes for Black students. In addition, du Pont commissioned a study of Delaware's education system that recommended consolidation of the 424 separate school districts into a more manageable system.

When du Pont spoke in Sussex County, the opponents of reform claimed that he was importing foreign ideas into Delaware schools. He was also vilified for advocating removing control of schools from local to state agencies. Critics charged that du Pont's plan would create a state-run educational system that would be unresponsive to the will of the people. People were dismayed at the increased taxes needed to finance the school improvements. In Sussex, the plan was attacked as "undemocratic, autocratic, oligarchic, un-American." To some critics, the placing of state controls on schools created a "benevolent despotism, absolutely controlled by a few persons and entirely irresponsive to the will of the people."

Many of the reforms suggested by du Pont were quickly enacted into law; but this sudden success led to a backlash. A special session of the state legislature repealed many of the reforms; but the legislature left intact the centralization of the state school system. With a control mechanism in place, changes could be made at an acceptable pace. During the next two decades, schools were modernized and new buildings were constructed. Although they have undergone major renovations, school buildings constructed in Lewes, Milton, and Rehoboth over a half-century ago are still in use. Following World War II, Delaware's tri-part school system was grudgingly desegregated; and the final contentious step in the consolidation of the state's education system was begun. Thanks to Pierre du Pont, Delaware schools were no longer a "state and national scandal."

CHAPTER 9. BETWEEN THE WARS

HELL BY COMPASS

Submarines usually make every effort to evade detection; but in September, 1920, Lieutenant Commander Charles M. Cooke worked, hoped, and prayed that someone would see his. The 231-foot long S-5 was one of the United States Navy's newest submarines; and as Cooke sailed the freshly-commissioned vessel through calm ocean waters near the mouth of Delaware Bay, he began to drill his men on rapid-submergence procedures. Cooke ordered the crew of the S-5 to practice a crash dive. The alarm sounded twice and the crew filed quickly through the small hatch in the conning tower to the control room below. After the hatch was pulled shut and secured, the S-5 began to dive.

The test was suddenly interrupted by an unexpected torrent of water which flooded the control room. Cooke immediately ordered the crew to resurface. The ballast tanks were emptied, but the vessel continued to plunge toward the ocean floor. Water deluged the crew as they struggled to make sure that all valves had been properly shut. The main air induction valve was open! When the offending valve was closed, the surge of water stopped; but the S-5 continued its descent. A few minutes later, most of the crew members were knocked off their feet as the submarine struck the ocean floor.

The water cascading through the S-5 had caused considerable damage to the vessel's vital electrical equipment; but the hull was intact. The submarine was stranded 170 feet below the ocean's surface. With limited air, no power to move, and their boat half-filled with water, the crew of the S-5 had no way of communicating with those on the surface. Cooke devised a bold plan to extricate his men.

Cooke ordered the after-ballast tank cleared of water. This gave the stern buoyancy; and the after end of the submarine began to lift off the ocean floor. As the stern rose, water trapped in the vessel's engine room began to flow to the forward compartments, as the crew retreated toward the stern. The sub's massive bank of batteries were stored in a room under the forward crew's quarters. Seawater would react with the battery acid to create chlorine gas, which could kill the crew within minutes. To prevent this, as each compartment filled with water, bulkhead hatches were sealed shut.

When the after end began to lift , the water flowed forward, accelerating the rise of the stern. An unexpected volume of water cascaded through the vessel and trapped several men near the batteries. As the S-5 approached a vertical position, the trapped men had difficulty climbing from one compartment to the next. A quick-thinking crewman fashioned a rope out of shower curtains, and the trapped men were able to lift themselves out of the battery room. Once the last man was out, the hatch was latched tightly shut; and the deadly gas was sealed off from the rest of the submarine.

All 37 crewmen of the sub were able to make it to the stern of the vessel. Once the S-5 had stabilized in a nearly upright position, Cooke crawled back — or up — into the tiller room, where he could hear waves lapping against the side of the submarine. Cooke tapped on the side and listened to the sound. He concluded that about 17 feet of the S-5 extended above the surface of the ocean, but the nearest hatch to the outside was 35 feet below the surface.

With the S-5 standing on its nose and swaying in the gentle roll of the ocean, one of the sailors used a hand drill to cut a hole through the steel plates that formed the skin of the S-5. The tiny hole allowed a small stream of fresh air into the submarine. After an electric drill was located, the crew worked in shifts to enlarge the hole. The sea had not yet destroyed all of the submarine's battery power; but the drill was not properly grounded. Each drenched sailor took turns drilling while an electric charge coursed through his body. After several hours of this, when the sailors had extended the diameter of the hole to four inches, they lost the remaining electrical power. Working in shifts, they continued to attack the small opening with a hacksaw blade and the hand drill. After 30 hours of work, the crew of the S-5 had enlarged the opening to six by five inches. The stranded sailors spotted passing steamers through the small "window" in the sub's stern.

The steamer SS *Alanthus* was sailing past the mouth of the Delaware when a lookout spotted something odd and alerted the captain. The cone-shaped end of the submarine was canted at an odd angle and the *Alanthus* changed course to investigate what appeared to be an uncharted buoy, from which appeared a hand waving a shirt attached to a short length of pipe. The captain of the *Alanthus* had a small boat lowered so that the mysterious buoy could be investigated further. As the sailors from the *Alanthus* neared the stern of the S-5, they spotted a face looking out from the "window" in the submarine.

One of the sailors from the *Alanthus* called out: "What ship?"

Commander Cooke replied "S-5."

"What nationality?" the sailor asked.

"American," Cooke answered.

The sailor from the *Alanthus* continued the interrogation, "Where bound?"

To which the impatient Cooke replied, "Hell, by compass!"

After one of the hull plates of the S-5 was pried loose, all the men from the submarine were able to escape the submarine that threatened to entomb them. Attempts to salvage the submarine failed; the empty hulk of the S-5 remains on the ocean bottom near the mouth of the Delaware Bay.

THE GENERAL'S DAUGHTER'S BIGGEST BATTLE

In March, 1920, Mary Wilson Thompson led an army into Dover for what many believed was the final battle of a long campaign. Thompson was no stranger to combat. Her father was James Harrison Wilson, a Civil War general who was an excellent organizer and a daring leader. Mary Thompson inherited many of her father's qualities; and when the war over women's suffrage reached Delaware, armies of rival partisans invaded Dover. With only one more state needed to ratify the 19th Amendment guaranteeing women the right to vote, throngs of demonstrators marched through the streets and around the State House. Suffragists wore yellow jonquils as they marched through the streets singing songs and chanting slogans. Opponents of the amendment, who sported red roses as their symbol, were equally vociferous. Both groups festooned the streets with banners, held raucous rallies and ardently argued their cause. Those who believed that Delaware would be the battleground where women's suffrage would finally triumph had not reckoned with the combat skills of Mary Wilson Thompson.

The women's rights movement began in the 19th century; and for decades, the idea of women's suffrage was met with ridicule and resistance; but by the beginning of the 20th century, it appeared success was within reach. In the wake of corporate and political abuses, a wave of governmental reforms swept the United States. The Federal Constitution was amended to provide for the direct election of senators, the levying of a federal income tax and the prohibition of alcoholic beverages. The final reform amendment called for women's suffrage.

One by one, states ratified the 19th Amendment; and by March, 1920, only one more state was needed for the amendment to become part of the Federal Constitution. A special session of the Delaware legislature was called to consider the question. Some Democratic legislators opposed the amendment because they believed it would create a legion of women Republican voters. Others, who wanted a quick repeal of Prohibition, thought that the new women voters would be reluctant to favor the return of legal alcoholic beverages to the United States. Thompson opposed the amendment because she believed the women of Delaware were against it.

Thompson avoided arguing the merits of the amendment. Instead, she turned the issue into a question of state's rights. The people of Delaware were proud of their independent opinions; and they resented attempts by outsiders to sway their views. With the streets of Dover awash with boisterous out-of-state demonstrators, it was not difficult for her to convince the Delaware legislators to take their time before voting on ratification of the amendment.

Although the state Senate approved the measure shortly after the special session convened, Thompson was able to prevent a vote in the House of Representatives. When the legislature adjourned without approving the amendment, Thompson declared: "The death knell of women's suffrage has sounded." She was a bit too optimistic in that, but she had at least managed to stop it for the time being; the suffragist forces turned their attention to Tennessee, which approved the measure several months later, and women acquired the right to vote.

Historian Richard Carter wrote of Thompson: "She was a person of almost ferocious competence and skill. Had she lived in a slightly later age, she could easily have won election to high political office (had she wished to pursue it). Yet she refused to consider that women should be made the political equals of men. She was a paradox of the passing of the Victorian era from Delaware."

Defeated in her battle against the 19th Amendment, Thompson looked for other wars to wage; and she found one in Rehoboth Beach. Mosquitoes had long been the bane of those living in the coastal region. In the 18th century, a visitor to

Cape Henlopen observed: "The people are afflicted with an evil, not much unlike, and almost as severe as, some of the plagues of Egypt. I mean the inconceivable swarms of mosquitoes and sand flies which infest every place, and equally interrupt the tranquility of the night and the happiness of the day. Their attacks are intolerable upon man as well as beast. The poor cows and horses in order to escape from these tormentors stand whole days in ponds of water with only their heads exposed."

When the first Europeans arrived in the coastal area, they had been battling mosquitoes for centuries. Ancient Romans claimed that if a person slept in a room with a pig, the mosquitoes would attack the pig instead of the person. Not wishing to lie down with their swine, Americans protected themselves by applying concoctions of natural oils distilled from sassafras, vanilla, eucalyptus and other plants. Proponents of such lotions claimed that a single application, combined with abstinence from bathing, repelled mosquitoes (and others) for weeks.

When Thompson arrived in the region, the insects made most outdoor activities unbearable. When she went outside to tend to her garden, she donned a hat, swung a scarf around her neck, pulled on gloves, and wrapped her ankles with newspapers. Even thus encased, Thompson could work for only a short time in her garden before she had to retreat behind her screens. The situation seemed hopeless, until Thompson met a visitor who had returned from Central America, where a successful mosquito control program had paved the way for the construction of the Panama Canal.

Thompson learned from her visitor that the Panama insects, which were infamous for spreading deadly diseases, had been vanquished by the draining of ponds, swamps, and other mosquito habitats. Armed with a battle plan, Thompson declared war on the mosquitoes of coastal Delaware. She organized a campaign designed to rid Rehoboth Beach of any place where mosquitoes could breed. Thompson started by organizing a long overdue cleaning of the resort, starting with the accumulated trash on the dunes. In the center of town, Thompson had the old railroad racks removed. The resort's old electric plant was torn down; and an open-air concert area was created near the boardwalk. She had the ponds in and around the resort cleared of rotting leaves and trees and stocked with fish that helped keep the mosquito population in check. Canals were cut through the marshes to help drain the excess water.

By the 1930s, Thompson's work had drastically reduced the number of mosquitoes in Rehoboth, but significant areas in southern Delaware were still plagued by the insects. To control mosquitoes over such a wide area, Thompson needed an army of workers. At that time, the Great Depression had put many people out of work, and the Civilian Conservation Corps was created by President Franklin Roosevelt to provide employment for single men ages 18 to 25. The corps worked on reforestation, road construction, soil erosion and outdoor projects. The corps' camps were organized along quasi-military lines. Thompson had found her army.

She went to Washington, DC to lobby for C. C. C. camps for southern Delaware Her efforts were successful, and camps were established at Lewes and Slaughter Beach. Each camp had a set of wood-frame buildings that included barracks, a medical office, a mess hall, officers' quarters, a recreation room and a warehouse. Each camp was staffed by 200 men who received room, board and $30 a month, which was sent home to support their families.

On the second anniversary of their work in coastal Delaware, C. C. C. workers erected a simple pile of 1,200 pieces of sod dug from the tidal marshes as a monument to their efforts. When the mound on Broadkill Beach Road was completed, it stood twelve feet high and measured twenty feet in diameter. The sod monument was topped with a long pole that held a sign proclaiming: "This mound, within sight of the first (Civilian Conservation Corps) mosquito control work in Delaware, begun December 5, 1933, is dedicated to those workers loyalty and efforts have made this work a success." Mary Wilson Thompson's army had won a victory that would have made her father proud.

LOOK AT THE CHRISTMAS I COULD HAVE HAD!

Two centuries after Captain Kidd's pirate band made its nocturnal visit to the sands of Cape Henlopen, the deep hum of a powerful engine carried a group of modern freebooters past the dark dunes at the mouth of Delaware Bay. On Saturday, November 21, 1930, no lights shone from the low vessel that steered well away from the Delaware Breakwater and continued up the bay. Aboard the fast-moving boat, several men watched for any signs that they had been seen. Open water beckoned them forward; but six miles from Lewes, the boat shuddered to a halt when it grounded on a sandbar. The crew quickly determined that their vessel was stuck fast. They could hardly sit there until the next high tide. They did not panic; nor did they make any attempt to call for help. Instead, they methodically began throwing their cargo of illegal alcohol overboard. After

150 cases were pitched into bay, the boat was light enough to slide off the sandbar. The bootleggers made no attempt to retrieve the illicit cargo that now littered the surface; they quickly made their way to shore and deposited the remaining cases of liquor in an unoccupied shanty. Then they abandoned their boat and disappeared into the dark Delaware night. Several hours later, a duck hunter from Lewes happened upon the shanty. He was about to enter the shack but decided against it and continued on his way.

In 1919, the 18th Amendment outlawed the manufacture, sale or transportation of intoxicating liquors and ushered in a dozen years of Prohibition. During that time, numerous bootleggers and rumrunners would find refuge in the remote dunes of Cape Henlopen. Some began their run to the Delaware coast in Canada, where they loaded little boats with metal containers filled with liquor. Rectangular metal boxes were easy to stack, but they made a terrible racket when they banged together; so each tin was shrouded with a cloth sack. That also prevented the tins from reflecting light that would alert the revenue agents to the bootleggers' presence.

When the rumrunners reached the mouth of Delaware Bay, they would stay outside the three-mile limit, where they were safe from interference from the Coast Guard. When night fell, the tins were loaded into small boats for the final run to shore. After they reached the beach, the bootleggers would load the containers onto trucks that would carry the drink to speakeasies in Washington, Baltimore, and Philadelphia.

No one can tell how much illegal alcohol landed on Cape Henlopen during Prohibition. Most of the time, the bootleggers unloaded their cargo and disappeared without a trace. On one occasion, a Coast Guard patrol boat spotted a rumrunner close to Cape Henlopen and well within the 3-mile limit. They sped to intercept the bootleggers, who attempted to outrun the patrol boat. Seeing that they could not make it to sea, the rumrunners turned and attempted to escape by heading into the bay.

They dashed to the mouth of Lewes Creek, where they turned into one of the streams that flowed from the Great Marsh. The Coast Guard patrol boat was unable to negotiate the narrow channels of the marsh, and that gave the rumrunners time to hide their cargo in the wetlands. When they returned to the bay, they were stopped by the Coast Guard; but with the incriminating cargo safely ashore, the Coast Guard had no choice but to release the men.

The bootleggers who ran aground in November, 1930, were part of an seasonal invasion between Thanksgiving and Christmas, bringing liquor for the holiday season. They were not captured, but the Coast Guard seized the abandoned boat and fished most of the jettisoned alcohol out of the Delaware Bay. Some of the floating containers were missed by the Coast Guard and drifted onto the Delaware beach, where they were "rescued" by thirsty beachcombers. As for the shack packed with alcohol, it was discovered and confiscated by the Coast Guard shortly after the duck hunter had decided to pass it by. When he learned that he had missed a shanty full of booze, he moaned: "Look at the Christmas I could have had!"

IT'S GONE!

On April 13, 1926, a small group of government officers was having a leisurely lunch on a ship not far from Lewes harbor. The group was steaming toward Cape Henlopen, where they were to inspect the foundations of Delaware's grand old lighthouse. The constant erosion of sand had left the Cape Henlopen Lighthouse perched near the edge of a high dune; the tower had stood for a century and half, and there seemed to be plenty of time to eat lunch before starting the inspection.

In the 17th century, when the Dutch colonists arrived in Delaware, the cape was a smooth round hump on the south shore of the bay. When the Delaware Breakwater was built in the 19th century, the great stone barrier interrupted the natural flow of sand around Cape Henlopen. The sand began to migrate northward, and the cape began to extend a finger toward the mouth of the bay. At the same time, the sand seemed to be swept from the beach, and the coast began to shift steadily westward. When the Cape Henlopen Lighthouse was constructed, it stood on a high bluff well away from the surf; but in 1926, the waves were lapping at the base of the sand hill that supported the revered beacon.

The lighthouse continued to be a significant aid to navigation; and the government believed that the venerated structure should be preserved. Thus, a commission was appointed to inspect the lighthouse. While the commissioners calmly ate their lunch, one of the officials took a pair of binoculars and began a long-range inspection of the tower. It seemed to be leaning a little more than usual. A few seconds later, lunch was interrupted by the curt announcement: "It's gone!" The Cape Henlopen Lighthouse had crumpled into a pile of stones that slid down the slope of the dunes.

BATTLING DEPRESSION

During the 1920s, southern Delaware experienced several years of drought. By the end of the decade, the water table had fallen considerably; and in October, 1929, dark clouds filled with cinders and ashes floated over the Great Cypress Swamp, spread over southern Sussex County and drifted toward the beach. The swamp had caught fire. Fires in the swamp occurred almost annually and burned a few hundred acres of undergrowth before they were extinguished. This fire was different. The drought had caused the peat and turf that lined the floor of the swamp to dry out. The peat was as much as ten feet thick; and the fire slowly ate its way through this layer of turf that had been dried by the lack of rain. As the flames wormed their way through the dry undergrowth, the fire consumed the centuries-old peat-coated cypress logs that had once been the backbone of southern Delaware's shingle industry. As each cypress log was consumed by the fire, the once-thriving shingle industry took another step toward extinction. At the time, it was reported that "The fire in many sections has eaten its way several feet into the ground. Rabbits and all kinds of wild game are hastily leaving the devastating fire, and it is said large numbers of snakes have been driven out and can be found on the outskirts of the swamp."

The fire in the swamp was another blow to the economy of Sussex County, which, along with the rest of the country, was mired in the Great Depression. Over the years, the farmers of southern Delaware had responded to changing conditions by raising tobacco, grain, peaches, and strawberries and other crops. During the late fall, when farm chores were minimal, many families manufactured holly wreaths to decorate their homes during the holidays. When the railroad provided a quick and reliable means of transportation, residents discovered that there was a wide market for their wreaths and during the Depression, the Du Pont Highway enabled farmers to truck their holly creations to wholesale florists, department stores and distant destinations.

By the 1930s, the town of Milton became the center of much of the holly wreath work; and one of the town's large wreaths was hung in New York's Radio City Music Hall. During the Depression, wreath production was so important to the Delaware economy that the holly was designated the state tree.

In 1931, the economy of southern Delaware was given a small lift by the celebration of the 300th anniversary of the arrival of the Dutch colonists at Lewes. The first Dutch settlers had sailed from Horn, Holland; and the committee that coordinated the celebration decreed that, "There shall be built at Lewes a small building which shall represent as faithfully as possible the type of architecture of the town hall of Horn." The new building would contain a museum and space for public meetings. The completion of the Zwaanendael Museum and the tri-centenary celebration provided only a temporary stimulus to the depressed local economy. Local committees were established to help those who could not find work; and in January, 1932, Marcy C. M. Elliott of the Sussex County Unemployment Relief Committee summarized reports from across the county: "Relief working the several communities of the county seems to be well taken care of judging from the various reports submitted, but it is apparent as we get deeper into the winter months that increased effort on the part of the communities should be made to provide funds for their relief organizations supplemental to the small sum which can be distributed by the County Relief Committee."

According to Elliott, most of the committees focused their efforts on providing food and clothing to children in public schools. By November, 1932, it was obvious that the patchwork system of committees and local organizations was insufficient to take care of the growing number of those in need. After some wrangling, the state authorized a $1 million bond issue to help the unemployed. In Sussex County, farmers were so short of cash that they resorted to bartering to obtain the goods that they needed. A number of local stores accepted chickens, eggs, milk and other produce in lieu of cash.

As the people struggled to make ends meet, the economy of southern Delaware was given an unexpected boost by a shy, moody chemist named Wallace Carothers. The Du Pont Company was America's premier manufacturer of explosives; but after World War I the company began to diversify. Teams of scientists were hired and allowed to experiment freely. In 1928, Carothers was named to head a team of chemists who were to conduct basic research in the hopes that some of their discoveries might have practical applications.

For several years, the Carothers team turned out a steady stream of scientific papers and patents. The chemists were particularly interested in the way in which molecules united to form long chains. Such chains of molecules were found naturally in rubber and resins. Carothers worked produced a chain of molecules that could be turned into the first practical synthetic fiber. The Du Pont company began work on a plant in Seaford to produce the new fiber, and the construction project immediately improved the employment situation in southern Delaware. While the factory was under construction, the company debated what to call the synthetic thread. Several names that included "Du Pont" were considered. The name "Delawear" was also suggested and rejected. Finally, the invented word "nylon" was chosen to emphasize the new fiber's synthetic character.

To further emphasize that the new substance was not based on any natural fiber, "nylon" was advertised as being from three simple raw materials: coal, air and water. On October 24, 1939, shoppers gathered early in the morning at the entrances to several department stores in Wilmington. They talked excitedly about the new product that was to revolutionize women's fashions. At last, the doors swung open; the shoppers surged forward and streamed down the aisles. Elbowing their way to the hosiery counters, they quickly snatched up their three allotted packages marked simply, "Nylon." As one newspaper reported, nylon stockings were "...given a clamorous reception by Wilmington women."

The introduction of nylon revolutionized the fashion industry, led to a host of new products, and gave a further boost to the economy of southern Delaware; but Wallace Carothers did not share in the public acclaim. Behind the public face of the modest and unassuming research scholar was a private man who was ill at ease in large groups. At times, Carothers was a witty conversationalist; but he sometimes lapsed into periods of melancholia. In spite of the efforts of family, friends and medical advisors, his spells of depression became worse. He withdrew from his interests in reading, music and tennis. In early 1937, when the first facilities for the production of nylon were nearing completion, the death of his sister plunged Carothers into a deep despair from which he did not recover. On April 29, 1937, Wallace Hume Carothers lost his battle with depression and took his own life.

SOME SOILS BECOME SOUPY

On a summer day before World War I, some 300 shovel-toting farmers from Baltimore and Indian Hundreds gathered near a shallow spot in the dunes that had once been the Indian River Inlet. For centuries, the coastal bays had been inhabited by numerous fish that made these waters an angler's paradise, but by the beginning of the 20th century, the bays had begun to die. Instead of the clear, healthy waters that were alive with fish and crabs, the bays waters were choked with grasses and covered with a stinking green algae. Not only were the bay waters dying, but the Indian River Inlet had silted closed. The waterway that had once been deep enough for use by coastal traders was now little more than a depression in the dunes. Without the regular exchange of water through the inlet, the coastal bays had become stagnant. For two days, the shovel brigade attacked the sands until they had opened a narrow, shallow inlet that allowed water to flow between the bays and the ocean. As quickly as they had created the inlet, the wet sand along the sides of the channel began to slide back into the waterway. Within two days, the Indian River Inlet had silted shut again.

A second attempt to dig a wider channel proved more successful; and the new inlet remained open longer; but it was still not very deep. Horse-drawn wagons could ford the new waterway without much difficulty, and only very small boats could use it as a passage to the sea. A larger inlet would have to be constructed if the bay waters were to be restored to health. The United States government had built a canal across Panama; surely a channel could be cut across the dunes from Indian River Bay to the Atlantic. High explosives had been used to pulverize the rock of Panama; and the Hercules Powder Company published a manual entitled, "Hercules Dynamite on the Farm" that detailed how drainage ditches could be safely blasted through fields. Among other things the publication boasted, "A few years ago, dynamite was considered an economical agent for ditching only under conditions where machinery or handwork could not be used. Today, as a result of improved methods of blasting, dynamite is rapidly being recognized as an economical method of constructing ditches either in swamp or open country. Ditch blasting is the best known method of constructing an open ditch."

Again, coastal residents descended upon the coast; and this time, they were led by the Indian River Inlet Commission, which had convinced the Hercules Power Company to donate a ton of dynamite for the project. After the tops of the dunes were scraped off, a rudimentary channel was dug, and the explosives were planted. The dynamite workers advised the onlookers to take cover, and some went all the way back to Burton Island to keep clear of the blast. The dynamite was detonated, and a loud "whoosh" sent sand and water skyward. As the debris returned to earth, water began to flow freely through a 60-foot wide inlet that had been blasted across the dunes. Success appeared at hand, but the Hercules manual had warned: "Some soils become soupy when saturated, and in this condition, no matter how much dirt is blasted, the muck will slide in from the sides, replacing practically everything blasted out. Under these conditions, explosives are not recommended."

Within a short time, the sandy sides of the Indian River Inlet had again flowed into the channel and blocked the waterway. The coastal bays continued to stagnate until 1937, when a deep inlet finally was cut across the barrier island and stabilized by stone jetties that extended into the Atlantic, preventing the sand from accumulating in the new waterway.

RED HANNAH

On February 13, 1932, families from across Sussex County rose early and braved the winter wind to reach Georgetown in time. Such an event had not taken place in southern Delaware for over a quarter century, and everyone was eager to get a good view of the festivities. According to one report: "More than two thousand people, men, women, and children, some of the women with babies in their arms stood crowded about the wire enclosure surrounding the new Sussex County Jail, located at the Almshouse farm two miles from Georgetown, Saturday afternoon, in a chilly February wind, waiting from 10 o'clock until 1:30 to see 5 prisoners whipped."

By the middle of the 19th century, many states had abolished physical punishment for criminals, but Delaware's whipping post and the pillory continued to play a prominent role in the state's justice system. In Delaware, the pillory consisted of a perpendicular beam, perhaps twenty feet high, that rose from an elevated square platform. Four and a half feet above the platform, a thick plank ran through the upright beam. On each side of the plank there were holes through which the culprit placed his arms and head. The criminal had to stand on the platform, bent over with his arms and head held in place by the pillory, and in this awkward position endure hours of jeers and insults from those who had gathered to witness his punishment.

In 1874, *Appleton's Journal* described a criminal sentenced to Delaware's pillory: "The man in the pillory, helpless, red with shame, exhausted ever so early, tried to laugh, and to look as if he did not care. The attempt was a wretched failure. He winked his inflamed eyes at his fellow prisoners, and spat every few seconds upon the platform. The yoke was so low that he was obliged to bend considerably, and this made him weary. He changed from one leg to the other, and took all manner of positions. He wore yellow pantaloons, heavy boots, a white shirt, a dark coat, and a black hat. He was about twenty-five years of age, and was suffering penalty for burglary and uttering a threat to kill."

After the burglar had done his time in the pillory, he was taken to the whipping post, which bore the infamous nickname, "Red Hannah." The prisoner's shirt was removed, and he placed his hands in two iron loops on either side of the post. With the man thus embracing Red Hannah, the sheriff administered the flogging with a whip that had a long yellow handle connected to nine leather thongs. Each thong was as thick as a pencil, and they were about as long as the handle. In 1874, the sheriff gave the burglar ten lashes; but the blows were so slight that they did little damage to the man's back. According to *Appleton's Journal*: "The on-lookers expressed great displeasure. This was child's play! This was the worst sort of foolery! There were no shrieks! There was no blood! ... At the tenth blow, and when the sheriff dropped his arm by his side, there was a general titter. The prisoner's back was flushed, and no more. Had he worked in a sunny cornfield half a dozen hours, his flesh would have received a deeper discoloration. Had some only smiled on the sheriff's daughter, she would have blushed a finer red than that."

The practice of flogging was discarded in southern Delaware shortly before World War I, but in 1932, it was decided to reinstate the punishment in Sussex County. Plans were made to stretch a canvas shield around the whipping post in order to make the flogging as private as possible. However, the law required the floggings to be public; and the shield was not erected. The sheriff who was to deliver the February 13 flogging mentioned above had reservations; but after an hour's delay, he decided to proceed. Joseph Smith, who had been convicted of stealing four chickens, was led from the jail and shackled to the whipping post. Smith was 57 years old, and the sheriff delivered the five blows lightly. After Smith was led away, the four other prisoners were brought out. All had been convicted of similar crimes and each was given five lashes by the sheriff. As the prisoners disappeared from view, the families of Sussex County made their way home. Floggings remained a part of Delaware justice for several decades. The last whipping occurred in 1952; and the practice was officially removed from the books in 1972.

ARTISTS FIND A HOMESTEAD ON THE COAST

When the artist Howard Pyle refused to allow Ethel Pennewill Brown to attend his regular art classes, he had nothing against the Wilmington teenager except the fact that she was a female. Pyle once commented: "I can't stand those dammed women in the front row who placidly knit while I try to strike sparks from an imagination they don't have. The pursuit of art interferes with a girl's social life and destroys her chances of getting married. Girls, are after all, only qualified for sentimental work."

Although Brown could not attend Pyle's daytime classes, females were allowed to attend the artist's evening lectures. During these informal sessions, Pyle recognized Brown's talent and she soon became part of his inner circle of students. Pyle often asked Brown to take new female students under her wing, and she became a friend of Pyle and his family. Many years later, Brown would write, "The contact I had with Howard Pyle and his wonderful spirit has meant so much in my life. More than any other gift, almost, I have had."

Following World War I, Brown joined the horde of vacationers who spent their summers at the beach, where the clean, bright air of Rehoboth made the resort the ideal place for her to paint. On October 7, 1922, Ethel married William Leach at St. Peter's Episcopal Church in Lewes. Will was also an artist; but he lacked Ethel's drive to paint. In the ensuing years, most of Ethel's time would be devoted to painting, while William spent more time maintaining the modest rental properties that the couple owned in Rehoboth. The Cape Henlopen Lighthouse was one of the couple's favorite subjects; and when the lighthouse collapsed in 1926, Will Leach was one of the first to reach the fallen tower. The Leaches proudly displayed the lighthouse door in their Rehoboth home for many years; and eventually they donated it to the Zwaanendael Museum in Lewes.

After Ethel arrived in Rehoboth, she became friends with developer Henry W. Conant, who came to town in 1923. Conant bought 150 acres of land on the south side of town. His tract lay between Philadelphia Street and Silver Lake, and it stretched from the beach to the planned Rehoboth Beach County Club Golf Links adjoining the Lewes and Rehoboth Canal. The Conant development sat on elevated land that promised homeowners excellent views of Silver Lake and the Atlantic Ocean. Conant dubbed his development "Rehoboth Heights;" and he urged buyers to "Picture yourself in a summer vacation spot amid pleasant shades at the edge of the lake and ocean in the deep waters of which many a good fry disports himself, ignorant of the mission he is to perform for you, your family and friends at your cottage table, when the summer sun warms an expanse of sandy beach that has no superior along the Atlantic Coast, where vast stretches of pine woods allure your steps with their depth and solitude."

Conant priced his 50- by 100-foot lots from $400 to $1,000. Buyers were required to put 20 percent down, and they paid 5 percent a month on the balance. Conant assured buyers that "Rehoboth beach is growing and expanding;...The lots in Rehoboth Heights are offered at an unusually low price. It is safe to predict that they will be worth twice as much in less than two years."

Two years after Conant began selling lots in Rehoboth Heights, the road from Georgetown to the resort was paved and a drawbridge was constructed over the canal. The improved roads encouraged more vacationers to visit Rehoboth, and Conant's development quickly sold out. The growing popularity of Rehoboth Beach convinced Leach that the resort could become an important center for the arts; and in 1928, she found the Annual Summer Art Exhibitions at the Village Improvement Association in Rehoboth Beach. The success of the annual exhibitions and the growing artistic community convinced another developer, Colonel Wilbur Corkran, his wife, Louise, and others to establish the Rehoboth Art League, which was housed in The Homestead, the oldest structure in the resort. The Homestead had been constructed in 1743 by Peter Marsh, who reputedly came to the beach to look for Captain Kidd's treasure. The Corkrans restored the old home, where the Art League would display work by new artists alongside treasures painted by Ethel Pennewill Brown Leach and her former teacher Howard Pyle.

FIRE IN THE HOLD!

"Fire in the hold!" The most frightening alarm for a ship at sea was passed by the crew of the passenger liner *Mohawk* as the vessel steamed southward along the New Jersey coast. A winter storm was brewing, but the passengers were unconcerned about the weather or the wisps of smoke that drifted through the ship. The jolly travelers had embarked at New York City on New Year's Day, 1925, and the ship was headed for Jacksonville, Florida; even the first scent of smoke failed to unnerve them.

The fire had started in the ship's aft hold, and the crew worked feverishly to put it out. The fire continued to burn, however; and fanned by the vessel's movement, a fire at sea could quickly destroy the ship. On the other hand, if they used too much water to douse the flames, they could sink the ship. Faced with this dilemma, the *Mohawk*'s crew calmly had the radio operator call for help.

At Lewes, the tugs *Mars* and *Kaleen* were working in the harbor when they received word that the *Mohawk* was on fire. They steamed out of Lewes along with the Coast Guard Cutter *Kickapoo* that was stationed at Cape May. The larger passenger liner *Persian* also diverted its course. As the rescue vessels sailed into the Atlantic, the winter storm closed in. Aboard the burning passenger liner, Captain James Staples weighed his options. He could swing the ship around and head back to New York, but turning the ship about in the rough seas would only spread the flames faster. By continuing to steam forward, he could use the wind to help keep the flames in the back of the boat; so he decided to steam toward Lewes.

The fire on the *Mohawk* reached several automobiles that were stored in the ship's hold. The flames ignited the tires, and clouds of black smoke began to billow through the ship. While the crew continued to fight the flames, some officers circulated among the passengers to assure them that help was on the way. The passengers accepted these reassurances; and they behaved as if there was nothing amiss.

After Captain Staples passed Cape May, he turned the *Mohawk* into Delaware Bay. The burning liner was now surrounded by several vessels eager to help; but the storm was so violent that Staples continued to steam ahead in search of calmer waters. When the *Mohawk* reached the shoals about ten miles from Lewes, the ship suddenly listed sharply to starboard and tossed many of the passengers off their feet. The jovial mood had eroded; but there was still no panic.

The storm and the stricken ship's steep list prevented the crew of the *Mohawk* from launching its lifeboats. The liner *Persian* hovered nearby, but it could not get close enough to rescue those aboard the burning liner. Finally, the Coast Guard cutter *Kickapoo* edged near enough to direct a fire hose onto the liner's stern, where the flames were greatest. As the passengers sang songs to distract themselves from the danger, the captain came to the dining room to reassure them. As the passengers listened intently, some noticed wisps of smoke rising from the captain's shoes.

The rescue vessels had edged close to the *Mohawk*, and some passengers were able to climb down Jacob's ladders to the tug *Kaleen*. Gangplanks were run between the cutter *Kickapoo* and the *Mohawk*; and some passengers made the perilous transfer to the Coast Guard vessel. One way and another, through brave work, good luck and level-headedness, all of the liner's 290 passengers and crew were safely removed; a few were found to have suffered broken bones but there were no major injuries.

The liner *Mohawk*, a modern vessel, was claimed by fire; the schooner *Mary G. Farr* was a throwback to earlier times. It slid down the ways at Milton in 1863 when the Civil War was at its height. The 129-foot long vessel was one of the largest ever constructed at Milton. The two-masted schooner was destined for the Atlantic coastal trade that included ports between Boston and Jacksonville. On New Year's Eve, 1885, Captain Conwell of Milton, part owner of the *Mary G. Farr*, took on a load of corn in Baltimore and set sail for Providence, Rhode Island. In all likelihood, he sailed north up Chesapeake Bay through the Chesapeake and Delaware Canal, down Delaware Bay, past Cape Henlopen, and into the Atlantic for the trip up the coast. After the *Mary G. Farr* reached the open waters, a snow storm struck somewhere north of Cape Henlopen. Crew members worked the sails, watched the sea, and huddled around the coal stoves as the wooden schooner tossed and turned in the heavy waves.

On the New Jersey shore, a member of one of the life-saving stations spotted a light at sea. He watched carefully to see if it was a flare signaling for help. The surfman alerted the rest of his crew; and they rolled the rescue equipment to the edge of the beach. As they watched, the light grew more intense, brighter and larger. This was no flare; it was a vessel burning at sea. Aboard the *Mary G. Farr*, the crew frantically battled the blaze. Their cries for help were heard on the beach, but the sea was so rough that the life-saving crew could not launch the surfboats. The surfmen could only help if the burning schooner edged close to the sand; but as the schooner was blown closer to shore, a large wave rolled it over, extinguishing the fire but tossing the crew into the frigid waters. By daybreak, there was nothing left but a burnt mass of tangled timbers. The body of Captain Conwell was found on the beach. There were no survivors.

Nearly a half century later, during Prohibition, bootleggers frequented the New Jersey beaches much as they used the Delaware coast. Stray containers of illegal whiskey were cut adrift and washed up on the beach. Revenue agents were on constant guard to snatch these cans of illegal booze. In November, 1929, revenue agents raided a bootleggers' cache of bottles in New Jersey and noticed that one bottle had a note in it. They broke open the bottle and discovered that the note was not written on paper, but on a piece of fabric that had been torn from a rain slicker. Scribbled on the fabric were the last haunting words of a sailor facing a fire at sea: "Aboard the *Mary G. Farr* — Fire gaining in the hold. Can no longer ride out gale. About to take to the long boat. God help us all."

CHAPTER 10. WORLD WAR II. PEARL HARBOR ECHOES ON THE COAST

As a youngster, George A. Penuel, Jr. delivered freshly-baked rolls from his mother's Millsboro bakery. Young George used his bicycle to pedal through town with each batch of baked goods. In 1939, Penuel joined the navy; and two years later, he was a member of the crew of the destroyer *Shaw*, which was undergoing repairs in Pearl Harbor, Hawaii.

On December 7, 1941, the sailors on the ships of the American fleet were going through their normal morning routine. After sending an American flag fluttering aloft to the sounds of the *Star Spangled Banner*, the sailors used this quiet Sunday to address Christmas cards to friends and family back home. Penuel was looking forward to a day of shore leave in Honolulu when the first of Japanese attack planes appeared. At first, the Japanese pilots ignored the *Shaw* and focused their attack on the larger American battleships. Once they were sure they had inflicted damage on these targets, the Japanese turned to other targets.

Normally, the *Shaw* would have slipped her moorings and attempted to steam out of trouble; but the destroyer was undergoing repairs in a floating drydock. The *Shaw* was high, dry and immobile. The crew of the destroyer attempted to fire back at the enemy planes but, to their dismay, the sailors discovered that some of their ammunition was so old that the charges failed to fire. Usually, in such cases, the defective explosive would be rolled over the side into the sea; but the *Shaw* was encased in a dry-dock. The defective shells had to be left, unprotected, on the exposed deck.

On the other side of the world, along the Delaware coast, the week after Thanksgiving marked the beginning of the Christmas shopping season. Radio was the center of home entertainment, and families gathered in the evening to listen to the adventures of the Lone Ranger, the comedy of Amos and Andy, and the music of Fred Waring. George Penuel's parents were driving to Milford when they heard the news of the attack on Pearl Harbor on the car radio.

The cascade of bombs that fell on the *Shaw* started a fire that the crew could not contain. When the fire reached the forward magazine, it set off an explosion that sent a fireball several hundred feet high over Pearl Harbor. The explosion was so great that it distracted the other American sailors from the Japanese attack for a moment. The *Shaw*, the dry-dock, and all aboard were blown to bits and buried at the bottom of Pearl Harbor, including the body of the Millsboro delivery boy, George Penuel.

The American ships were still burning at Pearl Harbor when workers began arriving for the 4:00- to-12:00 shift at Seaford's new nylon factory. Workers were buzzing with the news of the attack on Pearl Harbor when the foremen called to an emergency meeting to plan for the factory's defense. Although no one seriously expected the Japanese navy to come sailing up the Nanticoke River to shell the Seaford plant, there were concerns about sabotage. Workers were dispatched to patrol the perimeter of the plant.

The nylon plant had been churning out the artificial fiber since it had first opened. In its first year of operation, 64 million pairs of nylon stockings were sold. In addition, nylon from the Seaford plant replaced silk that was used in parachutes, tires, clothing and hundreds of other wartime products. The Seaford plant's importance and Delaware's historic location on the shipping lanes had caused the government to continually improve its coastal defenses.

During World War I, Fort Saulsbury was constructed about a dozen miles up the bay near Slaughter Creek. The fortification at Slaughter Beach was named after Willard Saulsbury, a US Senator and Attorney General of Delaware. Fort Saulsbury's four 12-inch guns could fire nearly to the New Jersey shore; but by 1940, it was apparent that this installation was insufficient to protect the Delaware Bay. In 1940, work began at Cape Henlopen on a massive fortification that would guard the mouth of the Delaware. Sprawling over 1,011 acres, the new installation contained a series of concrete gun emplacements, barracks, officers' quarters, mess hall, storage bunkers, and other facilities. The emplacements for the fort's guns were hidden in the cape's dunes. Some of the larger weapons were capable of firing a one-ton shell over 25 miles; and a series of concrete observation towers were constructed along the coast to house spotters who determined the effectiveness of each shot. During the day, lookouts in the towers could spot warships that ventured close to the Delaware coast. In addition, the fort was equipped with several 6 million-candlepower searchlights that could be used to illuminate any enemy vessel that attempted to approach the bay at night. The new fort was christened "Fort Miles" in honor of General Nelson A. Miles, an important Civil War general who had served in the army for more than half a century.

ENEMY RAIDERS RETURN TO THE COAST

On December 16, 1941, while the United States was reeling from the attack on Pearl Harbor, a German submarine left its European port and headed for the east coast of the US as part of what the German high command called Operation Drumroll. The fleet of U boats had orders to sink any vessel they encountered in the shipping lanes along the coast; and the steady stream of ships using Delaware Bay made waters around Cape Henlopen an attractive hunting ground.

Crews on American merchant ships were well aware of the threat posed by enemy submarines. Sailors talked and kidded each other as they sailed along the coast, hoping to reach the sanctuary of Delaware Bay. At the end of January, 1942, some of these voyages were interrupted by the dull sound of an exploding torpedo, followed by a mad scramble to get the lifeboats into the water. As one seaman who was torpedoed in coastal waters recalled: "Everything happened so quickly that we had no chance to get scared or think about what might happen. We just worked to get the lifeboat overboard."

Sometimes the torpedo only wounded its target, and the submarine would surface to finish the job with its deck guns. Just after midnight on February 2, 1942, the oil tanker *W. L. Steed* was rocked by a terrifying jolt as a torpedo exploded into its starboard side. As the *Steed* began to go down, its oil ignited and flames lit the cold Atlantic sky. The crew manned the lifeboats; and soon they were pulling away from the burning ship. In the eerie dark, the men in the lifeboats spotted the silent hulk of a German U-boat: "Just then a large submarine, estimated at about 2,000 tons painted a light gray, with guns forward and abaft her conning tower, appeared on the port side. Men immediately manned the guns, the forward one appeared to be 4-inch and the after one a trifle smaller. They started shelling the ship." As the tanker slipped into her watery grave, the German sub disappeared as silently as it had appeared.

With their ships torpedoed out from under them, sailors found themselves clinging to hope as they bobbed on the Atlantic swells. During some attacks there was enough time to radio a distress call, and sailors from these ships could be confident that help would be on the way. Then they would pass the time telling stories, joking and firing an occasional signal flare. Other attacks were so fast that little could be done. The small Norwegian freighter *Hvoselff* was making its way along the southern Delaware coast when a German torpedo broke the ship apart; the *Hvoselff* went under in less than two minutes. The crewmen only had time to launch the lifeboat on the port side; the seven sailors in the lifeboat were able to pluck seven other crewmen from the cold waters but the captain and five other crew members were killed in the attack. The fourteen Norwegians in the lifeboat were stranded in the cold and dark, miles from the Delaware shore, and no help was on the way. Knowing that the American coast lay due west, the sailors began to row in that direction. The seamen took turns at the oars and after thirteen hours, they splashed ashore at Fenwick Island.

Crews of vessels that were torpedoed off the Delaware coast who managed to make it into lifeboats had an excellent chance of being rescued by other vessels. These seamen were often taken to Lewes, where the Red Cross waited with dry clothes, warm blankets and hot coffee; those who were seriously injured were taken to Beebe Hospital for treatment. But, others were not so fortunate. The crew of the torpedoed tanker *W. L. Steed* had managed to climb aboard three lifeboats, but they became separated in the dark. As they floated about, the weather turned bad, snow began to fall, and the seas were running high. One by one, the men began to die. Eventually, all three lifeboats were discovered by rescue ships; but only four sailors out of a crew of 38 had survived.

THE LUCK OF JACOB JONES RETURNS

In the early years of the 20th century, the Navy named a new destroyer after Jacob Jones, the hard-luck Lewes captain who survived a failed medical practice, the death of his wife, and imprisonment by the Algerian pirates to become one of the Navy's outstanding officers. After the United States entered World War I, the *Jacob Jones* was dispatched to Great Britain; and on December 6, 1917, the *Jacob Jones*, under the command of David Bagley, was the trailing vessel in a squadron of six destroyers steaming southwest of England. The other destroyers had passed over the horizon and left the *Jacob Jones* alone when a

German submarine fired a torpedo at the American warship. It blasted a large hole in the after end of the destroyer and within minutes, the stern of the *Jacob Jones* was under water. The torpedo had also wrecked the ship's electrical power, and the *Jacob Jones* could not call for help.

Bagley was convinced that his ship was doomed, and he ordered the *Jacob Jones* abandoned. Some of the men were able to scramble into the ship's boats; others simply jumped over the side. As the destroyer's stern settled, the depth charges rolled off the deck into the sea. Moments later, the depth charges began to explode and killed many sailors in the water. The *Jacob Jones* Quickly disappeared beneath the waves.

The survivors struggled in the cold water for several hours, when a British rescue ship unexpectedly appeared. The commander of the German U-boat had gallantly radioed the position where he had torpedoed the *Jacob Jones*. Although sixty-four out of the 103 crewmen aboard the destroyer died, more would have perished had it not been for the action of the German captain of the U-boat.

Following the sinking of the *Jacob Jones*, another destroyer was named for the Delaware naval hero. At the beginning of World War II, the second *Jacob Jones* was affectionately called "Jakie" by its crewmembers and it was one of the few American warships assigned to protect the North Atlantic coast. As the *Jacob Jones* cruised the Atlantic in February, 1942, the destroyer pushed through the same waters where the ship's namesake had defeated the British sloop-of-war *Frolic* during the War of 1812. Suddenly, a torpedo exploded, blowing a large section of the stern right off the ship. As the "Jakie" began to sink, the sailors flung life rafts into the cold Atlantic and dived over the side.

The depth charges on the sinking *Jacob Jones* began to detonate and hammered the men struggling in the frigid water. Within an hour, most of the sailors were dead. When a rescue vessel arrived, only eleven sailors out of a crew of nearly two hundred could be found. Since then, the United States Navy has not named another warship after the unlucky *Jacob Jones*.

BLACKNESS DESCENDS ON THE COAST

Within days after the declaration of war, a meeting of community leaders was held in Lewes to organize civilian defense efforts. Plans were made to establish first aid stations on the outskirts of Lewes so that if the town were attacked, the Beebe Hospital would not be overwhelmed with minor injuries. In addition, an automobile corps was proposed to evacuate schools during an attack. Finally, work was begun on blackout procedures that would eliminate all onshore lights that could guide enemy ships and planes to coastal communities. The first large-scale test of air raid readiness came on January 28, when the Rehoboth Beach area held a major blackout exercise. On that snowy evening, representatives of the police and fire departments were joined by newly-appointed air raid wardens to observe how coastal residents responded to the blackout. At 7 p.m., all vehicular traffic in Rehoboth Beach, Henlopen Acres, and westward to Midway came to a halt. The cars and trucks sat motionless with their lights out. All the homes were dark. According to one report, had an enemy aircraft been flying over that part of the Delaware coast: "They would have looked down on a countryside in which the only light came from the whiteness of the snow which had fallen early in the evening, and which gave a ghostlike appearance to the streets that were devoid of all signs of normal life. They would not have known it, but down below them would have been a population of hundreds of people, ready to meet any emergency and not in the least afraid."

After three minutes, the test came to an end; and the exercise was rated a success. There was, however, one unexpected source of light. At that time, radios were major pieces of furniture and many featured large illuminated dials. The air raid wardens discovered that the radio dials were bright enough to be seen from a great distance.

In order to alert citizens to an impending air raid, Rehoboth Beach installed a new alarm on the roof of City Hall intended to "wake all sleepers within a distance of two miles."

Coastal residents were advised to prepare for an attack by preparing a safe room in their houses, obeying the blackout regulations, and keeping a store of water and sand available to fight fires caused by incendiary bombs. In addition, residents were admonished to always carry a gas mask while walking or riding. If a raid materialized, residents were to turn off all running water, gas and electricity before seeking shelter. If driving, coastal residents were advised to stop immediately, park the car and seek shelter. If they were riding or driving a horse, it should be tied to a post by the halter lead. After an air raid, they were not to leave their shelter until the all-clear had been sounded on the town siren. In addition, the air raid wardens carried a hand bell that also was used to indicate that the attack was over. When the danger had passed, residents were to check pilot lights to prevent a gas explosion; they were directed to remain at home, and

"...avoid interfering by standing about in crowds in order to satisfy your curiosity."

Following the first air raid drill in January, 1942, people became accustomed to the wail of the air raid siren. As the months passed and the first summer visitors arrived in Rehoboth, they noticed that the dark shadow of war had descended on the resort. Streetlights were shielded on the ocean side so that they would not be seen from far out at sea. Motorists driving in the resort were instructed to use only their parking lights. Oceanfront buildings were equipped with blackout shades; and on the boardwalk, businesses erected light baffles on doorways that opened toward the sea. To enable emergency vehicles to negotiate the darkened streets, the people of Rehoboth whitewashed the lower portions of tree and poles to make them more visible. Throughout the conflict, war-weary vacationers would continue to visit the Delaware seaside resorts but the subdued lighting generated a subdued mood, under the constant reminder that enemy submarines could be lurking off the coast.

When the sailors from the Norwegian freighter *Hvoselff* successfully rowed to shore after their ship was torpedoed, they received a friendly reception from the residents of Fenwick Island; but their feat demonstrated how easy it would be for the enemy to come ashore, as well. German submarines could venture to within a few miles of the coast and launch a small boat that could carry a spy or saboteur to the beach. To intercept enemy agents slipping onto the beach, a kennel was constructed at the Rehoboth Beach Coast Guard Station and K-9 patrols of the coast were begun. At first, sentries walked the sand each night with their dogs. Horses were soon brought in, and then the Coast Guard began mounted patrols.

In the case of many coastal residents, the obsession with security extended to distrust of their neighbors. During the first months of the war, several people notified the authorities of people they thought were acting suspiciously. The FBI directed an investigation by state and county police forces in Delaware and Maryland. On March 13, the authorities made coordinated raids at nearly two dozen locations across the Delmarva Peninsula. The agents confiscated: "over 400 rounds of ammunition, numerous rifles, shotguns, shortwave radios, cameras and miscellaneous items such as photographic development equipment, ammunition belts, a blackjack, swastika flag, pennants, and swastika armbands." One "enemy alien" was arrested in Delaware, and a second in Maryland. Under wartime regulations, enemy aliens were not allowed to own the type of equipment that was seized. There was no direct evidence that the two arrested

187

men were spies, but such raids did little to calm people's jitters and they continued to keep a close eye on each other, fearing that enemy agents would slip into the country by landing on one of Delaware's dark beaches.

A SUSPICIOUS SHADE OF GREEN

The Delaware wing of the Civil Air Patrol was established a week after the attack on Pearl Harbor. The destruction of American merchant ships had convinced military authorities to give permission for the Civil Air Patrol (CAP) to fly submarine hunting missions. Among the first to fly were planes from the Rehoboth Beach Base. Members of the patrol purchased their own uniforms and supplied much of the equipment needed to keep the planes flying. The patrol base at Rehoboth Beach was constructed of donated lumber. The pilots using the Rehoboth Beach airfield flew single-engine Stinson 105s and Fairchild 24s. Two aircraft, with a pilot and co-pilot each, would fly cover over convoys as they made their way along the coast. If a submarine was spotted, the location would be reported to the Rehoboth Beach airfield, where the radio operator had a special telephone line that was connected to the army air corps stationed at Dover. A B-25 would be dispatched from Dover to bomb the sub. The CAPs flights from Rehoboth Beach demonstrated their value almost immediately, when an enemy submarine was spotted stalking a ship not far from the mouth of the Delaware Bay.

The planes flown by the CAP had no sophisticated equipment; some pilots even carried inflated inner tubes as life preservers. The lack of modern navigation instruments made it difficult to pinpoint the location of any U-boat they sighted; and the Army bomber from Dover would often arrive long after the German submarine had slid safely beneath the waves. Beginning in July 1942, the planes of the Civilian Air Patrol were equipped with small depth charges and bombs. At Rehoboth Beach, the bombs were painted bright yellow; but after flying missions over the Atlantic, the pilots noted that the noses of their bombs were covered with a suspicious green smudge. Could someone have been tampering with their gear? The culprit was found — the bombs were picking up grass stains during the take-offs and landings on the unpaved field.

THE EXPLAINER CORPS DEFENDS THE COAST

In May 1942, all the residents of Sussex County went back to school. People who had not been in a classroom for decades reported to their local elementary schools to do their part in the war effort. Each person, young or old, was required to register for a mandatory rationing program that would reserve critical foodstuffs, such as sugar, and consumer items made from vital materials (iron, steel, cooper and aluminum) that were needed by the armed forces. After the registration was completed, ration books were issued that contained coupons that were required to make a purchase. The registration list for the first ration book would be used for subsequent books; anyone who failed to register would be unable to buy scarce materials for the duration of the war. When coastal residents registered for the ration program, they were required to present an inventory of their current stock of rationed goods. Those who had stockpiled critical items had the excess deducted from their first book of ration coupons. The first ration book contained coupons for sugar, coffee and shoes; but as the war wore on, other items would be rationed as well.

Rationed foods were assigned a point value, and each person was allowed 48 "points" of canned and processed foods each month. In 1943, the War Production Board issued ration tables based on standard sizes, and manufacturers were prohibited from deviating from these sizes. The introduction of standard-sized containers should have made wartime shopping easier; but shoppers needed to weigh prices, sizes and ration points before deciding what item to buy. For example, a 19-ounce can of tomatoes sold for 12 cents, and a 28-ounce can went for only 2 cents more; but the smaller can required 16 ration points and the larger can required 24 points. Arithmetically-challenged shoppers were paralyzed by the sudden complexity of buying their everyday groceries; but during the first week of the program, an "Explainer Corps" of specially trained women who were well-versed in the intricacies of the rationing system were stationed in the stores to answer questions.

The Explainer Corps helped launch the rationing system, but the ration points for controlled items was adjusted frequently and consumers were expected to keep informed of the latest regulations. To help shoppers sort out what they needed in order to buy restricted items, some grocery stores placed a ration point tag next to the price tag on the shelves. As the war went on, consumers kept track of changes in the program by following the Civilian War Calendars that were published in the local newspapers. The calendars indicated items being rationed, the ration coupons needed to buy the item, the point value of rationed foods, and the current status of various products.

Rationing aimed to distribute hard-to-get items fairly, but some items were nearly impossible to get. By the start of World War II, the thousands of automobiles that crowded into Rehoboth Beach, Bethany Beach, and Fenwick Island had driven railroad passenger service from the southern Delaware landscape. When the Japanese attack on Pearl Harbor cut the United States off from its principal source of rubber, a moratorium was placed on the purchase of new tires. Each state was allotted a certain number of new tires; and Delaware divided its allotment among the state's three counties. In April, 1942, the results of these calculations were announced and the people of Sussex County learned that they were collectively allowed a total of eighteen new tires a month. Car owners became experts at repairing old tires.

Those lucky enough to own a car with a decent set of tires still had to contend with gasoline rationing. Every car was issued a sticker with the letters A, B, C, or T. "A" stickers were initially allowed four gallons of gas a week, but later in the war it was reduced to three gallons per week. "B' and "C' stickers were for drivers whose occupations were considered critical to the war effort, and they were allowed more gas. "T" stickers were for trucks, which were allowed unlimited fuel to ensure that the economy continued to function. In Delaware, a top speed limit of 40 mph was placed on cars as an additional measure to conserve fuel.

The wartime restrictions reduced the number of cars registered in the state by 10 percent; but it did not stop people from driving to the seaside resorts. At least, now the cars packed with vacationers had no problem finding places to park.

Scrap drives were conducted by the Delaware Salvage Committee to recover critical materials from old items. Metal, rubber, cooking fats, rags, and paper were collected and recycled into war goods. Caught up in the patriotic spirit of the campaign, one young coastal resident later confessed that he had taken several pots and pans from his mother's kitchen to donate to the drive. A more significant accumulation of scrap lay a short distance off Cape Henlopen where the remains of old shipwrecks yielded valuable metal. A single hulk recovered near Lewes produced 3500 tons of scrap metal.

In August, 1942, the salvagers turned their eyes to the eight heavy cannons that had been installed along the canal in Lewes as a memorial to the defenders of the town during the War of 1812. In addition, the park had a small six-pounder cannon that was reputedly taken from a pirate ship that had been abandoned in Lewes Creek. Tradition had it that the small gun was used to celebrate Abraham Lincoln's re-election during the Civil War; and that it had to be buried on a farm on Pilottown Road to keep it out of the hands of the town's Confederate sympathizers. Although it appeared for a time that the old cannons would be sacrificed to the scrap drive, enough alternate sources of critical metals were found to save these historic pieces from destruction.

By the beginning of November, 1943, the prospects for a traditional Thanksgiving dinner looked bleak. Thanksgiving turkey was a deeply-ingrained tradition that traced its roots to the beginning of the American colonies. Benjamin Franklin thought so much of the bird and the sustenance that it had given the early settlers that he wanted the turkey to be declared the American national bird rather than the Bald Eagle. The war year 1943, however, was not a good year for the nation's turkey population.

Two years of war had drastically reduced the nation's poultry supply. During 1943, more than 33 million turkeys were raised in the United States, but one out of every ten was consigned to the armed forces. Furthermore, strict price controls and difficulties getting feed, young birds, and eggs had driven many turkey farmers out of business. With the approach of the holiday, the War Price and Rationing Board reminded buyers that the price of turkeys was strictly controlled. The highest price to be paid for drawn turkeys (a bird from which feathers, head, feet, entrails and craw ware removed) was 63 cents a pound. The price for dressed turkeys (one from which the feathers had been removed, but the head, feet and entrails were left intact) was limited to 53 cents per pound; and live birds were 48 cents a pound.

On the East Coast, less than half the turkeys needed for the traditional Thanksgiving feast were available. A flourishing new industry in the region helped fill the gap; and it was started by Cecile Steele of Ocean View.

In 1923, Steele was surprised when her regular shipment of chickens arrived. Like most folks in the coastal region, she used her chickens to produce eggs. The Ocean View resident was expecting her usual delivery of 50 chicks; but 500 young birds were delivered instead — ten times the number of chickens that she needed. Nevertheless, Steele took the birds to her little red chicken house and raised them. At that time, chicken was more expensive than hamburger; and most people considered it a premium meat. Young chickens that were tender enough to be fried or cooked in the oven were traditionally a by-product of the egg industry. Broilers were a few of the choicest young birds culled from the farmyard flock, and they commanded high prices. Those families who were affluent enough to eat broilers generally reserved chicken for a special weekend meal. Cecile Steele cared for her young chickens for 16 weeks; and when the birds had reached 2 pounds, she was able to sell most of the broilers for a profitable 62 cents a pound. Her success convinced Steele to order more chicks to raise as broilers.

Word of Steele's lucrative chicken business spread to her neighbors; and by 1937, Sussex County was producing 16 million broilers a year. The coastal region's moderate weather was ideal for raising chickens; and the abundant forests and lumber mills produced inexpensive lumber for the construction of chicken houses. Within two decades, Sussex County emerged as the leading chicken growing area in the world. In April 1943, the Eagle Poultry company opened a new plant in Frankford that featured innovative equipment for processing chickens. Up to this time, workers removed only the bird's head and feathers; but the Eagle plant's new evisceration apparatus enabled workers to quickly remove the head, feet and entrails. The new machinery enabled the plant to process 10,000 birds a day.

An army travels on its stomach, as they say; and during World War II, the stomachs of American soldiers were often filled with chicken. Without chicken, the food supply for the armed forces would have been stretched dangerously thin. In the coastal region, military contracts during World War II gave an additional boost to the area's broiler production. In addition, the military's use of chicken meat helped change the eating habits of many servicemen who had seldom eaten chicken before. Chicken retained some of its glamour as a premium food; and the broiler's ready availability made it a perfect replacement for turkey. In the weeks before Thanksgiving 1943, a Salisbury newspaper reported: "Tom, Turkey, the big bird that is symbolic of the nation's holiday dinner, will be missing from more lower shore dinner tables on Thanksgiving than every before, but the pride and joy of the shore, the broiler, will be a likely substitute."

SUMMER OF '44

The first sight of German soldiers traveling the roads of Sussex County was quite a shock; but the summer of 1944 brought a number of astonishing events to southern Delaware. When the war began, coastal Delaware was considered a critical defensive area; and prisoner of war camps were banned from the region. Continued labor shortages and success in driving the German submarines from coastal waters prompted a reconsideration of that policy; and in 1944, the first German prisoners began to arrive at camps established at Lewes, Georgetown and Fort Saulsbury. The use of the captured soldiers was heavily regulated, and the prisoners proved to be effective workers. Many of the German soldiers were employed in the area's burgeoning broiler industry, whose labor demands were constantly growing at a time when the number of available workers was shrinking.

The German POWs had just begun to appear in southern Delaware when the summer vacation season began at Rehoboth Beach. Shortly before 8 o'clock on the morning of June 6, church bells began ringing. As the bells echoed through the town, residents switched on their radios to learn that the D-Day invasion of France had begun. People gathered to discuss the news which by mid-day could be heard blaring from the open windows of most homes. In the evening, the audience at the Auditorium Theatre listened to a short prayer and then stood to sing the *Star Spangled Banner*; and at the Blue Hen Theatre, the audience stood and bowed their heads as they listened to the radio broadcast of President Franklin Roosevelt's D-Day speech as it was played over the theater's sound system.

The success of the D-Day invasion made the summer of 1944 the most encouraging since the war began. But, that did not mean that all vigilance could be dropped. By September, when the freighter *Thomas Tracy* steamed steadily along the Delmarva coast, most vacationers had gone home. During the first years of World War II, ships had kept as close to the shore as possible to avoid the deadly German submarines. By 1944, the convoy system and other measures had driven nearly all enemy vessels from Delaware waters. The threat to the *Thomas Tracy* came from a different quarter. Labor Day marked the end of the vacation season but it also marked the beginning of the hurricane season. As the *Thomas Tracy* steamed along, a vicious hurricane roared into Delaware waters.

Weather forecasting during World War II was more art than science. Without satellites, weather radar, computer simulations and other devices, forecasters relied on ground reports, experience and intuition to predict the arrival of storms. A fast-moving hurricane could engulf a ship with little warning. The storm that hit Delaware in September 1944 ripped through Fenwick Island and Bethany before overtaking the *Thomas Tracy* near Rehoboth Beach. The storm's hundred-mile-per-hour winds and the raging seas drove the *Tracy* hard toward the beach. On shore, the waves crashed onto the Rehoboth boardwalk, splintered the planks and sent chunks of timber flying. As the *Thomas Tracy* was thrown toward the shore, the ship's engines failed.

When the storm abated, rescuers rigged lines to the stranded ship and they were able to use a breeches buoy to ferry the crew ashore. The vessel, however, could not be saved. The ship's hull had been driven deeply into the sand. The ship was nearly broken in half. The wreckers cut the *Thomas Tracy* down to the waterline, and the lower portion of the hull was left in the sand. Ironically, the *Thomas Tracy* had settled on top of the hulk of the *Merrimac*, the barge that had been swept ashore during the closing months of World War I and likewise stuck so fast in the sand that she could not be salvaged.

WELCOME TO THE HARBOR OF REFUGE

By May 1945, Germany was caught in the vise of the American and Russian armies. As Adolf Hitler struggled to hold onto his rapidly shrinking territory, the Nazi forces were driven to desperate measures. Admiral Karl Doenitz, the commander of the German navy, decided to launch Operation Seawolf. He ordered the few submarines that were still operational to cross the Atlantic and attack the American coast. A few well-placed shells might disrupt civilian life enough to force the American navy to divert a substantial number of ships from Europe to home waters. Among the vessels that headed westward was the submarine U-858, which was commanded by Thilo Bode.

The Allied counter-intelligence network began to pick up hints of the operation. These fed quick-spreading rumors that the Germans planned to shell the East Coast, that buzz bombs would be launched against American cities, and that people along the coast would be plunged into the war zone.

Powered by diesel engines, the U-858 spent most of the time cruising on the surface. When Bode wanted to submerge, he had to stop his diesel engines and switch to battery power. This would allow him to run under water for several hours. Although this was enough time to attack an unarmed merchant ship, he would need a lot of luck to outrun a well-armed destroyer. Poor weather kept most Allied search planes on the ground as Bode crossed the Atlantic but as he steamed toward the Mid-Atlantic coast the weather cleared, and the American planes took to the skies. One of them spotted the *U-858*. Bode quickly dove, but American navy ships quickly began to converge on his position. The Americans fired several depth charges, but none damaged the *U-858*. Bode managed to evade the destroyers and steer his boat to safety. But after eluding the American naval forces, Bode and his crew received a devastating message — Hitler was dead. The war was over. Commander Bode decided to surrender his ship. After surfacing, he radio Allied forces who again converged on the submarine. As the Germans waited to give themselves up, they threw most of their ammunition overboard, then feasted on whatever remaining rations they had aboard. Shortly afterwards, a small flotilla of American ships arrived and the Germans surrendered.

The *U-858* was piloted to Lewes, where it was anchored near the Delaware Breakwater. While a helicopter whirled overhead and a small army of photographers snapped pictures, the crew of the German U-boat was ferried ashore. According to the *Delaware Coast News*, the crew of the *U-858* "...were shabby and dirty. Their hair was long and unbarbered. Several wore perky little goatees on unshaven faces, and some had weeks-old beards. But they stood stolidly and repressed emotionally and made snappy response(s) to one of the officer's commands to line up. Most wore soiled leather slacks, and heavy rubber boots. All were young, apparently in their twenties, while a couple appeared less than 18 years old. One or two had white Turkish towels worn scarf-wise around their necks."

The war with Germany was over, but the *Delaware Coast News* recalled the early days of the conflict when enemy submarines prowled coastal waters, and "More than 252 of their victims back in the early part of 1942 were landed here from twelve of the sinkings off the New Jersey and Delaware coasts, the largest contingent of the U-boat survivors at any one Eastern port. The bodies of many more who had died from their vigils aboard frail lifeboats were also brought ashore at Lewes."

WE HAD TO FIGHT THESE GUYS

At the start of World War II, the 198th and 261st Coast Artillery of the Delaware National Guard had inherited the tradition of defending the Delaware coast. At the beginning of the war the 261st, which included more than 300 men from southern Delaware, garrisoned in the newly-constructed Fort Miles, Fort Saulsbury near Slaughter Beach, and guns on the other side of the bay at Cape May. On the other hand, the 198th was destined for a more distant post, code-named "Bobcat."

In the early months of the war, Japanese forces spread far and wide across the Pacific Ocean, and it was to this theater that 198th was dispatched. As they were transported to the south Pacific, they learned "Bobcat" was the island of Bora-Bora, located 150 miles southwest of Tahiti. It was not known if the Japanese had occupied the island, and the Delaware troops went ashore with their weapons at the ready. They soon discovered that they were alone on an island with friendly natives, but no electricity, and no roads; and thankfully, no Japanese soldiers.

Over the next year, the 198th turned the tropical island into a modern military installation. The troops were not under attack and their major problem was getting enough food to eat. After several months of a diet of canned and powdered food, a ship arrived with fresh provisions. A member of the unit recalled: "We even had a parade and marched down to the dock to escort the pork chops or whatever it was."

The 198th spent a year on Bora-Bora before it was posted to other assignments in the Pacific. By this time, transfers and replacements from other states had changed the character of the unit; and it was no longer dominated by Delaware soldiers. Unlike early wars, military units lost much of their regional flavor, and Sussex County men were scattered in units throughout the armed forces. They fought and died in the Atlantic and Pacific, in Africa, Europe and Asia. George Penuel of Millsboro had died at Pearl Harbor at the war's beginning; and Ensign James R. Kelly of Lewes was there at the end.

When President Harry Truman announced the surrender of all Japanese forces on August 14, 1945, the news kicked off a celebration along the Delaware coast. Alerted by wailing air-raid sirens, people rushed into the streets. At Rehoboth, the fire department paraded every piece of equipment it had through the streets. As people cheered, motorists blared their horns and others banged on pots. When the news reached the Dinner Bell Inn, diners stood silently; and some wept as the National Anthem was played.

Two weeks later, the formal surrender ceremony was to take place on the battleship *Missouri*; and Ensign James Kelly had a ringside seat. Kelly was the son of Delaware River pilot, and he had been commissioned in June, 1944. After some fleet duty in the Atlantic, he was dispatched to the Pacific and participated in several actions in the Philippines. In September, Kelly was the Junior Officer of the Deck aboard the destroyer *Nicholas*, which was part of the American fleet that had gathered in Tokyo Bay. Around 7:00 in the morning on September 2, the *Nicholas* rendezvoused with a Japanese destroyer that carried the emissaries who were to sign the surrender documents. After the officials were transferred to the American destroyer, the *Nicholas* steamed out to the U. S. S. *Missouri*, where the official Japanese surrender would take place. Ensign Kelly escorted the Japanese officials aboard the American battleship; and he watched as they signed the surrender documents.

In January, one of Kelly's cousins, Ensign Leroy I. Evans, Jr., had died in an airplane crash; and after the surrender ceremonies, Kelly remained bitter about the war. He wrote his parents about the Japanese whom he encountered: "It is hard to keep from being friendly with them. I am not going to have anything to do with them, however, Roy died because we had to fight these guys."

Chapter 11. Into the Modern World

Had Enough!

In 1946, World War II was over, peace had arrived on the Delaware coast, and the supporters of Senator James M. Tunnell eagerly awaited the fall elections. Tunnell hailed from a prominent Sussex County family that had played an influential role in the Democratic party of southern Delaware. In 1940, his unflinching support of President Franklin Roosevelt's New Deal convinced Delaware voters to send Tunnell to the United States Senate. Tunnell had supported Roosevelt's handling of the war; and Tunnell had worked diligently to assist servicemen and their families. By the time Germany and Japan were defeated, Tunnell had become one of Delaware's most respected political leaders. The coming election appeared to pose no threat to the honest, hard-working senator.

John J. Williams, on the other hand, was a chicken-feed dealer. Born in 1904 to a farming family in Bayard, Williams was the ninth of eleven children. After attending Frankford High School, which he left after the 11th grade, Williams settled in Millsboro, where he operated a feed company, established a hatchery, and farmed 2,000 acres of nearby land. Williams was a pillar of Millsboro; but outside the small Sussex County town, he was unknown. Nonetheless, the politically inexperienced Williams declared his intention to challenge James Tunnell and run for the United States Senate.

In her biography of Williams, Carol E. Hoffecker remarked that "James Miller Tunnell, Sr. could have posed as a model for what Delawareans thought a

United States Senator should be. He seemed born to politics. Tall and distinguished looking, the scion of a prominent Democratic family in eastern Sussex County, the Senator was a major land owner in his native Baltimore Hundred, an astute member of the Sussex bar, and an excellent debater." Tunnell was also John Williams' lawyer.

The neophyte Republican, however, was disturbed by the myriad New Deal programs that had spawned a growing federal bureaucracy and an endless web of government regulations. During the war, Williams had observed firsthand how price controls had created a black market in the broiler industry; and he was concerned with President Harry Truman's apparent reluctance to end wartime economic regulations.

When the Republicans held their state convention in August, veteran politicians had little interest in volunteering to be the sacrificial lamb put up to run against Tunnell. There was a concern that nominating the unknown Williams might make a farce of the Senate race, but the Millsboro businessman's quiet demeanor and straightforward manner appealed to many Republicans, so they went ahead and nominated him.

Armed with a "war chest" of $6,500, Williams began his quest against Tunnell. After buying pins, posters and newspaper advertising, Williams began a grassroots campaign that stressed his simple manner and direct approach to politics. Delaware was a state where candidates could drive from border to border in just a few hours; and voters expected to meet political candidates firsthand. Williams went door-to-door and talked to voters; he appeared at meetings of local organizations and talked to voters; he attended chicken dinners and talked to voters; and when all else failed, he stood on street corners and talked to voters. Williams railed against the Federal government's "cockeyed rules" that attempted to control prices and economic production. In addition, he attacked widespread government waste that he believed was being covered up by the Democratic-controlled Congress. He capitalized on the distrust of government bureaucracy with the simple slogan, "Had Enough!"

Delaware voters responded; and when the votes were counted, the obscure Millsboro feed merchant had defeated the incumbent Tunnell by nearly 12,000 votes. Not only was the Williams campaign effective, it was also economical. He was able to return $1,070.28 of his "war chest" to the Republican National Committee.

When Williams entered the US Senate in 1947, Truman was president, the Cold War had begun; and some government agencies were bloated. When an informant told Williams that there was a tax-fixing ring in the Bureau of Internal Revenue, the senator quietly investigated the charges. After many months of work, he exposed several corrupt Internal Revenue officials in a scandal that rocked the Truman administration.

In the years that followed, Williams built a reputation as a tireless worker who doggedly uncovered government waste and corruption. Williams did much of the investigative work himself, though his Senate staff was never larger than eight employees. When he reported his findings to the Senate, he spoke in a voice so quiet that some senators called him "Whispering Willie." He was so scrupulously fair that he also became known as "Honest" John Williams and the "Conscience of the Senate." In 1952, Williams was considered as a running mate for Republican presidential nominee, Dwight Eisenhower; but Williams declined. After serving four terms in the Senate, Williams retired, in 1971, to Sussex County, where he resumed the simple, unassuming lifestyle that he had known before his first election. He had had enough of Washington politics.

INVIGORATING VISITS TO THE COAST

In August, 1946, Harry Truman had been in office a little over a year; and during that time, he had presided over the end of World War II in Europe, the dropping of the atomic bombs on Japan, and the beginning of the Cold War. Faced with widespread labor unrest and rising economic difficulties at home, Truman saw his popularity sink to a new low. In an effort to gain a short respite from the rigors of the presidency, he decided to take a short vacation.

On August 16, Truman and a small group of advisors boarded the presidential yacht, *Williamsburg*, for an 18-day cruise. The *Williamsburg* and an escort vessel sailed down the Potomac River and up the Chesapeake Bay. When the ship reached the entrance to the Chesapeake and Delaware Canal, Daniel D. Dunlop came aboard to guide the vessel through the canal and down the Delaware Bay. According to the ship's log: "About this time the President and his party donned bathing suits, to enjoy the sun on the flying bridge. The President waved at various groups assembled on the shore, and greeted ships as they passed us on our way through the Canal. On leaving the flying bridge, he stopped by the navigating bridge to greet the pilot. Mr. Dunlop, although only 40 years of age, is the senior pilot of the Pilot Association, Bay and River Delaware, having piloted in these waters since 1929, without mishap. The ships piloted by him include some of our largest battleships, though he told us he considered taking the President through the channel one of the greatest privileges of his career."

The presidential yacht reached the Harbor of Refuge inside Cape Henlopen just before 5:00 in the evening; and the *Williamsburg* and its escort vessel dropped anchor in order that the presidential party might enjoy a short swim. President Truman, accompanied by one of his advisors and his personal physician, climbed down the port gangway and dived into the cool waters of Delaware Bay. After splashing about for ten minutes, Truman led the group back to the *Williamsburg*. According to the ship's log, "At 1710, the swimming party, completely refreshed, returned aboard."

Two years later, Truman again faced monumental difficulties. The Republicans had gained control of both houses of Congress and they seemed poised to oust Truman from the White House. In July 1948, the Democratic National Convention nominated Truman for a second term; but the President's stand on civil rights prompted the delegates from thirteen Southern states to storm out of the convention. The Southern "Dixiecrats" nominated Strom Thurmond as their candidate for president; and the hopelessly divided Democratic party appeared headed for a sure defeat. Before he began his campaign for reelection, Truman decided that he needed another trip to the coast.

On August 20, 1948, President Truman began a cruise during which he would circumnavigate the Delmarva Peninsula. A thick fog surrounded the yacht as the president began his vacation voyage; but by the time the *Williamsburg* reached the C & D Canal, the weather began to clear. As the *Williamsburg* steamed through the canal, the President was greeted by people who lined the shore, piers, and bridges along the way, giving him a warm reception.

The *Williamsburg* did not reach the Harbor of Refuge until nearly sundown, and Truman decided to forego another swim in Delaware Bay. Instead, the President enjoyed dinner aboard the yacht while it lay at anchor near Cape Henlopen, and then watched a movie.

The next morning, the entrance to Delaware Bay was enshrouded in fog; but at 9:00 am, the *Williamsburg* got under way. The presidential yacht rounded Cape Henlopen and headed southward along the Delaware coast. According to the log: "During the late morning, a small bird appeared on the fantail. Its colors, yellow and black, gave it the appearance of a canary. It flitted about the deck and on occasion would leap in the air to gulp bugs flying about. Our presence on the fantail seemed not at all to disturb the bird...In the early after noon, the bird was seen about the flying bridge, and then it disappeared — as mysteriously as it came aboard."

The playful little bird, the pleasant cruise down Delaware Bay, and the warm reception by those who spotted the presidential yacht helped to rejuvenate President Truman. Following his vacation on the Delaware coast, Truman returned to Washington and won reelection in one of the greatest upsets in American political history.

COLD WAR IN LEWES

A frigid winter wind blew across Cape Henlopen as a gray Soviet warship steamed toward the mouth of Delaware Bay. In March 1949, the first chill of the Cold War had frozen the hopes for peace. Following World War II, Germany had been occupied by the United States, Great Britain, France, and the Soviet Union. Although the city of Berlin was within the Soviet occupation zone, sections of the German capital were divided among the four occupying nations.

At first, the Soviet Union had guaranteed the three Western powers access to Berlin; but in June 1948, Joseph Stalin blockaded the roads to the city. President Harry Truman responded to the Soviet challenge by initiating an airlift of supplies to Berlin. By September 1948, the airlift was carrying 4,500 tons of food and other supplies into Berlin every day. Throughout the winter, the Berlin blockade and the airlift continued. Tensions remained high on March 10, 1949, when the Soviet cruiser *Murmansk*, accompanied by the transport *Molotov*, steamed defiantly into Delaware Bay.

Around noon, word was received in Lewes that the Soviet cruiser was approaching the bay; and a Coast Guard cutter led a small flotilla of boats seaward to intercept it. Aboard the *Murmansk*, the Soviet crew stood rigidly at attention as the cruiser began to reduce speed. At the bow, the Soviet naval ensign featured a red star edged in white contrasting with the solid red field of the flag. Within the star, a small white hammer and sickle proclaimed the workers' sovereignty in the Communist state. After the *Murmansk* dropped anchor about five miles north of Cape Henlopen, the crew stoically ignored the Coast Guard cutter and other small boats from Lewes that encircled their warship. A 20-knot wind whipped across the bay as government officials, reporters, and others aboard the American vessels waved to those aboard the

Murmansk. None of the Soviet sailors smiled, waved or acknowledged the presence of the small American vessels.

The relationship between the Soviets and the Americans had not always been this cold. During World War II, the two countries had allied to defeat Hitler, whose Wehrmacht had driven deep into Russia. The city of Murmansk, on an arm of the Arctic Ocean, was one of the few ports left unconquered by the Germans; and the United States had funneled vital war materials to the Soviets through Murmansk. To help protect the Arctic shipping lanes America lent the Russians fifteen warships, one of which was the U.S.S. *Milwaukee.*

The *Milwaukee* was renamed the *Murmansk* when it arrived in the Soviet Union. After serving in World War II, the ship remained in the Soviet Navy until 1949, when the Soviets decided to return the ships that the United States had lent them. The *Murmansk* was the first of the vessels to return to American waters. Given the tensions generated by the blockade of Berlin, the American authorities had decided that the ship should be received with as little pomp and ceremony as possible. The Soviet sailors transferred to the transport *Molotov;*. as the Soviets left the ship, a crew of American sailors took control of the *Murmansk.* After the exchange had been completed, the *Molotov* turned and sailed into the Atlantic for the long voyage back to the Soviet Union.

Aboard the *Murmansk*, the American sailors quickly went to work stripping the vessel of any sign of its Russian use. The Stars and Strips replaced the Russian flag, and the Soviet-style white waterline stripe was painted over. After the name *Murmansk* on the ship's stern was replaced with *Milwaukee*, the ship was ready to begin the short trip to Philadelphia, where the vessel was to be scrapped, anyway; and this chapter in the Cold War would come to an end.

DISASTER WITHOUT WARNING

Storms have always been a fact of coastal life. Long ago, in October 1693, Lewes was still a small colonial village when the area was struck by a storm that battered the dunes and blasted new channels between the coastal bays and the ocean. These new waterways soon silted closed, but the 1693 storm demonstrated the damage that wind and water could wreak on the coast.

A half-century later, Lewes had grown into a much larger town and its harbor was frequently filled with sailing ships. In 1749, a hurricane passed over Cape Henlopen and did considerable damage to the area. Several vessels that had taken refuge in Lewes harbor were blown ashore; and a channel was gouged across the neck of Cape Henlopen that allowed shallow draft boats to take a short cut to the sea. Elsewhere along the coast, the storm uprooted trees and damaged farmhouses. In September 1775, a hurricane pounded the Delmarva Peninsula. Fortunately, the center of the storm passed west of Sussex County and this lessened the damage along the coast. The easterly winds, however, drove water up Delaware Bay and created some of the highest tides on record. A resident of Philadelphia reported: "We had a hard gale of wind from N.E. to S.E. which occasioned a prodigious high Tide so that a number of Stores on the wharfs were overflowed, and great quantities of sugar, Salt &c were lost and damaged and we hear of great Devastation in many parts of the county by the washing away of banks and overflowing of meadows. Carrying away bridges, mill-dams, stores and spoiling of the roads &c &c."

In 1821 and 1846, the coastal area was battered by severe hurricanes. After each storm passed, the damaged was repaired; but after the Civil War, the establishment of the seaside resorts that eventually extended from Rehoboth Beach to Fenwick Island created additional potential for disaster. Before the resorts were built, few people lived within sight of the sand dunes. A storm could erode the dunes, and the ocean could flow across the beach into the bay without doing significant damage to man-made structures. In these pre-resort years, time and tide often replaced the sand, and the beach returned to its normal state.

In addition to tropical storms, the Delaware coast is often battered by low pressure systems that do damage even though they do not pack hurricane-force winds. The counter-clockwise movement of these winter weather systems produces strong north-easterly winds that earn the storms the sobriquet "north-easters," or more commonly, "nor'easters." As they travel up the coast, the steady winds of a nor'easter can drive the ocean over the dunes and into the streets of the coastal resorts. During the first week of March 1962, two low pressure systems combined to create a nor'easter that stalled off the Delaware coast, and the storm had several days to drive the ocean water toward the shore. While the storm surge was building, the moon reached its perigee, the shortest distance from Earth. The closeness of the moon intensified the spring tides; and the slow-moving storm deluged the Delaware coast with a succession of four or five astonishingly high tides.

"Disaster without any forewarning," the *Delaware Coast Press* reported on March 8, 1962, "struck the Rehoboth Beach, Lewes and Dewey Beach area on Tuesday and Wednesday of this week causing damage to properties estimated at over $10 million. The havoc was so great it belies the imagination...it was the worst flood and windstorm ever to strike this area." Up to six feet of water stood on Bay Avenue, and several feet of water covered Savannah Road from the Lewes and Rehoboth Canal to the beach. The bridge across the canal had been undermined by the storm, and the roadway was unsafe to use. Lewes Beach would be isolated until the floodwaters subsided.

Much of the Rehoboth Beach boardwalk was reduced to a series of neatly-spaced pilings. The storm ate the front off the Henlopen Hotel; and most ocean-front buildings had been damaged. At Dewey Beach, the ocean had breached the dunes, and the storm water cascaded through the resort to Rehoboth Bay. The damage was widespread: "Sinks, refrigerators, chairs, cinder blocks, boats and other debris littered Dewey. Oceanfront homes were severely damaged and in some cases, gone out to sea." During the height of the storm, the highway from Dewey Beach to Fenwick Island was under water. At Fenwick Island, the waves washed over the barrier island and continued into the coastal bay. For a time, an ancient inlet just north of town was re-opened to the sea. Many beach cottages in Fenwick Island were destroyed, and nearly every structure in the resort sustained some damage.

After the storm passed and the tide subsided, coastal residents went to work repairing the damage. It was only a few months before the start of the summer vacation season and an army of workers descended on the resorts. When the first summer visitors arrived, a few storm scars were still visible; but the resorts were back in business.

LITTLE CRITTERS THAT MADE IT BIG

When the first Dutch colonists arrived along the coast in the early 17th century, they found a dead whale on the beach and others cavorting around their ships. Whaling was expected to help sustain the colony, and whales there were; but the disaster at Zwaanendael ended hopes of a whaling station on Cape Henlopen. Instead, the settlers of the Delaware coast were content to scavenge the bay for a more lowly beast: the oyster.

The European settlers discovered mounds of oyster shells left by the Native Americans; and they quickly developed a taste for oysters, themselves. The settlers ate their oysters fried, stewed, and a variety of other ways. William Byrd of Virginia noted in his diary that he had a breakfast of "Pickled oysters and chocolate." Although few followed Byrd's breakfast menu, during the 18th century Delaware oysters were in great demand; and by the beginning of the 19th century, residents of Sussex County were using a small fleet of sloops and schooners to harvest them. Unlike the shallow-draught skipjacks and bugeyes that sailed the Chesapeake Bay, the oystermen on the Delaware Bay needed vessels with more substantial hulls that could withstand the high winds and waves that blew past Cape Henlopen during the winter months, when oyster collection was at its peak.

Although most early oystermen used long rake-like tongs to gather the bivalves, others used crude dredges to collect them. The early dredges were made of wood with a row of iron teeth to rake the oysters from the bottom of the bay. The loose oysters were collected in a rope netting that was attached to the back of the dredge. In the 19th century, the dredge developed into an all-iron affair, including the collection bag, which was made of a chain-like mesh. The dredge and its catch was hoisted aboard the vessel by a hand-operated wooden windlass.

After the catch was aboard, the crew of the oyster boat placed the shellfish into baskets, which could be hoisted aboard a buy boat for the trip to shore. Time was of the essence to prevent the tasty critters from spoiling. When railroad lines were established between New York City and the New Jersey oyster ports, much of the oyster business moved to the north side of the bay. The Delaware legislature attempted to keep the business on its side of the bay by requiring all oyster boats in the bay to be licensed in Delaware or to have captains who were citizens of Delaware.

So many oysters were harvested in the first half of the 19th century that in 1852, the Delaware state legislature limited the length of the oyster season. Oystering was prohibited from May 1 to August 10. During the first year that the law was in effect, August 10 fell on the second Thursday of the month; and on that day, a crowd collected to celebrate the opening of the oyster season. The celebration became known as "Big Thursday," and it developed into an annual event. The night before Big Thursday, families would gather at their favorite oystering dock so that they would be on hand when the first boats arrived. Some of the oysters were set aside to be taken home; and others were cooked immediately. While the oysters were being prepared, the crowd sang, danced and played games.

In the early 20th century, Big Thursday celebrations were sometimes marred by rowdiness; and just before World War II, the carousing was halted.

At the same time, many of the oyster beds had been depleted by over-harvesting, and those that were left were attacked by the microscopic MSX parasite that invaded Delaware Bay. In recent years, the Delaware oyster has made a comeback. In addition, more genteel celebrations of Big Thursday have been revived; and the day may come when mounds of oyster shells once again will appear along the Delaware coast.

The European settlers were quick to recognize the value of oysters; but it took a long time before any use could be found for horseshoe crabs. Long before the dinosaurs vanished from the earth, the horseshoe crab had developed into a near-perfect creature. Although styled a "crab," it is related to scorpions, ticks, and land spiders. The horseshoe crab's hard shell enables it to roam the ocean floor in search of food, safe from predators. As it moves along the bottom, it kicks up a cloud of debris that includes worms, mollusks, dead fish and other edible morsels. Since it has no teeth, the crab uses its legs to crush the food, which it adroitly passes into its mouth

Horseshoe crabs live along the North American coast from Mexico to Canada, but the population is concentrated in the mid-Atlantic region, where the Delaware coast hosts the creature's annual mating ritual. Like college students on spring break, thousands of horseshoe crabs head for the beach. The males arrive first, and they wait near the edge of the surf for the larger females. As a female passes by, a male reaches out with its first pair of legs and grabs onto the female's shell. The two crabs continue a short distance up the sand. Every few feet, the female scrapes out a hole where she deposits up to 20,000 eggs. As the couple moves on, the male fertilizes the eggs.

After the mating ritual is completed, the crabs return to the ocean and the waves cover most of the eggs with sand. A few eggs remain on the surface of the beach, where they become food for the estimated one million birds that stop along the coast on their migratory journey from South America to Canada. Some of these birds eat enough horseshoe crab eggs to triple their body weight before they continue northward.

The eggs that are buried by the action of the waves take about a month to hatch. A week later, the young crab molts its first shell, and it is ready to explore the ocean for food. As horseshoe crabs grow, they molt about once a year for the first ten years of their lives. Most of the shells found on Delaware beaches are the discarded shells from molting crabs.

Before the European colonists arrived, Native Americans hunted the horseshoe crab for food. They also used the shells as scoops, and they used the creature's spiny tail as a tip for spears. In the 19th century, it was discovered that pulverized horseshoe crabs made excellent fertilizer and pig feed. The mass spawning habits of the crabs made them easy to harvest; and during the first half of the 20th century, the population of horseshoe crabs was dramatically reduced.

In recent times, it has been discovered that a horseshoe crab's white blood cells contain a lysate that can be used to detect endotoxins, which are poisons produced by infectious bacteria. In addition, blood from horseshoe crabs has been used to diagnose a form of spinal meningitis. The study of the electrical impulses in the horseshoe crab's optical nerve has also led to a better under-standing of how human eyes function; but for many years scientists were puzzled as to why horseshoe crabs needed to see at all. Although they would move away when a shadow passed over one of their eyes, horseshoe crabs have no known predator. In addition, the crabs spend most of their time feeding on the ocean bottom where there is little light. They appear to feed by feel, not by sight.

Scientists who studied the habits of horseshoe crabs created concrete castings of female crabs and forms of random size and shapes. They placed these castings near the edge of the surf and watched as the male crabs arrived. The males ignored the random shapes; but when the males spotted the concrete shape of a female crab, they attached themselves to it in imitation of the mating ritual. The scientists concluded that at least one primary purpose of the horseshoe crab's complex eyes is to locate the females. The evolution of the horseshoe crab may have stopped millions of years ago; but during the late spring, the crabs that loiter along the surf are not much different from sup-posedly more advanced human critters who migrate to the beach.

In 1938, when Otis Smith arrived in Lewes, the oyster and horseshoe crab populations were in deep decline; and it had been centuries since the whaler's cry, "Thar she blows!" had been heard in this part of the Atlantic. Smith, however, saw large schools of valuable fish that others had ignored; and within a few years, his small fleet of boats would bring back to Lewes more fish than the whalers ever dreamt of carrying. During the 18th century, colonists in Sussex County were aware of the vast schools of menhaden that inhabited coastal waters, but the early settlers considered the fish too oily to eat. Although some of Delaware's early settlers used oil from menhaden as a substitute for whale oil in their lamps, the colonists found extracting oil from several thousand small men-haden was far more difficult than rendering several hundred barrels of oil from a single whale.

In the 19th century, the processing of menhaden was mechanized so that the oil could be extracted economically and efficiently, and the bones and other remains turned into fertilizer. Later, it was discovered that fishmeal could be used in animal feed. Because Lewes lay along the migratory routes of the menhaden, its location made it the ideal place to build fish processing plants.

When Otis Smith came to Lewes, he saw that the plants were using antiquated techniques. The seine nets used by the fishermen captured thousands of wildly flopping fish that had to be laboriously brought aboard the small boats and carried to the plants where pitchfork-wielding crews unloaded the catch. Even the most careful crews sometimes spiked the feet of fellow workers as they pitched the fish into bucket elevators. In 1938, Smith purchased the Harley Joseph processing plant, and he began an extensive modernization program. Smith introduced a small fleet of steel-hulled boats equipped with electronic units that calmed the fish once they were captured in the nets. And when Smith's boats reached the plant, the fish were unloaded by vacuum pumps that allowed the stevedores to use water hoses to float the fish into flumes that were built into the boat hulls.

Smith also improved the processing techniques by installing steam-tube dryers that dramatically reduced the odors that once emanated from the plants. In addition, Smith developed techniques for capturing the water that was used when the fish were processed. After the oil was separated from the water, the liquid was piped to evaporators that reduced the water to a salable product.

Smith's techniques were such a success that his company's holdings to grew to include plants in Canada and South America. The company also had several shipyards to build and maintain its fleet of fishing vessels. Lewes became the leading fish processing port in the country. Following World War II, Sea Coast Products built a large processing plant on the bight of Cape Henlopen. The area was prone to storms, but the 14-story Sea Coast plant was designed to last for hundreds of years. The reinforced concrete walls were up to 18 inches thick. In addition, the interior walls were interconnected in a way that gave the building enormous strength and stability. The plant could withstand the strongest hurricane.

In its heyday, the Lewes menhaden fleet of more than two dozen fishing vessels were crewed by more than 500 fishermen. The boats worked in groups to set seine nets that could capture entire schools of menhaden in a single casting. In 1956, 360 million pounds of menhaden were landed at Lewes; but too much efficiency might not be a good thing. The Lewes fishermen soon devastated the menhaden population. Within two decades of the peak catch, the last menhaden processing operation closed. The Sea Coast plant that had weathered the March 1962 nor'easter without difficulty could not withstand the depletion of fish stocks, and the empty plant became an eyesore near Cape Henlopen.

On March 26, 1983, a crowd of curious onlookers gathered outside of Lewes to see what promised to be a spectacular show. Because it was still early spring, most folks in the crowd were local residents. This would be the biggest blast to hit town since the British bombarded Lewes during the War of 1812. There, near the landing area for the Cape May ferry, they were about to see the giant silos of the Sea Coast menhaden processing plant demolished. The enormous structure was to be blasted from its foundation by 700 pounds of explosives. An earlier blast had already leveled the plant's tall chimney, and as the appointed hour the excitement and anticipation in the crowd increased. The minutes shrank to seconds, and the signal was given. A few moments later, tell-tale puffs of smoke and dust appeared at the base of the building. As the sound of the explosion reached the crowd, the plant began to tilt. Everyone strained for a clear view of the imminent collapse — but the building stopped moving. The dust settled around it, and the building remained frozen in place. The saga of the tower too tough to die had begun.

After the first explosion failed, the head of the demolition company, Bell Shellhouse, laconically remarked, "We'll have to pack 'er again."

As the crowd waited, another 700 pounds of explosives were placed in the building, Again the signal was given, the charges were ignited, and the dust flew. The powder boomed, but the building refused to budge. A third try was announced for the next day. Anther 700 pounds of dynamite, another explosion, another cloud of dust, but the leaning tower of Lewes refused to collapse. A recess in the proceedings was called.

After studying the situation for several weeks, the dynamiters decide to blast away at the plant's interior walls. On May 10, the blast cut through and the great building toppled over on it is side. For the next few weeks, a crane fitted with a wrecking ball worked to reduce the structure to manageable chucks of concrete that could be carted away. Once the site was cleared, vacationers had the Delaware beach to themselves again.

Bibliography

Abplanalp, Jean Murdock and Dougherty, Barbara Quillen. *Dewey Beach, History & Tales.* Milton: Harold E. Dukes, Jr., Publisher, nd.

Alexander, Edward Porter, ed. *The Journal of John Fontaine, An Irish Huguenot Son in Spain and Virginia, 1710-1719.* Williamsburg: The Colonial Williamsburg Foundation, 1972.

Anderson, Enoch. *Personal Recollections.* Wilmington, 1896.

"Attack on Lewistown," *National Intelligencer.* April 16, 1813.

Bagley, Admiral Worth. "Torpedoed in the Celtic Sea," *Naval History.* May/June, 1997.

Barney, Mary, ed. *Biographical Memoir of the Late Commodore Joshua Barney.* Boston, 1832.

Bartholomew, Robert E. "War-Scare Hysteria in the Delaware Region in 1916," *Delaware History.* Spring-Summer, 1998.

Beach, Jack. *This was Rehoboth Beach, Flotsam, Jetsam and Trivia.* Lewes: Media Associates, 1993.

Bendler, Bruce A. "Ann Elliott Versus Robert Twilley: Securing a Family's Freedom," *Delaware History.* Vol. XXVII, #3, Spring-Summer, 1997.

Benson, Barbara E. "Delaware Goes to War," *Delaware History.* Vol. XXVI, #3-4, Spring-Summer, 1995, Fall-Winter, 1995.

Biographical and Genealogical History of the State of Delaware. Chambersburg, PA, 1899.

"Blasters Even Score With Silo," *Delaware Coast Press.* May 18, 1983.

Blockson, Charles L. ed. *The Underground Railroad.* New York: Berkley Books, 1987.

"British Freighter Sinks Off Lewes Wednesday," *Delaware Coast News.* March 6, 1942.

Brittingham, Hazel D. "Joshua Fisher — The Man and His Family," *Lewes, Delaware 2001.* Dover: Lewes Chamber of Commerce & Visitors Bureau, 2001.

———. *Lantern on Lewes.* Lewes: Lewestown Publishers, 1998.

——. "The Port of Lewes," *Del-Mar-Va Heartland*. Fall, 1991.

——. "Thoughts on a Theme: Mosquitoes," *Peninsula Pacemaker Magazine*. June, 1991.

Bryan, E. D. "The Confederate Raider *Alabama*: A Lewes Connection," *Journal of the Lewes Historical Society*. Vol. IV, November, 2001.

Bryant, Tracey L. and Pennock, Jonathan R. *The Delaware Estuary: Rediscovering a Forgotten Resource*. Newark, Delaware: University of Delaware Sea Grant College Program, 1998.

Burgess, Robert. "The 73-Year Story of the Sailing Ram," *Sunday Sun Magazine*. February 4, 1962.

Carter, Dick. *The History of Sussex County*. Rehoboth Beach: Community News Corporation, 1976.

——. "Return Day, Party or Politics," *Del-Mar-Va Heartland*. Spring, 1976.

Carter, Richard B. *Clearing New Ground, The Life of John G. Townsend Jr*. Wilmington: Delaware Heritage Press, 2001.

Chance, Elbert. "Matthew Wilson — Professor, Preacher, Patriot, Physician," *Delaware History*. Vol. #3, April, 1963.

Charles, Joan. *Mid-Atlantic Shipwreck Accounts to 1899*. Hampton, VA: Joan Charles, Publisher, 1997.

Clark, William Bell; William James Morgan, Michael J. Crawford, eds. *Naval Documents of the American Revolution*. Vol. 1-10, Washington: U. S. Government Printing Office, 1964-1996

Cole Family Records. Photocopies, author's collection.

Conner, William H. and deValinger, Leon Jr. *Delaware's Role in World War II*. Wilmington: Delaware Heritage Commission, 2003.

"Co-operation Given 'Position,'" *Delaware Coast News*. January 30, 1942.

Copper, Constance J. "Make It Do or Do Without: Delawareans and Rationing During World War II," *Delaware History*. Vol. XXVI, #3-4, Spring-Summer, 1995, Fall-Winter, 1995.

——. and Cone, Ellen. "Defending the Delaware Home Front During World War II," *Delaware History*. Vol. XXVI, #3-4, Spring-Summer, 1995, Fall-Winter, 1995.

Copper, Linda. "Women's Suffrage Battle Was Fought in Delaware," *Looking Back, A Century of Life in Downstate*, Frank Fantini Coordinator, Dover: Delaware State News, 2000.

Cordingly, David. *Under the Black Flag*. New York: Harcourt Brace & Company, 1995.

Cox, S. S. "The Life Saving Service," *The North American Review*. May, 1881.

"Crowd of 2000 See Five Negroes Lashed at Whipping Post," *Delaware Coast Press*. February 19, 1932.

"Cypress Swamp Fire Swept Over 5000 Acres," *Delaware Coast News*. October 26, 1929.

"D-Day Proclaimed by the Rigging of Church Bells," *Delaware Coast News*. June 9, 1944.

DeCosta, B. F. "Captain Kidd-Why He was Hung." *The Galaxy*. Vol. 7, Issue 5, May, 1869.

De Vries, David Pietersz, *Voyages from Holland to America*. Online at http://134.76.163.65/agora_docs/4309TABLE_OF_CONTENTS.html.

"Dim-Out Regulations Must Be Obeyed," *Delaware Coast News*. May 15, 1942.

Dudley, William S. ed. *The Naval War of 1812, A Documentary History*. 2 Vols. Washington: Naval Historical Center, Department of the Navy, 1985.

Eldred, Tom. "Carpetbagger Tried to Buy Senate Seat," *Looking Back, A Century of Life in Downstate*, Frank Fantini, Coordinator, Dover: Delaware State News, 2000.

——. "CCC: Mosquito Control and Much More," *Looking Back, A Century of Life in Downstate*, Frank Fantini, Coordinator, Dover: Delaware State News, 2000.

——. "Delaware in World War I," *Looking Back, A Century of Life in Downstate*, Fran Fantini, Coordinator, Dover: Delaware State News, 2000.

——. "Early Lessons from the CCC," *Looking Back, A Century of Life in Downstate*, Fran Fantini, Coordinator, Dover: Delaware State News, 2000.

——. "German POWs Aided Delaware Farm Efforts," *Looking Back, A Century of Life in Downstate*, Frank Fantini, Coordinator, Dover: Delaware State News, 2000.

——. "The Great Depression," *Looking Back, A Century of Life in Downstate*, Frank Fantini, Coordinator, Dover: Delaware State News, 2000.

——. "1930 Fire Ravaged Great Cypress Swamp," *Looking Back, A Century of Life in Downstate*, Frank Fantini, Coordinator, Dover: Delaware State News, 2000.

Emilio, Luis F. *A Brave Black Regiment, History of the Fifty-Fourth Regiment of Massachusetts Volunteer Infantry*. Boston, 1891.

Estes, J. Worth. "Commodore Jacob Jones: A Doctor Goes to Sea," *Delaware History*. Vol. XXIV #2, Fall-Winter, 1990.

"European Phase of War Ended May 6th," *Delaware Coast News*. May 11, 1945.

"FBI Arrests Two Aliens on Shore," *The Salisbury Times*. March 14, 1942.

Fetzer, Dale and Mowday, Bruce. *Unlikely Allies; Fort Delaware's Prison Community in the Civil War*. Mechanicsburg, Pa.: Stackpole Books, 2000.

Foner, Hilip S. *Blacks in the American Revolution*. Westport, CN: Greenwood Press, 1976.

"Forest Fire Sill Raging in Lower Sussex County," *Delaware Coast News*. August 15, 1930.

"40 Sub Attack Survivors Land Safely At Lewes," *Delaware Coast News*. February 6, 1942.

Frank, William P. *Caesar Rodney, Patriot*. Wilmington, Delaware: Delaware Heritage Commission, 1992.

Franklin, Benjamin. *Journal of Occurrences in My Voyage to Philadelphia.* Online at http://odur.let.rug.nl/-usa/D/1726-1750/franlin/voy/ht

"Frigid Formality on Part of Russians Is Keynote of Return of Milwaukee," *The Public Press and Delaware Coast News.* March 10, 1949.

Gannon, Michael. *Operation Drumbeat.* New York: Harper Perennial, 1991.

Garraty, John A and Carnes, Mark C. eds., *Dictionary of American Biography.* New York: C. Scribner's Sons, 1988.

Garrison, J. Ritchie, Herman, Bernard L., Ward, Barbara McLean, eds. *After Ratification, Material Life in Delaware, 1789-1820.* Newark, Delaware: Museum Studies Program, University of Delaware, 1988.

Gentile, Gary. *Shipwrecks of Delaware and Maryland.* Philadelphia: Gary Gentile Productions, 1990.

"German U-Boat Crew Landed at Fort Miles," *Delaware Coast News.* May 18, 1945.

Gilmore, Jann Haynes. "Ethel Pennewill Brown Leach: Delaware Artist of Time, Place, and Season," *Delaware History.* Vol. XXVIII, #2-3, 1998-1999.

Haden, Amy, *Victorian Lewes and Its Architecture.* Lewes: The Lewes Historical Society and The Preservation Trust, 1986.

Hall, Clayton Colman, ed. *Narratives of Early Maryland, 1633-1684.* New York: Charles Scribner's Sons, 1910.

Hancock, Harold B. *Delaware During the Civil War, A Political History.* Wilmington: Historical Society of Delaware, 2003.

———. *Delaware Two Hundred Years Ago: 1780-1800.* Wilmington: The Middle Atlantic Press, 1987.

———. *The History of Sussex County.* No place of publication: Sussex County Bicentennial Commission, 1976

———. "Lewes and the American Revolution," paper given at Lewes Historical Society Seminar, July, 1979.

———. "A Loyalist in Sussex County: The Adventures of J. F. D. Smyth in 1777," *Delaware History.* Vol. XVI, #4, Fall-Winter, 1975.

———. "The Revolutionary War Diary of William Adair," *Delaware History.* Vol. XIII, #2, April, 1968.

—— "Thomas Robinson: Delaware's Most Prominent Loyalist," *Delaware History.* Vol. IV #1, March, 1950.

Harder, Leland, "Plockhoy and His Settlement at Zwaanendael, 1663." *Delaware History.* Vol. III, #3, March, 1949.

Hayman, John C. *Rails Along the Chesapeake, A History of Railroading on the Delmarva Peninsula, 1827-1978.* Pittsburgh: Marvadel Publishers, 1979.

Hercules Dynamite on the Farm, Ditch Blasting. Bradely, Illinois: Lindsay Publications, 1990.

Herman, L. Bernard. *Architecture and Rural Life in Central Delaware, 1700–1900.* Knoxville: University of Tennessee Press, 1987.

Hewitt, Arthur and Spears, John R. *Signals of the Sea* and *Heroes of the Surf.* Silverthorne, Colorado: Vistabooks, 1996.

Hickam, Homer H. *Torpedo Junction, U-Boat War Off America's East Coast, 1942.* New York: Dell Publishing, 1991.

Higgins, Anthony, ed. "Mary Wilson Thomson Memoir," *Delaware History.* Vol. XVIII, # 1-3, Spring-Summer, 1978, Fall–Winter, 1978, Spring Summer, 1979.

Hoffecker, Carol E. *Honest John Williams, U. S. Senator from Delaware.* Newark, Delaware: University of Delaware Press, 2000.

———, ed. *Readings in Delaware History.* Newark, Delaware: University of Delaware Press, 1973.

Hume, Audrey Noel. *Food.* Williamsburg: The Colonial Williamsburg Foundation, 1978.

Hurley, George and Suzanne. *Shipwrecks and Rescues Along the Barrier Islands of Delaware, Maryland and Virginia* Norfolk/Virginia Beach, Virginia: The Donning Company, 1984.

"Jacob Jones, U.S.N." *International Magazine of Literature, Art, and Science.* Vol. 1, Issue 8, August 19, 1850.

"John H. Mulholland and his Bentwood Spoon," *Milford Historical Society News Letter.* Fall, 1995.

Jones, Carlton. "When Sail Struck Steel — And Sank It," *Sunday Sun Magazine.* August, 8, 1991.

Jones, Frank Morton, ed. "Description of the Cypress Swamps in Delaware and Maryland States," *Delaware History.* Vol. III, #3, March, 1949.

Kelley, James A. "A Big-War Industry in a Small Town," *I Remember When: The World War Periods...at Home and Abroad.* Dover: University of Delaware Press, 1981.

Kern, John R., "The Election Riots of 1787 in Sussex County, Delaware," *Delaware History* Vol. XXII, #4, Fall-Winter, 1987.

Knox, Dudley W., ed. *Naval Documents Related to the Quasi-War between the United States and France.* 7 volumes. Washington: U. S. Government Printing Office, 1935-1938.

———. *Naval Documents Related to the United States Wars with the Barbary Powers.* 7 volumes. Washington: U. S. Government Printing Office, 1939-1945.

Kyle, Mary Pat. *Fenwick Island: Ice Age to Jet Age.* Fenwick Island: Mary Pat Kyle, Publisher, 1995.

Laird, Marnie. "U-Boats off Delaware," *Delaware Beach Life.* June, 2004.

Lencek, Lena and Bosker, Gideon. *The Beach, The History of Paradise on Earth.* New York: Viking, The Penguin Group, Penguin Putnam Inc., 1998.

"Lewes Historic Cannon May Have to Be Sacrificed," *Delaware Coast News*. August 21, 1942.

"Lewes Navy Officer Saw Japs Surrender," *Delaware Coast News*. September 21, 1945.

Log of President Truman's Vacation Cruise August 16-September 2, 1946. Online at Truman.library@nara.gov.

Log of President Truman's Vacation Cruise in the Chesapeake and Delaware Bays, August 20-29, 1948. Online at Truman.library@nara.gov.

Mabie, Hamilton. *The Memorial Story of America*. Philadelphia, 1894.

Marine, William M. *The Bombardment of Lewes by the British, April 6 and 7, 1813*. Wilmington: The Historical Society of Delaware, 1901.

Marshall Dr. George. *Memoir of Brigadier-General John Dagworthy*. Wilmington, 1895.

Martin, Roger A. *Tales of Delaware*. np, 1991.

Marvil, James E. ed. A Pictorial History of Lewes, Delaware, 1609–1985. Lewes: The Lewes Historical Society, 1985.

Marx, Wesley. "A Last Hurrah for Seagirt Monuments to Fun and Games," *Smithsonian Magazine*. September, 1982.

Marye, William B. "The Sea Coast of Maryland," *Maryland Historical Magazine*. Vol. 40, # 2, June, 1945.

Maryland Archives. Vol. 25. Online at http://www.mdarchives.state.md.us/

Meehan, James D. *Rehoboth Beach Memoirs...From Saints to Sinners*. Bethany Beach: Harold E. Dukes, Jr., Publisher, 2000.

——. *Bethany Beach Memoirs...A Long Look Back*. Bethany Beach: Harold E. Dukes, Jr. Publisher, 1998.

Merryman, J. H. *The United States Life-Saving Service — 1880*. Golden, Colorado: Outbooks, 1981.

"Meeting of Sussex County Unemployment Relief Committee," *Delaware Coast News*. January 8, 1932.

"Men Brought Ashore from Ill-Fated Vessel," *Delaware Coast News*. January 30, 1942.

Mills, Eric. *Chesapeake Rumrunners of the Roaring Twenties*. Centreville, Md.: Tidewater Publishers, 2000.

Moale, Richard. *Notes on Shipwrecks on the Maryland and Delaware Coast*. Westminster, Maryland: Family Line Publications, 1990.

Morgan, Edmund S. and Helen M. *The Stamp Act Crisis*. New York: Collier Books, 1962.

Morgan, Michael. "The Fighting 1st Delaware," *America's Civil War*. January, 1996.

Morison, Samuel Eliot. *The European Discovery of America, The Northern Voyages*. New York: Oxford University Press, 1971.

Mullin, Gerald. *Flight and Rebellion, Slaver Resistance in Eighteenth-Century Virginia.* New York: Oxford University Press, 1974.

Munroe, John A. *History of Delaware.* Newark, Delaware: University of Delaware Press, 1979.

Murray, Aubrey P. *Millsboro Honor Roll World War II.* Millsboro: Aubrey P. Murray, 1989.

Nathan, Roger, E. *East of the Mason-Dixon Line, A History of the Delaware Boundaries.* Wilmington: Delaware Heritage Press, 2000.

"New Year's Rum Seized As Boat Dashes for Shore," *Delaware Coast News.* December 30, 1932.

Noble, Dennis L. *That Others Might Live, The U. S. Life-Saving Service, 1878–1915.* Annapolis, Maryland: Naval Institute Press, 1994.

Norton, Oliver W. *Army Letters, 1861-1865.* Chicago: Oliver W. Norton, 1903.

Norwood, Henry. *A Voyage to Virginia.* Online at http://etext.lib.virginia.edu/etcbin/jamestown-browse?id=J1025

Nulty, William H. *The Road to Olustee.* Tuscaloosa: University of Alabama Press, 1990.

Official Records of the Union and Confederate Navies during the War of the Rebellion. 31 volumes. Washington, 1894-1927.

"One Hundred and Fifty Bags of Rum Picked Off Lewes Saturday," *Delaware Coast News.* November 28, 1930.

Orr, Robert Hunter, *A Small-Town Boyhood in the First State.* Robert Hunter Orr, 1999.

Osborne, Duffield. "Surf and Surf-Bathing," *Scribner's Magazine.* July, 1890.

Ostroski, Drew. "Captured Sub Came to Lewes," *Looking Back, A Century of Life in Downstate.* Frank Fantini, Coordinator, Dover: Delaware State News, 2000.

———. "Keeping the Flow During Prohibition," *Looking Back, A Century of Life in Downstate.* Frank Fantini, Coordinator, Dover: Delaware State News, 2000.

———. "Long Live the Du Ponts," *Looking Back, A Century of Life in Downstate.* Frank Fantini, Coordinator, Dover: Delaware State News, 2000.

"Patrolling Bay to Stop Invasion of Bold Rum Runners," *Delaware Coast News.* December 9, 1932.

Pearson, Eric A. *Bits & Pieces on Fabulous Cape Henlopen.* Lewes: Eric Pearson, 1991.

Peery, Lynn, ed. *Some Letters of and Concerning Major William Peery.* Strasburg, Va.: Shenandoah Publishing House, Inc., 1935.

Pepper, Dorothy. "The Fenwick Island Lighthouse," *Del-Mar-Va Heartland.* Fall, 1991.

Pleasants, Henry Jr. *The Tragedy of the Crater.* Eastern National Park & Monument Association, 1975.

Plowman, Terry. "Locals Recall 'Great Storm of 62,'" *Delaware Coast Press.* March 11, 1997.

"Presidential Yacht in Lewes Waters," *The Public Press and Delaware Coast News*. August 22, 1948.

Pyle, Howard. "A Peninsular Canaan," *Harper's New Monthly Magazine*. July, 1879.

———. *Howard Pyle's Book of Pirates: Fiction, Fact & Fancy Concerning the Buccaneers & Marooners of the Spanish Main*. Online at http://etext.lib.virginia.edu/modeng/modengP.browse.html

———. "Chincoteague, The Island of Ponies," *Scribner's Monthly*. April, 1877.

Quinn, Judith. "Traversing the Landscape in Federal Delaware," *Delaware History*. Vol. XXIII, #1, Spring-Summer, 1988.

"Radio Man's Heroic Work Praised by Skipper," *Delaware Coast News*. February 6, 1942.

"Rehoboth Beach Outlines Defense," *Delaware Coast News*. December 19, 1941.

Return Day 2000 Commemorative Program. np, nd.

Rollo, Vera F. *Maryland Personality Parade*. Vol. I , Lanham, Maryland: Maryland Historical Press, 1967.

Roosevelt, Theodore. *The Naval War of 1812*. New York, 1882.

Roth, Hal, ed. *The Entailed Hat by George Alfred Townsend*. Vienna, Maryland: Nanticoke Books, 2000.

———. *The Monster' Handsome Face, Patty Cannon in Fiction & Fact*. Vienna, Maryland: Nanticoke Books, 1998.

Scharf, J. Thomas. *History of Delaware, 1609-1888*. 2 volumes. Philadelphia, 1888.

Scheer, George F. and Rankin, Hugh F. *Rebels & Redcoats*. New York: Mentor Books, 1957.

Schonhorn, Manuel, ed. *A General History of the Pyrates by Daniel Defoe*. Mineola, New York: Dover Publications, 1999.

Sebold, Kimberly R. "The Delmarva Broiler Industry and World War II: A Case in Wartime Economy," *Delaware History*. Vol. XXV, #3, Spring-Summer, 1993.

Seibold, David J. and Adams, Charles J. *Shipwrecks and Sea Stories & Legends of the Delaware Coast*. Barnegat Light, New Jersey: Exeter House Books, 1989.

Seville, William P. *History of the First Regiment Delaware Volunteers*. Baltimore, 1986.

Shanks, Ralph and York, Wick. *The U. S. Life-Saving Service, Heroes, Rescues and Architecture of the Early Coast Guard*. Petaluma, California: Costano Books, 1998.

Shields, Jerry. *Gath's Literary Work and Folk and Other Selected Writing of George Alfred Townsend*. Wilmington: Delaware Heritage Press, 1996.

Sherry, Frank. *Raiders and Rebels, The Golden Age of Piracy*. New York: Hearst Marine Books, 1986.

Shomette, Donald. *The Hunt for HMS De Braak, Legend and Legacy*. Durham, NC: Carolina Academic Press, 1993.

"Shore's Pride And Joy Will Substitute for Tom Turkey," *The Salisbury Times*. November 23, 1943.

Skelcher, Bradley. *African American Education in Delaware: A History through Photographs, 1865–1930*. Wilmington: Delaware Heritage Press, 1999.

"$60,000 Worth of Liquor Captured by U. S. Coast Guards," *Delaware Coast Press*. November 20, 1931.

"A Soldier's Story: Thomas Lodge, 198th Coast Artillery," *Delaware History*. Vol. XXVI, #3-4, Fall-Summer, 1995, Fall-Winter, 1995.

Spears, John R. "Sand-Waves at Henlopen and Hatteras," *Scribner's Magazine*. Vol. 8, Issue 4, October, 1890.

Spruance, John S. *Delaware Stays in the Union*. Newark, Delaware: University of Delaware Press, 1955.

Stacton, David. *The Bonapartes*. New York: Simon and Schuster, 1966.

Stevenson, Jay. *Rehoboth of Yesterday Vol. II*. Millsboro: Jay Stevenson, 1981.

"Suggestions to Heed During Air Raids," *Delaware Coast News*. December 12, 1941.

"Survivors Tell of Seven Hours in Small Boat," *Delaware Coast News*. January 30, 1942.

Taggart, Robert J. "Pierre S. Du Pont and the Great School Fight of 1919-1921," *Delaware History*. Vol. XVII, #3, Spring-Summer, 1977.

Thompson, Priscilla M. "Navigation of the Delaware Bay, 1790-1830." *Delaware History*. Vol., #2, Fall-Winter, 1980.

Trapani, Robert. *Indian River Life-Saving Station...Journey Along the Sands*. Virginia Beach, Virginia: The Donning Company, 2002.

Terrell, Dan. *Eight Flags over Lewes*. Rehoboth Beach: The Duck Press, 1975.

———. *Room for One More Sinner*. Rehoboth Beach: Dan Terrell, 1984.

"Transportation Problems," *Delaware Coast News*, June 12, 1928.

Truitt, LeRoy B., "The Holly Wreath Industry," *I Remember When: Between the World Wars*. Dover: University of Delaware Press, 1981.

Tucker, Glenn. *Dawn Like Thunder, The Barbary Wars and the Birth of the U. S. Navy*. New York: Bobbs-Merrill Company, 1963.

Tunnell, James M. Jr. "The Manufacture of Iron in Sussex County," *Delaware History*. Vol. IV, #2, Sept. 1954.

Turner, C. H. B. ed., *Some Records of Sussex County Delaware*. Philadelphia: Allen, Lane & Scott, 1909.

Valle, James E. "Schooners of the Delaware Coast, 1880–1949," paper given at Lewes Historical Society Seminar, July, 1979.

Vaughan, Alden T. ed. *Chronicles of the American Revolution Compiled by Hezekiah Niles.* New York: Grosset & Dunlap, 1965.

"Victory Is Celebrated in Rehoboth & Lewes," *Delaware Coast News.* August 17, 1945.

War of the Rebellion: A Compilation of the Official Records of the Union and Confederate Armies. 128 volumes. Washington, 1888-1901.

Ward, Christopher. *The War of the Revolution.* 2 Volumes, New York: The Macmillan Company, 1952.

———. *The Delaware Continentals.* Wilmington: The Historical Society of Delaware, 1941.

Warren, T. Robinson. "Bay Shooting," *Scribner's Monthly.* December, 1876.

Warrington, C. W. *Delaware's Costal Defenses, Fort Saulsbury & A Mighty Fort Called Miles.* Wilmington: Delaware Heritage Press, 2003.

Webster, A. F. "The Delaware Penalties," *Appleton's Journal.* June 20, 1874.

Weslager, C. A. *Delaware's Buried Past, A Story of Archaeological Adventure.* New Brunswick, New Jersey: Rutgers University Press, 1968.

Wheeler, Richard. *Voices of 1776.* Greenwich, Connecticut: Fawcett Publications, 1972.

Williams, William H. *Slavery and Freedom in Delaware, 1639–1865.* Wilmington, Delaware: Scholarly Resources, 1996.

Wilson, E. Emerson. *Forgotten Heroes of Delaware.* Cambridge, Mass.: Deltos Publishing, 1970.

———. *Fort Delaware.* Newark, Delaware: University of Delaware Press, 1957.

———. "Lewes in the 19th Century," paper given at Lewes Historical Society Seminar, July, 1979.

Winslow, Julian D. *Sussex Awakens to the Toot.* Wilmington: Julian D. Winslow, 1999.

Made in the USA
Lexington, KY
09 November 2011